BRYAN LANKFORD is a leading Wiccan practitioner in the Dallas Pagan community. He has been trained as a High Priest in the McFarland Dianic Tradition, a Wiccan tradition founded in the early 1970s by Morgan McFarland, and has master standing in Old Path Wicca. He is the cofounder and High Priest of the OIC coven, an Old Path Wiccan coven that holds regular Circles of its own as well as performing rituals for the Dallas Pagan community.

Bryan has served as national co–second officer of the Covenant of the Goddess (CoG), an international organization for Wiccans, and as first officer of the Texas Local Council of CoG. Since its creation he has been on the board of directors of Betwixt & Between (B&B), a community center for Wiccans, Pagans, and others who follow alternative spiritual paths, and has taught the beginning Wicca class at B&B since 1998. As inter-faith officer for the Texas Local Council of CoG and interfaith director for B&B, Bryan lectures extensively about Wicca at colleges, universities, and private functions around the North Texas area helping thousands of people understand the truth about Wicca. Bryan is also a founding member of B&B's Civil Rights Division, which aids those who are experiencing reli-gious discrimination.

Since 1999 Bryan has been a member of the Thanks-Giving Square Interfaith Committee, which promotes dialogue and cooperation between people of all religions, where he represents the Wiccan faith in the Dallas area religious community. In 2000 he received international media attention when he gave the opening invocation at a Dallas City Council meeting.

Bryan has been frequently interviewed by the media and has been a guest on both secular and religious radio programs. He lives in Mesquite, Texas, with his wife and two children.

THE COMPLETE DEMYSTIFIED SERIES

Insulin Pump Therapy Demystified
by Gabrielle Kaplan-Mayer

Bipolar Disorder Demystified
by Lana Castle

Borderline Personality Disorder Demystified
by Robert O. Friedel, MD

Therapy Demystified
by Kate Scharff, MSW

Wicca
Demystified

A GUIDE FOR PRACTITIONERS,
FAMILY, AND FRIENDS

Bryan Lankford

MARLOWE & COMPANY ■ NEW YORK

In memory of Renda "Selket" Bowman.
She was my crone and my inspiration.

I hope I can live up to the example you set,
and I'm sorry I didn't finish this before you had to leave us.

∞

WICCA DEMYSTIFIED:
A Guide for Practitioners, Family, and Friends
Copyright © 2005 by Bryan Lankford

Published by
Marlowe & Company
An Imprint of Avalon Publishing Group, Incorporated
245 West 17th Street • 11th floor
New York, NY 10011-5300

AVALON
publishing group incorporated

LIBRARY OF CONGRESS CATALOGING-IN-PUBLICATION DATA
Lankford, Bryan, 1964–
Wicca demystified : a guide for practitioners, their family, and friends /
Bryan Lankford.
p. cm.
Includes bibliographical references (p. 244)
ISBN 1-56924-380-8 (pbk.)
1. Witchcraft. I. Title.
BF1566.L36 2005
299'.94--dc22
2005001002

9 8 7 6 5 4 3 2 1

Designed by Pauline Neuwirth, Neuwirth and Associates, Inc.

Printed in the United States of America

CONTENTS

INTRODUCTION

For whom is this book written?

AS CHILDREN TWO of the first questions we ask are "What is it?" and "Why?" We ask these questions to clear away the dark places of ignorance and let the light of knowledge shine its rays of understanding throughout our minds. As children we ask questions naturally and hungrily seek answers to all those mysteries we don't understand. However, as we get older, we change: we get lazy or complacent, we start to become satisfied with the knowledge we have, and our quest for new information slows down or stops completely. We stop asking "Why?" and delude ourselves into thinking that we already know all that's important to know. When this happens, those dark places of ignorance cease to be the realm of exploration, becoming instead places of evil and fear. Like old maps where the unexplored territories were labeled "Here There Be Monsters," we write off our own "unexplored territories" as dangerous places where something might consume us if we venture into them. Those things we don't understand are often feared as evil, and we vilify them not because they will hurt us but because it is easier to condemn than to learn and understand. The purpose of this book is to serve as a guide for those who have chosen to venture into one unexplored corner of their minds. We will push past the sign that reads "Here There Be Witches" and shine a light on Wicca.

Most people don't know much about Wicca, and unfortunately, some are more than willing to fill in their factual gaps with fanciful creations. This has led to any number of problems for Wiccans at home, work, and school. For example, I was the first Wiccan minister to give the opening invocation at a Dallas City Council meeting. At that time the invocation was a routine occurrence and few people gave it a second thought. This particular invocation, however, turned into a circus-like event complete with protesters, death threats, extra security, and coverage on every media outlet in the city. Why? Because it's easier and more exciting for some people to believe lies than to learn the truth.

I have always been fascinated by religion, not just one religion, but all of them, past and present. To me, it's intriguing to examine the myriad ways people perceive Deity, which partly explains how I became Wiccan. When I was a teenager, I began questioning the religious tenets I was being taught and began looking for my own answers to life's questions. Over the years this eventually led me to form my own set of religious beliefs, which I thought were mine alone. I thought I was following a religion of one until, by an odd set of circumstances, I found a book about Wicca and discovered others believed as I did.

Since 1998 I have done a great deal of interfaith work, which means I lecture about Wicca to groups interested in world religions, I work with other religious leaders to help plan multifaith events, and I counsel people who are having problems caused by those who misunderstand their religion. In all three instances, people have asked me to suggest a book that would provide factual information about Wicca; they want a resource to help someone understand Wiccan beliefs without teaching them how to be Wiccan. Now, back when I became Wiccan, only a handful of books about Wicca existed, and many of them could be found only in specialty stores. Nowadays entire sections of bookstores are dedicated to the subject of Wicca, so when I couldn't find a book explaining Wiccan beliefs to non-Wiccans, I was a bit surprised. I could see why people wanted such a book, but a suitable volume didn't seem to exist. I looked around in astonishment at the hundreds of books currently published about Wicca but was unable to find one I would recommend to someone needing that kind of resource.

Discussing this problem with Renda, a High Priestess and friend of mine who had been in Wicca since the early seventies, I told her we needed a book that gives people the basic information and answers the common questions about Wicca but doesn't try to teach them to be Wiccan and thereby give them more information than they want. She looked at me and said, "Why don't you write one?" Thinking she was joking, I chuckled and said, "Oh yeah, like that's going to happen." She gave me a look both penetrating and questioning, a look that seemed to peer into my soul and carefully examine all the motivations and reasons for my actions. It's a look few people can achieve but one she had certainly mastered. She simply said, "Why not? You said someone needs to write the book, and you're *someone*, aren't you? You've been studying Wicca since 1991, you're clergy in two different traditions, and you've spoken to more people and answered more questions about Wicca than most anyone else in this community." I thought, "She's *serious*," and said, "I can't write a book; I barely made it through high school English." Again with the stare, she said, "If you set limitations on yourself, they will be with you forever." Thus began my quest to give people the best possible tool with which to better understand the Wiccan religion and those who practice it.

If you've picked up or been given this book, it is probably because you are either interested in the possibility of pursuing Wicca as a religious path or you know someone who has told you they practice the Wiccan religion. A son or daughter, coworker, friend, or family member has shared with you something very personal about their life. Sharing this information is usually a very scary proposition. By disclosing that they practice Wicca, a person risks the real possibility of rejection, ostracism, and alienation from people they care about very much, and the closer you are to this person, the more they have risked by sharing their religious convictions with you. By opening this book, you are saying you are not going to condemn them for being different but instead are willing to try to understand their choice of religious paths. The purpose of this book is neither to convert you to Wicca, nor is it to convince you this is the way everyone should live their lives. The purpose of this book is to help you understand why someone would make this choice and to alleviate any fears or concerns you have about their religious practices. After reading this book, I hope people will understand Wicca is simply another variation in the wonderful diversity of world religions, not a sinister force to be feared and reviled.

I'm not asking everyone who reads this book to agree with everything I am presenting; I would be horrified if they did. Many of the answers I present here are questions for which there are no definitive answers. Questions such as why are we here, what happens after we die, and why is there evil in the world are eternal and life-defining questions because they determine how one views the world and interacts with the people in it. We seek the answers to these questions throughout our lives, and as we grow and mature, many of our answers change. As children, simple answers were given to us; however, most people outgrow those answers and seek answers that add more depth and meaning to their lives. Answering these questions for ourselves is part of life's adventure, and if the answers were obvious or handed to us wrapped in pretty paper with a bow, much of the mystery and purpose of life would vanish.

Answering life's eternal questions is a quest for our personal Holy Grail, and if Arthur's Grail knights rode out of Camelot only to find the Grail, swathed in a pretty pink bow, resting at the end of the drawbridge, the story would be a bit boring. Instead, the knights went out separately, each selecting their own dark place where there was no path to begin their quest.[1] Finding our own answers to the eternal questions is our life's quest; it is how we grow as people. These answers are our own Holy Grail, and we must seek these answers within the dark reaches of our own soul.

I am not presuming to claim my musings on the Wiccan religion should be the definitive viewpoint. Wicca has no sacred books. Every book about Wicca is that author's opinion about what Wicca is, and this book is no exception. Most Wiccans will disagree with at least a few of my views. What I am intending to present is a possible Wiccan answer to some difficult questions, and if you are looking for answers and you like any of my answers, use them. If you don't like my answers or feel they aren't right for you, then look within yourself and find your own answers. Try not to simply dismiss an idea offhandedly without considering it. If you don't agree with something I have written, decide why you don't agree. I find I often learn more when I disagree with something I have heard than when I feel the information is correct. Disagreeing causes me to explore the reasons why I feel the statement is incorrect. I try to explore my beliefs and ask myself not only why I think the original statement was wrong but also what I feel would be a more correct statement for me. By examining our beliefs and finding our own answers, great truths are sometimes revealed to us, and we more clearly understand our own spiritual path. If anything I write helps point you in the direction of your own answers, then I am happy to have helped.

Wicca Demystified is not a "Wicca 101" book; it will not teach you how to practice the Wiccan religion. The purpose of this book is not simply to give you knowledge of Wicca, although it will do that. The purpose of this book is to help give you an understanding of Wicca. Knowing someone has many levels: one can know another person as in "I have heard of them," "I work with them," "we went to school together," or even in an intimate sense. However, none of these levels of knowing will provide you with an understanding of that person. A person is more than their name, job, schooling, or whom they have . . . well, you get the idea. Knowledge of a person and understanding of a person are two different things. Knowledge gives one surface facts, paints a picture of the individual, and no matter how detailed or masterfully rendered that picture, it's still only two dimensional, leaving out the heart and soul of the person. Until you discuss personal philosophy with that person, know some of their hopes and dreams, their triumphs and defeats, you will never even begin to understand them. Understanding requires long talks in the middle of the night and tear-filled stories. In a similar way, Wicca is more than its holidays, rituals, and ethics; it is even more than the deities worshiped, although these are important. The understanding of Wicca is in the living, the connection to nature, the ideas on birth, death, and why we are here in the first place. Wicca's soul is in the people who practice it, their hopes, dreams, and reasons for walking a religious path so different from what many view as traditional.

In order for me to show everyone a part of Wicca's soul, I must show them a piece of mine, letting everyone see Wicca as I see it. Until you experience the world through Wiccan eyes, there is no way to truly understand Wicca. My goal is to make this book your eyes with which to glimpse the Wiccan world. I will share with you not only the form of Wicca, but also glimpses into its soul where you can, if only briefly, see the world as a Wiccan does and, through that, possibly understand Wicca. If at times I seem to be attempting to sway people to my point of view, I want to assure everyone this is not my intention. It's only my enthusiasm for the subject that may make it seem that way. People usually experience joy and find comfort in their religion. I want people, for a moment, to experience the joy, comfort, and peace Wiccans find in their religion. This isn't an attempt to bring people around to our point of view; rather, it's an opportunity for them to see why someone else might choose the Wiccan spiritual path.

There is no subject on which all Wiccans will universally agree; therefore, everything I am writing will not be absolutely correct for all Wiccans. Nonjudgmental discussion of different religious ideas can lead to rich and rewarding spiritual dialogues. I would never say a Wiccan who disagrees with me isn't a true Wiccan. Wicca believes there is room in the world for all religions. The religion you practice and the way you practice it is correct for you. There are many variations among the world's religions, and just as there are many denominations or sects within other religions, each one different, but all having certain characteristics in common, there are also many variations among Wiccans, and all of them are valid. A student beginning their study of Wicca is similar to an art student approaching a painting class. Everyone learns the basics of shape, shadow, color and perspective, but each person's finished work, like their Wiccan practice, should have its own style, reflecting their own background and talent. The practices of Wicca are as diverse as one artist's work from another even though they will all have similar techniques. The shades and hues of Wicca are varied enough to paint a sunset over a field of wildflowers. However, there are concepts that most Wiccan traditions share, and these commonalties are what I am presenting here.

This book is an interactive guide to Wicca and is divided into two sections. The first is a basic overview of Wicca, things you need to know in order to understand the basics of the Wiccan religion. The second section is in a question-and-answer format and covers more advanced topics. Many of the questions in the second section are possible Wiccan answers to spiritual questions with which all religions struggle. Each chapter in the first part is followed by a list of questions related to the material in that chapter, which are answered in the second part. Since this is an interactive book, you the reader get to choose your own path through the book. My intention is for people to read the answers to any questions they are curious about immediately upon finishing the chapter. However, some people may choose to read the first part of the book in its entirety, saving the questions until they have completely finished the first part. Other readers, only wanting the absolutely essential information, may choose to skip the questions entirely. The choice of how you utilize the questions in the second part of the book is, of course, entirely up to you.

Those of you who are reading carefully may have noticed that I am using forms of "they" as a gender-neutral singular pronoun rather than the more grammatically proper "he." Please don't write letters to inform me that this practice isn't grammatically correct; my wife, the English professor, has already quoted the correct rule to me. I have never liked using "he" because it seems to exclude half the population, even though people will argue that it is proper and not exclusionary. In response to the proper English people, I would like to point out that when I substituted "she" as the gender-neutral singular pronoun, I seemed to have a large percentage of readers wondering why I was only writing about women. The use of "they" as a gender-neutral singular, while not officially correct, has been gaining acceptance in business and professional writing in recent years. I thank you for your indulgence and for those English purists in the crowd, please try to keep the flinching to a minimum.

Wicca Demystified is an overview of Wiccan beliefs, practices, philosophy, and spirituality. A practicing Wiccan will probably find little surprising in this book. However, if you are trying to understand what Wicca is and why someone would follow this path, then this book is for you.

PART ONE

Basic Understanding

WHAT A PERSON NEEDS TO KNOW
TO GAIN A BASIC UNDERSTANDING
OF WICCANS AND THEIR RELIGION

ONE

The Beginning

What is all this about anyway?

The best place to start with any explanation is at the beginning, and the beginning of Wicca dates far back into antiquity. As far as can be told, people all over the globe have always had religious beliefs. Early people seemed to honor the spirits of the animals upon which they depended for survival. Hunter/gatherer societies worshiped deities of the Earth, the elements, and the animals they hunted. Their lives were tied to the Earth, and they respected the animals on which their existence depended. They developed rituals honoring the sacrifice of the animals who were their food, often offering the preys' blood back to the Earth in the belief that through the ritual the animal would be reborn to be hunted again.[1]

Time progressed, and religion became more involved as people changed from hunter/gatherer societies to agricultural societies. In an agricultural society, people worshiped both gods and goddesses representing not only the Earth but also the seasons, the weather, and the crops. People honored the changing of the seasons and the changing of life. Birth and death became sacred mysteries, and life happened within a "wheel"—the seasons of planting, growing, harvesting, and the dead of winter before the rebirth that came with the next planting season. Many people felt that since the Earth provided for them they were a part of the Earth, connected to the same cycle of birth, growth, death, and rebirth that governed the rest of the Earth. People felt all life was sacred and full of Divine energy, so people identified with Deity, believing Deity was a part of them as well as a part of all things.[2]

With the invention of mathematics, religion gained even more complex elements as people began to look toward the stars as well as Earth. Reasoning that the cosmos was the template upon which all life was built, people began to project Deity into the vastness of space.[3] Deity no longer was a part of the people; now gods and goddesses were located on mountaintops or in space. People began to no longer identify with Deity but viewed Deity in some relationship to people such as parent to child. With this shift from an internal to an external Deity, people were no longer viewed as part of Deity and could not be responsible for their own worship. The responsibility for religious observance usually fell to a professional priestly caste whose job it was to interpret the messages of Deity and relate them to the people.[4] Writing provided a means to record religious traditions and rules, which were recorded and interpreted again by the priests. The written texts enabled priests and warriors to carry religious beliefs far and wide, imposing them on conquered people, displacing the religious traditions of the indigenous people and forcing them to follow the religion of the conquerors. Valuing strength and power, the religions of the conquerors tended to become increasingly more and more patriarchal, relegating female forms of Deity to minor roles or removing them completely.

Obviously, the evolution of religion is much more complex than I have presented here and varies greatly depending on the culture. Through the years and with the world becoming more urbanized and industrialized, people have lost much of their connection with the Earth. Few realize when the seasons change, and growing food, tending animals, and other skills on which our ancestors relied to survive are completely unknown to most people in our modern technological world. The loss of a female version of Deity is also something of which many people are becoming acutely aware; some believe the world might be more peaceful if the male tendency toward aggression were tempered by the female energy of compassion. Many people have felt this separation from the feminine Divine and the world around them and have desired some way to reconnect with the Earth and Deity in a society they perceive as having become sterile and left them feeling hollow. Many people have begun to desire a system of worship that emphasizes both a reconnection with nature and an integration of both the feminine and masculine forms of Deity. This brings us to the environment that has led to the rise in popularity of Wicca.

Wicca is a religion that practitioners believe is both relevant to our modern world and honors the religions of our ancestors. Wicca encompasses many religious traditions that base their form of worship on Celtic, Egyptian, Greek, Scandinavian, African, Native American, Sumerian, or other ancient religions. Wicca bases its worship on these ancient traditions; however, many times reliable sources are scarce, and worshiping exactly as an ancient people, even if it were possible, would have little relevance to our modern society where television, cars, and electricity form a world which would be unrecognizable to the people who lived and worshiped thousands of years ago. The current forms of Wiccan worship are based on the mythology of these ancient traditions. The myths, concepts, beliefs, and practices used in Wicca are not new; the ideas are extremely old and have simply been adapted and reinterpreted to meet the needs of a modern world. Wiccans of various traditions have gleaned what they can from ancient traditions and formed the Wiccan religion into something meaningful to their life in the twenty-first century. This makes Wicca either one of the oldest religions on the planet or one of the newest, depending on one's perspective. Some Wiccans trace the roots of their tradition back centuries, others for only a few years. Regardless of the age and origins, current Wiccan traditions help people clear away the brambles from their life's path, making life more meaningful for them.

The Wiccan religion is not some exclusive club open to only a select few individuals. It's available to anyone who shares the Wiccan view of Deity and the world around us and who has a desire to be

Wiccan. Wiccans usually share the belief in a Deity that can be perceived as both a male God and a female Goddess and may be worshiped in groups, often called covens, or alone as a solitary practitioner. Wiccans share a reverence for nature and celebrate the cycles of the Earth. Wicca has a strong ethical structure based on a belief that everything has a right to exist if it follows a path of harmony, and nothing should be unnecessarily harmed. Wiccan traditions may differ in the names they use for Deity and the specific rituals used for worship. However, each tradition fulfills the spiritual needs of the people following that tradition, and one tradition is not intrinsically better than another. Wicca is an experiential religion; that is, the experience of spirit is very personal, and since no two people experience life the same way, no two Wiccans worship in exactly the same way. Two Wiccans may worship in a similar fashion, but each person's worship will be colored by their own life, making Wicca a very different spiritual experience for each individual. Wicca is nature-based, providing a link to the Earth many people feel is lacking in today's technology-based world. It honors both male and female deities, which some feel offers women and men a more balanced view of Divinity and could lead to more equality between the sexes. Wicca is a legitimate religion whose system of worship is uplifting, brings peace, and is spiritually fulfilling for its followers. Wicca provides practitioners answers to life's eternal questions of where we came from, why we are here, and where we are going. Worship is centered around eight holidays that are celebrated throughout the year, the cycles of the moon, and rites of passage that mark changes in our lives.

Wiccan, Witch, and Pagan

Before we get too far, I want to make sure everyone understands the difference between the words *Wiccan*, *Witch*, and *Pagan* because these three words will be used frequently if you have any interaction with someone who is Wiccan. Keeping the meanings of these words separate can be a rather daunting task for someone not familiar with the terms. I've even known quite a few people who were Wiccans,

Witches, or Pagans who really didn't know the differences between the terms and tended to use the words improperly. The confusion is easy to understand given the fact that some people toss the three terms around as if they were completely interchangeable, which they are not. The problem is all three terms are umbrella terms, and the groups they describe frequently overlap. For those who might not know, an umbrella term is a word which covers or describes several different groups; for example, the word musician is an umbrella term which covers anyone who plays a musical instrument whether they are a concert violinist or a kazoo player in a jug band. The diversity of groups sheltered under each of the umbrellas of Wiccan, Witch, and Pagan are as different as concert violinists are from kazoo players. Definitions of each term vary, and how many groups each term covers depends on which definition one uses.

Wiccan refers specifically to someone who practices some form of the Wiccan religion. There are many traditions in the Wiccan religion, each having differences in practice but similarities in ethical structure and worship. The different Wiccan traditions are similar to sects or denominations within other religions, each practicing the same religion but in slightly different ways. Therefore, people can be Dianic, Gardnerian, Celtic, Isian, Eclectic, or any of a host of other Wiccan traditions.

Witch refers to someone who practices magick. (The spelling "magick" is used to differentiate true magick from stage illusions.) If spell work or the use of energy is employed to cause changes to themselves or the world, then that person might refer to themselves as a Witch. Remember, *Witch* is a gender-neutral term and applies to both men and women. Vastly different groups can and do refer to themselves as Witches. Practitioners of Voodoo and Santeria, and even gypsies, might call themselves Witches even though there is no religious connection between them; each is a separate religion with vastly different practices and ethical structures. There are even some Christians, Jews, and Hindus who practice a form of magick and sometimes call themselves Witches. Therefore, witchcraft itself isn't a religion; rather, it typically refers to the use of magick within or outside of a religious structure. Within this book, however, since I am specifically talking about Wicca, the word Witch will refer to a Wiccan Witch unless otherwise noted.

The definition of the word *Pagan* varies widely based on what the person wishes to imply by its use. At various times Pagan may be defined as someone who isn't Christian, as people who aren't Jewish, Christian, or Muslim,[5] or even as the *Oxford Advanced Learners Dictionary* defines it, "a person who holds religious beliefs that are not part of any of the world's main religions."[6] The academic definition of Pagan is someone who follows either the Greek or Roman religions, but modern Pagans have expanded that definition to encompass Egyptian, Celtic, Sumerian, Nordic, or any number of other ancient religious traditions. *Pagan* has been used to describe idol worshipers and country dwellers;[7] Pagan can also be a term of nobility or used as a derogatory word for people the speaker considers ignorant, unclean, or perverse. There is obviously a great deal of disagreement in how the word should be properly used. A good definition for Pagan, at least from a Wiccan viewpoint, comes from *Wicca: A Guide for the Solitary Practitioner* by Scott Cunningham: "Today used as a general term for followers of Wicca and other magical, shamanistic, and polytheistic religions."[8] This definition, or one similar to this, would be given by most people who practice a Pagan religion. Therefore, like the word Witch, the term Pagan can refer to a number of differing religious groups that share some similarities in beliefs but have differences in practices, rituals, and ethics.

Many Wiccans use the terms *Wiccan, Witch,* and *Pagan* interchangeably because all three terms apply to Wicca and may be switched around if everyone understands they are working solely within a Wiccan structure. The problems start to occur when one tries to use these terms too loosely, shifting the context of the conversation into and out of a Wiccan structure, because:

- Not all Pagans are Wiccan
- Not all Pagans are Witches
- Wiccans are typically Witches
- Not all Witches are Wiccan
- Not all Witches are Pagan

Someone who follows a Voodoo path might call themselves a Witch and may or may not call themselves Pagan, but would never refer to themselves as Wiccan. A New Age practitioner might say they were Pagan, but probably wouldn't characterize themselves as a Witch or a Wiccan.

Too many differences in meaning exist between the words *Wiccan, Witch,* and *Pagan* for them to be freely used interchangeably. Each refers to its own subset of people or religious groups, which may or may not identify with one another. However, none of these terms intends to convey evil or violence and should hold no dread or fear for anyone.

When people learn someone has a different religious belief system, the natural question for them to ask is "So what do you believe?" While this is an easy question to ask, it is much more difficult to answer. Wiccan spiritual practices are personal and, therefore, somewhat different for each worshiper. Wicca is a system of worship that honors the Divine spirit within all things and defies being boiled down to one or two bullet points. Because Wiccan worship is based on each individual's experience of spirit, Wicca becomes not so much what a person believes but instead a part of who that person is. Asking what a Wiccan believes is rather like asking a person who they are. Someone could tell you their name, but that tells you very little about them, or they could tell you what they do for a living or for fun, and while that gives you more information about them, a person isn't defined by their job or hobbies. To get to know a person, one has to be around them, share the person's thoughts and feelings, hopes and dreams, and finally one would begin to understand something about who that person is.

Understanding Wicca is similar to understanding a person; until you live it, until you share the Wiccan path with Divinity, understanding why someone would follow Wicca is difficult, and any bullet-point explanation seems flat and sterile. Also, any answer I give will be completely valid only for me; other Wiccans will, quite probably, have similar beliefs, but they may vary on points. However, since it is the purpose of this book to explain what Wicca is, I will attempt to explain it from my perspective. The attempt is like an artist who, only equipped with a pencil, tries to capture the majesty of a rainbow. The artist knows from the onset that they can capture the form of the rainbow, but the hues and tones, the true beauty of the subject, are impossible to convey in a monochromatic medium. One has to personally experience the rainbow to truly know its beauty.

What I believe

What do you believe? This is such a simple question to ask, but the answer is complex, personal and, therefore, difficult to give. It's not that Wiccans don't know what we believe; it's that our beliefs are so much a part of who we are that finding the correct words or a good starting point can be a challenge. The following is a list of my personal beliefs, many of which are shared by a great number of Wiccans. Other Wiccans probably won't have exactly the same list, but their list will be similar on many points. This is the best way I know to answer the question in a bullet-point format. Some of the points may seem confusing, but I hope to clear up any quandaries as we go on.

- I believe the world is a place for us to learn; it is beautiful and perfect the way it is. The world is full of love and goodness, and the more people who perceive it that way, the more it will become so.
- Deity created nature, and therefore It reveals Itself through nature.
- We are all connected to everything around us; the fate of a forest or a deer is tied to our own.
- We are not our body. Bodies are born and bodies die, but our spirit is eternal.
- Divinity is without limits; It is not only everything we can imagine, It is more than we have the capacity to imagine.
- Deity is not male, female, animal, or human in form; It is simultaneously all of these and none.
- The Divine is one; the perceptions of the Divine are many. Just because two people's perceptions are different doesn't mean one of them is wrong.
- Deity is a part of everyone, but not everyone is the same, so we are free to perceive Deity in whatever form our culture, heritage, or conscience dictates.

- Belief in one's perception of Deity is not an excuse to suppress, harm, or enslave others. Everyone has the right to worship Deity in whatever way they see fit.
- We, like everyone and everything around us, are part of the Divine.
- All people are perfect in their own way; each person has a bit of Divinity inside them, and they should be honored for that reason.
- Life is how we honor Deity, and living life completely and to our full potential honors the Deity within.
- Love is the energy that runs the universe; anger and hatred are the absence of love.
- People are inherently positive, and they become negative when they are pulled from their natural connection to Deity.
- Good and bad are value judgments we put on events. Everything happens for a reason, and the Divine knows the "why" for all actions and events. We, however, lack the Divine's perspective to immediately see the reasons.
- Thoughts are things: what we think, we become, and the way we expect the world to be, it is. If we expect the world to be full of hardship, suffering will be what we find.
- In order to love and be kind to others, one first has to learn to love and be kind to oneself. It is difficult to understand others if we don't understand ourselves.
- If you can't find what you're looking for inside yourself, you will never find it outside yourself.

Wiccan beliefs are very personal and vary somewhat from individual to individual. Our beliefs are very important because they color how we perceive ourselves, other people, the world, and our place in the universe. Our beliefs become glasses through which we perceive life. If we believe the world is a place of joy and love, the lenses of our perception will lead us to see the world as such. When unfortunate events happen, we will simply choose to see them as opportunities rather than trials and everyone as a possible friend. If, however, the world is viewed as a place of suffering and evil, we will judge everyone and everything through those lenses, perceiving people's actions with suspicion and fear. Our personal beliefs and perceptions of the world are our own to choose, but they are influenced by our choice of Deity. The world around us is often seen as a reflection of Deity, so our perception of the world is colored by how we believe Deity relates to the world. Is Deity part of the world or separate from creation? Are people inherently good, or are they mired in evil? Do we cut ourselves off from those who believe differently, or do we dive into the world and experience the spectrum of humanity's beliefs? Our beliefs about the nature of Deity affect all these aspects of our lives.

For a deeper understanding of Wicca, please read:

Why did they have to tell me they were Wiccan? Page 91

Why did they hide the fact they were Wiccan from us? Page 92

What does the word *Wicca* mean? Page 98

Is Wicca a real religion? Page 99

Can anyone be a Wiccan? Page 102

Why do people change religions? Page 103

Is Wicca a cult? Page 106

Is the Wiccan religion safe? Page 113

Why would people call themselves a Witch? Page 114

Why would a person use myths in religion when myths aren't true? Page 128

TWO

Deity

What Wiccans worship

Throughout time people have worshiped Deity in every imaginable form. Goddesses and gods in forms ranging from human perfection to the fantastical have been honored by every culture on the planet. People have worshiped in isolation and in enormous groups, peacefully shared space with their neighbors, and fought bloody wars in the name of their deities. Every culture in recorded history has worshiped, honored, and sacrificed to their gods, and each usually believes its god(s) were the most powerful, correct, or true deities. However, no one has ever been able to prove any Deity has ever existed, much less that any one version of Deity was more correct than another. Voltaire provided a convincing argument when he said he believed in the existence of God because "I cannot dream that this watch exists and has no watchmaker."[1]

Unfortunately, however, as compelling as this argument may be, it still offers only his personal opinion without any empirical proof. Now don't get me wrong. I'm not trying to argue against the existence of Deity; I am trying to point out that no matter how strong an individual's personal convictions are, it is impossible to prove any of the various deities worshiped on this planet even exist, much less which one might be the correct variation. Belief in Deity has ultimately always come down to one thing—faith. Maybe Deity can't be proven for a reason. Perhaps, as Douglas Adams put it, God refuses to prove He exists, "for proof denies faith, and without faith I am nothing."[2] Now, while this argument may or may not be true, the point is that from an intellectual level, none of us knows for sure.

However, the fact that Deity can't be proven on an intellectual level has never stopped people from taking a leap of faith and believing in Deity on an emotional level, and, boy, do we get emotional about our vision of Deity! Some people seem to feel that if someone disagrees with the way they personally view Deity, then that person is not only wrong but is also dangerous. Debates, fights, and wars have erupted between people because of differing religious beliefs. In almost every conflict, each side firmly believes their view of Deity is either better or, more often, the only correct one. Both sides of every war have believed God was on their side, and winning the war is often viewed as a triumph of the victor's Deity, divine validation of the winner's political system, or confirmation that the winner was the one who was morally correct. This line of reasoning fueled the "might makes right" mentality of the Renaissance and the idea of the divine right of kings. Legal disputes were at one time settled by combat, reasoning that God would never allow a guilty person to triumph over a just person.

The common stand on differing viewpoints about Deity is an either/or stance, where either the first person is correct or the second person is; one has to be right and the other wrong, or possibly both are wrong. Consider for a moment another possibility: what if *both* of them could be correct? Impossible, some say; how could something be both when the two visions may differ radically? Consider again Voltaire's argument; there may not be the possibility of having a watch without a watchmaker, but could the watch, no matter how finely crafted, understand the watchmaker or the purpose it was created to serve? Our personified watch ticks on and moves in its crystalline regularity but has no real idea why. It doesn't understand its cogs or springs; the watch is happy just to live and tick and move its hands around in a circle envisioning that since it is formed in magnificent complexity, its creator must be some even more fantastic watch that formed all watches after its likeness. Could it be that we, like the watch, are incapable of understanding the vastness of our creator? Could every image and description we have for Deity be only a tiny fragment of the reality of Deity, whose transcendent magnificence is more than we have the possibility of understanding? I realize people are not watches and Deity is not a watchmaker, but ask yourself if you believe people are any more intelligent or aware than that watch is when compared to Divinity.

Wiccan view of other religions

There is a story used to describe Hinduism that also applies to Wicca. The story tells of an anthropologist who wanted to catalogue each and every Hindu deity. He went from village to village from the north of India to the south and compiled copious notes listing and describing tens of thousands of Hindu deities. His desire was to be thorough, and not wanting to miss even a single deity, he constantly asked people if anyone knew the exact number of deities worshiped in Hinduism. He was told that an ancient guru in the mountains was said to know the exact number of deities Hindus worship, so he found the correct peak and began the arduous climb, trying to find this reclusive teacher. Finally, he came upon the guru's cave; upon entering he sat down at the feet of the guru and asked him if he truly knew how many deities there are in Hinduism. "Oh yes," the guru replied, "I know how many there are." Licking his lips, the anthropologist waited for the answer, holding his breath in anticipation. "There is only one." The anthropologist was indignant; how could there be just one when he had notebooks full of names, not to mention legal pads and the backs of several receipts covered with notes? "Well, if there is only one," exploded the anthropologist, brandishing binders as several scribbled cocktail napkins floated to the floor, "which of these is the correct one?" "All of them," replied the guru, "Deity is one; our perceptions of Deity are many."

Like most religions, Wiccan theology can be discussed in concise terms that are easy to understand, or they can be debated in deep theological discussions that tend to obfuscate precepts to all but a few theologians. Because the purpose of this book is to explain Wicca in a way that is easy for everyone to understand, I am presenting a simplified version of Wiccan theology. Wicca doesn't view itself as being at odds with other religions because Wiccans typically see all religions' views of Divinity as a part of the whole, as if each view of Divinity were a piece of stained glass, beautiful on its own, but which if assembled correctly could create a stunning window revealing a portion of the majesty of Deity. Therefore, most Wiccans view all religions as valid for the devotee and every vision of Deity as correct—incomplete but correct. This is why Wiccans don't proselytize or worry about people disagreeing with our religious views; we can allow people to have a different religious viewpoint without believing it diminishes our own.

Wiccan view of Deity

Wicca has many perceptions of Deity, but ultimately there is only one. Throughout time, people have called this one transcendent Deity by many names; some call this Divinity the Great Spirit, the Is, the One, or the Order. It can be called by many names, but in this book, I am going to call this one power simply "Deity" or "Divinity." I am not going to call this one Deity *God* because, even though *God* is a title used for Deity, usually when that Deity is perceived as male, many in the Western world have come to view the title *God* as the actual name of Deity, and I don't want to appear blasphemous. Also, the word *God* frequently conjures up an image, especially in the Western mind, of an old man who is sitting in the clouds looking down upon us, and this is not the image I want to evoke. Wiccans perceive Deity to be manifested in both male and female forms. The archetypal female form is referred to as "the Goddess" and the archetypal male form as "the God." When I do use the word *God* within this book, I will be referring to either this archetypal male form of Deity or one of the many ways in which this male form of Deity can be perceived. It is not intended to refer to the specific Deity worshiped in the occidental religions by the Muslims, Jews, and Christians.

To Wiccans, this transcendent Divinity is the ultimate expression of Deity. It is not male or female, good or bad. It does not judge actions or events as right or wrong. It is more than we can possibly imagine, and Its only concern is that the universe functions in harmony. If we live our lives and walk in harmony with Deity, our lives go relatively smoothly, and things we consider good happen not because we are being rewarded for being "good" or because we belong to a certain religion, but rather because we are flowing in harmony with the rhythm of the Universe. Consider a river: it is always easier to flow downstream with the current than to try to swim upstream against it. The river carries everyone along equally; it doesn't matter to the river what race, religion, color, creed, or sexual orientation someone is. People can be any religion, and as long as they are flowing in harmony with the Universe, their lives will have fewer bumps. It is when they begin struggling and thrashing against the current that their lives become difficult.

Wicca is a nature-based religion that honors both male and female aspects of Deity as Goddess and God. Wicca views Deity as transcendent; that is, Deity is not only more than we have understood, but more than we can ever understand. As humans, we look into the universe and try to understand the universal order that controls the cosmos, but it is beyond our comprehension. Deity, to us, is at once everything and nothing; it is the duality of yin and yang, simultaneously all possibilities and their opposites. It is all things spiritual and material. The Universe itself is Deity, and everything in the universe is a portion of Divinity. Any deity that we, in our limited understanding, can imagine is possible because this Divinity is everything. Therefore, throughout time humanity has reached out into the cosmos and felt the presence of a goddess or god who is in "charge of" or who guides our existence, helping comfort us in a crisis, and indeed that god or goddess exists. When we focus upon or pray to that goddess or god, we receive the help, inspiration, or comfort we request, because as part of the One, that goddess or god becomes real for the person honoring it. One person can say, "I see Goddess as a mother, compassionate and comforting," and Deity answers, "I can be that." Another person says, "I see God as a father, strong and protective," and Deity answers, "I can be that also." Every vision of Deity can be real and vital, with none of them being any more or less real than the others. How can all of them be real? Because it's Deity. It always amazes me when people in one breath claim Deity formed the awesomeness of the universe and keeps it functioning smoothly and then in the next breath start to tell me all the things Deity can't be and can't do. It's Deity: It can do everything; It can be everything; and It can be and do everything simultaneously.

Trying to put into words something that can't adequately be explained and can only be experienced may leave people very dazed and confused. Explaining the transcendent with words is like trying to describe a Van Gogh painting to a person who is blind; having never seen color, they can't understand the changes in hue, and unseen sunflowers or stars would not affect them in the same way they affect others. The only way to understand Deity is to feel it, for one's spirit to experience what cannot be expressed in words. This experience of spirit is possible in all religions when a person moves beyond the form of the religion and touches the spirit inside. Divinity is the source of all emotion; It is pure love, compassion, and peace that is beyond the human limits of ego and personality and, therefore, doesn't care what we call It or what face we put on It.

Deity is more than we can comprehend, which makes people uncomfortable, so humanity anthropomorphizes Deity, puts human faces on the Divine, gives It personalities and emotions, and calls It Zeus or Gaia or Isis or a myriad of other names. Giving form to Deity makes us secure because, if Deity looks like us and acts like us, we can understand It, define our relationship with It, and use our perception of that relationship to make sense of everything that happens in the world. Deity can become our parent and we Deity's children, or Deity can become master and we Deity's servants. We want to relate to Deity in a form that is comfortable to us, and an incomprehensible transcendent is not comfortable to most people. A central theme to some religious beliefs is whether or not Deity created people in Its image or people created images of Deity to look like us. Either approach is simply an attempt to comprehend the incomprehensible, and to that end people have imagined that deities have human faces and human names. We give our perceptions of Deity our emotions, making them strong, angry, wise, vengeful, loving, and jealous. These emotions make the deities something we can relate to, and if we can relate to them, we imagine they, in turn, can relate to us. Putting a familiar face on Divinity makes us feel secure and special because Deity then becomes somewhat like us.

Every society has had its own deities, and most cultures think their deities are the true ones, the real ones, or are better than everyone else's. However, from a Wiccan point of view, all people have done is to metaphorically reach out and grab a part of Deity and anthropomorphize it into a goddess or god. This means every goddess or god that has ever been worshiped, prayed to, sacrificed to, or carved in stone is part of Divinity. Therefore, all goddesses and gods are true goddesses and gods, not complete, but a representation we, as humans, can understand. Therefore, while it may seem that Wiccans worship a plethora of divinities, we actually honor one transcendent Deity that Wicca perceives as both the Goddess and the God. These two forms of Deity have then been anthropomorphized into all the deities that have ever been worshiped on this planet.

Wicca defies being pigeonholed into any single type of relationship with Deity. Wiccans may view themselves as monotheistic, choosing to identify with the one transcendent Divinity. Wiccans may also be ditheistic, choosing to identify with the archetypal Goddess and God, seeing all images of Deity originating in these archetypal forms and themselves as part of the Goddess and God, their power flowing through them. Many Wiccans see themselves as polytheistic. Polytheistic Wiccans may believe the goddesses and gods are distinct spirits living on a higher plane, each having its own unique personality. These divine spirits choose to interact with people by choice and may take on a human appearance to better interact with people. These spirits are believed to be the source of the pantheons of deities worshiped by different cultures throughout the ages. Wiccans who worship in this way may choose goddesses or gods from any pantheon of deities worshiped by people throughout history or may choose to work with only one historical pantheon. Some even see themselves surrounded by the goddesses and gods who comfort, protect, and teach them, somewhat as people of other religions might see themselves surrounded by angels or saints. Wiccans could also be henotheistic, choosing one form of Deity to worship exclusively but not denying the existence of others.

Since most Wiccans view the elemental forces of Earth, Air, Fire, and Water to have a spirit or consciousness and may feel the animals, plants, and rocks all have a spirit, Wicca could be called animistic. Also, a great number of Wiccans see Deity as the Universe, which is one living creative force, and feel they, and everything else, are all parts of this Deity, which would make Wicca pantheistic. Wiccans are free to view Deity in whatever way they are most comfortable. Each option is acceptable, and one often finds Wiccans using each view of Deity at different times. Often a person who is pantheistic or who usually honors the Goddess as an archetypical form will assign a name to Her when there is a specific need, choosing a name of a goddess who has been viewed to control that energy. For example, if a woman has a sick child, rather than ask the archetypical Goddess, a mother might appeal for healing to Brigit, Isis, or Kuan Yin, Goddesses known through mythology for healing and compassion.

How perceptions affect actions

As humans, the way we perceive Deity affects the way we view and interact with the world around us. In Wicca the perception of Deity is very different from the way Deity is usually viewed in Western religions. In typical Western understanding, Deity is viewed as the creator; people, other animals, and the Earth are its creations. They are separate from Deity, and each person is his or her own unique individual separate from all others. As individuals we determine what our relationship to Deity is and live our lives according to how we view that relationship. Wicca usually sees Deity as both the creator and the creation. The difference between the Western and Wiccan creation myths is that in the first, God spoke and it was; in the second, Deity imagined and It became. All things were created from

Deity and are therefore part of Deity, and each person is connected to every other person and to everything around us by that shared Divine spark. Wiccans believe if a person wants to see Deity—look around. Deity is in everything, and like a mosaic, the more people, animals, and things one assembles, the more clearly Deity is seen. Deity is in all things; we identify with the Divine in everything and live according to that identification.

Wicca also views Deity as something both imminent and personal. To us the Divine flows through and touches everything. Deity is not something people are separated from and to which they are trying to return. Deity is all around us and part of us. Our spirits are part of the Divine, and therefore Divinity is within us. From a Western viewpoint this sounds very odd. It sounds egocentric, as if Wiccans are saying we are God. However, what we are saying is not that we are a part of Divinity and no one else is; we're saying *everyone* and *everything* around us is a beautiful and valuable part of the Divine. The birds, trees, rocks, and platypi are all part of Divinity. From this viewpoint, everyone has a connection with the Divine rather than feeling separated from It. The Divine, to us, is something of which we are a part. Wicca has an identification with Deity rather than a relationship to it, and we try to manifest It in our lives. To Wiccans, being spirit-filled is not something that comes from without; it is something that comes from within. Every day we try to behave more like the Divinity of which we are a part and to respect other people, even if we don't agree with their views because we are honoring the Divinity within them, and by honoring the Divinity within them, we honor us all.

It's a matter of perspective. When a person walks into a garden, do they see themselves as a separate entity that has entered the garden, or do they see themselves as becoming a piece of that garden? What defines the garden? To me the garden is more than a hydrangea or rose bush; it's more than the ceramic gnome or willow tree. The garden is not one thing; it's the totality of all, including the people. When we enter that garden, we and the garden are one. We become a piece of it, and it becomes a piece of us.

Dallas' Arboretum is an absolutely breathtaking garden; of course, calling the Arboretum a garden is like calling Buckingham Palace a house. When I go there, the experience is not the plants or trees; it's not the statuary or fountains; it's not the birds, squirrels, or butterflies—it's all of that. The Garden is comprised of the children squealing with laughter as they run on the grass, the wonder of a child as they watch a butterfly softly land on the petals of a flower, the ecstasy of a couple holding hands like young lovers even after years of marriage, the enraptured expression of an elderly lady as a breeze carries the fragrance of azaleas past her wheelchair, my wife walking with me because the flowers are always more stunning when she is there, and me, a piece of this garden which is ever changing, vibrant and fantastically different every second of every day. This garden with all its beautiful parts is a piece of Deity, which is a dynamic combination of every person, flower, bird, tree planet, star, and galaxy in the universe.

Wiccan view of nature

Because Wiccans view all of nature as part of Deity, some people get the mistaken idea we worship nature. Wiccans do not worship nature; we revere nature as part of the Divine and honor it. We believe the seasons of the Earth and the cycles of the moon are metaphors for the Goddess and the God. Yes, we realize the moon is a large rock orbiting the Earth and the sun is a huge ball of burning gas. Wiccans don't worship the sun and moon as objects; we revere them as symbols of the Goddess and the God. Imagine you wake up one morning disheveled and grumpy. As you lumber to the kitchen complaining about the lack of coffee, your spouse says, "Boy, are you a bear this morning." She doesn't mean you are actually transforming into a bear; she is speaking metaphorically. In the same way, someone who says the moon is the Goddess and the sun is the God is speaking metaphorically. We view the changing of the seasons and length of days as a symbol of the life of the God. The monthly cycles of the moon are symbols of the Maiden, Mother, and Crone aspects of the Goddess.

All life to us is sacred, and we truly believe we are only strands on the web of life. What we do affects not only us but everyone and everything around us as well. Therefore, we try to walk as softly upon the Earth as we possibly can, knowing the Earth is our Mother, who gave birth to us and will give birth to our great-grandchildren if we don't destroy Her ability to sustain us.

The Triple Goddess

She is Artemis, She is Cybele, and She is Hecate. The Goddess is one, but her names and forms are many. Wicca is sometimes criticized for having many different deities; however, this is a misunderstanding of Wiccan theology. Wiccans typically view all goddesses ever worshiped in any culture on Earth as aspects of the same Goddess. People want to believe we are so important to Deity that we were made to look like It. Almost every culture's deities carry the physical characteristics of the indigenous people who worshiped them. Oya, the African Goddess of the Wind, is dark skinned, resembling the Yoruban people who worship Her, while the Goddess Tonantzin resembles the Central American people who worshiped Her as the Earth Goddess before the arrival of Spanish invaders on that continent.

Throughout time, many women have sought the Goddess in their culture. Today, many women still seek the Goddess in part because for so long they have been denied a Deity who is female, one they feel will better understand what it is like to be a woman, and their spirit cries out for Her. People need to feel Deity relates to them and their lives. Because of this, the Goddess has three primary aspects, that of the Maiden, the Mother, and the Crone. This ancient female trinity allows a woman to see the Goddess within herself at any age. These three aspects of the Goddess are archetypal images of women and therefore appear in the goddesses of almost every culture around the world throughout recorded time. Within each of us, women and men, is part of each aspect of the Goddess waiting to share Her wisdom; the Goddess's influence has shaped how people have viewed Deity from the beginning of time.

The Goddess as the Maiden is the young carefree aspect of womanhood. She is the sprouting plants and the blooming of the flowers. She is the girl in love who braids flowers into her hair and the young woman pregnant with her first child. She is the Muse who inspires creativity and the first light entering an infant's eyes. She is the potential within all things. Her season is late winter and spring, when life is returning to the world. Her symbol is the waxing crescent phase of the moon, which is growing toward motherhood. The Maiden form of the Goddess is essentially the same whether She is the Anglo-Saxon Goddess Eostre or the Roman Goddess Lucina.

The Goddess as the Mother is one of the most pervasive images of Deity throughout the mythologies of the world. This aspect of the Goddess is the primordial Mother who gives birth to children and suckles them at Her breast. She watches over families and children. She is a Goddess of hearth and home. The Mother is the Earth in the summer and the harvest as she pours forth the food that nourishes us. She is the Goddess of artists, weavers, and potters who are creating things born in their imaginations. Her symbol is the full moon, which bathes the world in Her radiance. Whether she is the Iroquois Goddess Ataentsic or the Egyptian Goddess Isis, she is Mother.

The Goddess as the Crone is the aspect most feared by people, because She is old age and death. The Crone represents the wisdom gained through a lifetime of experience and the patience to wait. She is the matriarch watching over Her family, protecting them from mistakes. She is the power of the storm and the stillness of the grave. She holds death in one hand, but in the other she holds the keys to rebirth and regeneration. In many cultures, the Goddess of Childbirth is a crone; she is the grandmother who walks with people through the veil separating life from death, carrying people from this life into the next. Her time of year is from the final harvest through winter, when the Earth is barren and life is harsh. Her symbol is the waning crescent of the moon as it approaches its dark. Whether She is the Celtic (Kel-tic) Goddess Cerridwen or the Hindu Goddess Kali, she is the Crone.

Aspects of God

The aspects of the God, which have been worshiped throughout time, reflect the various male roles in society. Most of the male deities can be divided into the broad categories of the Hunter, the

Warrior, the Sage, the Trickster, and the Sacrificial God. Each aspect of the God is an archetypal form of maleness, and gods of each type are typically found in most cultures around the world. Each culture has similar male roles, and those cultures have male deities who watch over, protect, and guide the people who fulfill those roles in society. If we, as a society, still worshiped pantheons of deities for those things important to the male life, I am sure we would have gods of sports and finance. Shrines would be built to the computer gods, and we would pray to whatever Deity would keep the grass from needing to be mowed. Our lives would be affected by "Murray," the god of cars and parking, and "Asphalta," the goddess of highways. As with the Goddess, Wiccans typically view all versions of male deities ever worshiped as archetypical aspects of the God-form who is Himself, along with the Goddess, part of the one universal Deity. Therefore, any aspect of God in which people believe becomes real because it is a part of the One and we give it our energy.

Think of the Hunter; for many people this word conjures up images of Robin Hood, wearing green tights and striding through the forest carrying his bow with his quiver over his shoulder. Hunter Gods, however, are rarely viewed as wearing spandex. Gods of the hunt are usually depicted as man and animal hybrids showing their connection not only to man but to the forest as well. When there are goddesses of the hunt, they are usually completely female, and they befriend the animals, protecting them. However, gods of the hunt are typically both man and animal, hunter and prey. They are at once the hunter stalking the stag and the stag whose blood is shed to sustain life. Their stories are of man hunting nature and of nature hunting man because the hunt was a game between man and the animals, which man did not always win. Nature is respected, and the animal that dies is honored for the sacrifice it is making.

The hunter who takes too much or becomes presumptuous finds himself becoming the prey. The Hunter God is the lord of the forest, sometimes referred to as the Horned God because He is usually depicted with antlers or horns to show His connection to nature and the prey, not because He is an image of the Devil. Wicca doesn't have deities who are all evil; for that matter, we don't have deities who are all good either. The gods of an old religion often become the images used for the demons of a newer religion. Ancient images of the Horned God were perverted into Satanic images, and as religion changed, these benevolent images of Deity were twisted and made to seem evil. The Celtic God Herne and the Greek God Pan are both images of the Horned God, who is at once the spirit of the wild places, the hunter, and the prey who dies so we may live.

War has been an unfortunate part of mankind's history, and gods of war find themselves toward the top of many of the ancient pantheons of deities. The War God is a valid aspect for a pantheon of deities because people need to defend themselves or fight when necessary. However, when a people's pantheon of gods is dominated by a god or gods of war, the mentality of the people reflects that, and the society becomes violent. Nomadic tribes who were followers of war gods swept in from harsh deserts or northern climates and pillaged or conquered peaceful communities. Mythologies in the conquered lands would be altered, so the deities of the invading culture would either dominate the earlier deities or replace them completely. Warrior cultures maintained a "might makes right" mentality. They believed their gods taught them that whatever they could take was divinely promised to them and that their god would help them to stomp the weak as long as they obeyed him exactly. War gods were often cruel and jealous, sometimes ordering their followers to decimate villages to the last child. An interesting contrast to the blood lust of male war gods was the Goddess of War, like the Greek Athena, who usually taught that war was for defense and unnecessary violence was to be avoided. A lot can be told about a culture by the violence of its gods, but there is hope that the gods of war are losing their hold on society and the more peaceful gods are returning. Whether it is the Greek God Ares or the Hindu God Indra, they are the embodiment of war.

The Sage is the old man sitting on the mountaintop waiting to dispense wisdom to those with the skill and courage to reach him. Human sages are the older men who have survived the hunt or the battles and now teach others what they have learned along that path, and the Sage aspect of the God is much the same. In mythology, sage gods are very often the kings of the gods; they fought monstrous foes and conquered enemies of staggering proportions, usually before mankind existed. Their battles often resulted in the formation of the Earth and/or the creation of humans. Now they leave the majority of the fighting to the younger gods, coming out of retirement only in dire emergencies. The Sage is the Greek God Zeus, who defeated the Titans in an epic war resulting in the creation of humans, or the Norse God Odin, who slew the frost giant, Ymir, and formed the world from its body. The Sages often bestowed upon humans some gift to be used in the quest for wisdom, as when Odin won the Nordic runes, which are used as a tool for wisdom and divination, and then released them to the gods and humanity.[3] The gift of the Sage is the wisdom gained through the hardships of life, and the wise seek the Sage's wisdom rather than having to personally learn it from the harsh experiences of life.

One of the most pervasive images of the God is as a sacrificial entity. Women are necessary to the survival of humanity and are, therefore, indispensable. Fewer men are necessary to propagate the next generation, so one could view them as more expendable. This might be the reason men became adapted to the more dangerous occupations because their loss would affect society as a whole to a lesser extent than would the loss of women. This is reflected in the characteristics of Deity: the Goddess is usually viewed as eternal, changing Her form from one aspect to the other but never dying, while the God is a sacrificial entity who dies so that humanity will continue to live, is buried or somehow given back to Mother Earth, and is reborn in some way. The Goddess is the Earth, and the Earth is eternal, but the God is the crops grown to be cut down. This image is carried into our culture as Father Time, who dies at midnight to be replaced by Baby New Year. The sacrificial God was the Assyro-Babylonian God Tammuz, who was killed with the harvest, making the world barren; the Goddess Ishtar had to descend into the underworld to bring him back, restoring life to the world. The Egyptian God Osiris's death and rebirth caused the Nile to flood, fertilizing the land. Attis, who was worshiped in Rome beginning early in the second century BCE, was crucified on a pine tree, where his blood flowed down to save the Earth, and resurrected a few days later.[4] All of these and many more have been worshiped as sacrificial gods who give their lives to replenish the Earth so humanity can continue to live.

Trickster deities are in the pantheons of most mythologies to keep us from taking life too seriously. They are the sacred fools, the divine court jesters who force us to laugh at ourselves. The Trickster Gods and Goddesses play pranks on people and cause accidents when people become too full of themselves. They poke fun at the pretentious, lampoon the sacred, and exalt the profane. Tricksters are frequently believed to be shape-shifters who will even impersonate the other deities on occasion, leading people into mischief. Tricksters aren't evil. They're mischievous, and in many myths they end up becoming the butt of their own jokes. Tricksters help us to remember not to take ourselves, or life in general, too seriously. Whether it's the Native American Coyote or the African Ananse, they are mischief, mayhem, and practical jokes; they are Tricksters.

Just as all aspects of Deity have their own unique characteristics and spheres of influence, each goddess and god also has its own type of rituals and way it can be honored. Perceiving Deity as Oshun, a Mother Goddess of love and sweet things, a person may honor Her by placing a bowl of honey on Her altar. In a ritual someone might honor Brigit, a creative Mother Goddess of the arts, by composing poetry or choreographing dances. A community may have a ritual reenacting Persephone, a Maiden Goddess of spring, returning from the underworld to celebrate the changing seasons. When events seem to meet with unexpected obstacles, people might ask Ganesha, the smoother of obstacles, or Eris, a Trickster Goddess, to help clear the way. Deity can be honored in a variety of wonderful ways and in a rainbow of forms, each having its own unique rituals and ceremonies, allowing people to find not only a face of Deity that comforts them, but also a unique form of worship that speaks to their soul.

For a deeper understanding of the Wiccan view of Deity, please read:

THREE

Ethics

An it harm none . . .

Life is filled with moral decisions. Do we scream at the person who accidentally bumped us in line, keep the wallet we found that was filled with money, or sneak our kids' Halloween candy? Every day we must wend our way through these and many other ethical pitfalls. Part of a religion's job is to help people traverse these moral minefields. Religions have compiled rules, composed poems, and created mythic stories to give people tools to use in an attempt to provide guidance when deciding between right and wrong. The moral compass Wicca uses is called the Wiccan Rede, a single rule applied in all cases. The Wiccan Rede states, "An it harm none, do as you will."[1] At first glance this seems very permissive, and some people have criticized the Wiccan Rede, thinking it allows people to indulge any hedonistic whim that strikes them; however, this assumption is incorrect.

The Wiccan Rede is not a "do what feels good and forget about tomorrow" philosophy. The Wiccan Rede doesn't refer to our base nature's will to indulge the physical but to the spirit's will to be itself, as Shakespeare says, "to thine own self be true."[2] People need to be true to themselves; trying to be true to anyone or anything else is living a lie. People must live according to their own will and not be swayed by peer pressure or by people around them who may want them to do other than what they feel is right. Therefore, people should follow their dreams and live their lives to the fullest as long as they don't hurt anyone or anything by thought, word, or deed— including themselves—emotionally, physically, psychologically, or spiritually. Harming none refers not only to other people but also animals, plants, and the Earth itself. This is the reason some Wiccans choose to be vegetarians, work to protect the environment, and seek to remedy social problems.

"An it harm none, do as you will." Harming nothing with thought, word, or deed is a difficult goal to which to aspire, and we frequently fall short of that goal, but when we do, we try to learn from those mistakes and keep going, attempting not to misstep in the future. However, it is important to aspire to not causing harm with thought, word, or deed because each is destructive in its own way. The fact no physical harm is done does not excuse harmful words or thoughts.

Words can slice like a sword or crack like a whip, and words chosen in anger can leave deeper scars than any physical injury ever will. It's a funny tendency of the human psyche to disregard compliments, thinking the person was only being nice, while agonizing over spiteful comments and criticisms and taking these negative images to heart. Poorly chosen words can crush a person's spirit or destroy their self-image. Hurtful comments tend to haunt our minds by lurking behind every compliment, causing us to doubt ourselves.

Wicca teaches that thoughts are things; this is one of the basic principles of magick. Our thoughts have energy that travels from us into the world, causing changes in our environment. If we think hateful thoughts about people, that harmful energy will be directed toward them and affect them in subtle ways. Destructive thoughts should be viewed as no less damaging than hitting someone with a hammer. Anger and aggression are not only harmful to the person on the receiving end of that negative energy, but they're also harmful to the thinker. Studies have shown anger causes changes in the body that damage a person physically, making them more emotionally volatile and mentally unstable. There is an old Chinese proverb that says a person who seeks revenge should dig two graves. The first one is for their enemy, but the second grave is for themselves because the hatred and destructive or harmful thoughts will kill the body and poison the soul.

Peace and harmony with ourselves and our surroundings is the goal of the Wiccan Rede; however, the Rede does not require someone to be a pacifist. Many Wiccans serve in the military, and most Wiccans believe it's acceptable to use force to protect one's own life or the lives of others. The Wiccan Rede requires people to evaluate their choices, try to determine the ramifications of their actions, and make amends if their choices negatively impact another.

The Wiccan Rede is actually very restrictive and even more encompassing than the ethical structure of many other religions. It gives people the ability to use their free will to evaluate situations. This forces people to take responsibility for their thoughts and actions and accept the consequences of their decisions. The Rede also teaches people to use their brains and not pass the buck. The majority of the ethical teachings of other religions can be derived from the Wiccan Rede. Not only are rape, murder, lying, cheating, and stealing all against the Wiccan Rede because they harm others, but also cruelty or neglect to animals, and even throwing cigarette butts on the ground, would be against the Wiccan Rede because such actions harm the Earth. All people have the right to make decisions for themselves, and every viewpoint has the right to exist if it can find a path of harmony and balance within its surroundings.

The concept of the Rede is ancient and can be found at the core of many other ethical teachings. "Live and let live" is essentially a variation of the Wiccan Rede, and "Play nice" is a kindergarten incarnation of the concept. One of the earliest written variations on the Rede dates from the early fifth century and reads *Dilige, et quod vis fac,* or for those of you who, like me, are a bit rusty with Latin: "Love, and do what you will." This was, surprisingly, penned by Saint Augustine in tract 7 on the gospel of Saint John.[3] The concept of the Rede is fundamental to people getting along in society, and I think the world would be a much friendlier place if everyone respected each other's right to live as they wish.

The Rule of Three

Choices, choices, choices—life is filled with them. Most of the choices we make are positive, but every once in a while, we make choices we later decide are unfortunate. Sometimes these are accidental, and we wish desperately to press some cosmic rewind button and undo our stupid mistakes. However, some people purposely make choices they know are harmful to others. What happens to these people? Religions have various answers to this question. Some say the offending individual will be reborn in a circumstance where they will be punished for the misdeeds of their former life. Other religions believe unrepentant individuals will be punished after they die, and some people are comforted by the thought that "bad people" will get what they deserve in the afterlife. Wicca doesn't believe people are punished in the afterlife, and some people think this means Wiccans believe they can do whatever they want, no matter what the Rede teaches. People sometimes think it doesn't matter what Wiccans do, because there are no consequences for breaking the Wiccan Rede. It would be easy to think this, and people have criticized Wicca with this exact, and very incorrect, statement.

Wiccans believe everything we do has consequences, and our actions are punished or rewarded here in this lifetime, not in the hereafter. Actions are punished or rewarded by the Rule of Three. The Rule of Three states that whatever energy people put out, for good or ill, will be returned multiplied by three. This isn't intended to be an exact measure of return. It simply means if people do positive things, positive things will come to them, but if they do harmful acts, harmful energy will return. This concept has been handed down through the ages, being altered slightly as it passed from generation to generation. The adages "what goes around comes around," "he'll get his," and "he who lives by the sword, dies by the sword" are all variations of the Rule of Three. This doesn't mean everything people do is going to come back exactly the same way. If someone steals something, three items might not be stolen from them, but something may happen to them that is worse than their theft. It could be a plague of smaller problems or that negative karma may just build up and catch them all at once.

The cosmic books will always balance in the end. People can't lie to the Fates and pass something off as an accident. Deity knows the intentions behind every action. People "reap what they sow" and "have to pay the piper" eventually. On the other hand, "good things do happen to good people." As these clichés show, people are aware that the energy a person sends into the Universe is returned in kind. This is not to imply that every "bad" circumstance that happens in a person's life is a punishment for some transgression. Sometimes problems are personal growth experiences, and we are supposed to learn a lesson as we, hopefully, live through and solve the problem.

Wiccan values

Currently there is a great deal of talk about "values." People are pontificating about values and America's loss of values. Some people say if we taught values in school, crime would stop, people would get along, the national debt would disappear, and Uncle Albert would regrow hair. This sounds great, and I am in favor of teaching values— as long as they are generic values common to all faiths.

Unfortunately, people often mean not that we should teach generic values but that everyone should be taught *their* particular religion in the public schools. People who want their religion taught in schools tend to have the attitude that minority religions shouldn't get a say, because, being in the minority, people who follow these religions should go along with what the majority wants. What such people fail to consider is what it would be like for them if *they* were in the minority, say in a Muslim country where their children would be immersed in the Islamic culture. Their children could hear Islamic prayers at public functions, celebrate Islamic holidays, and be taught that the teachings of Islam are more correct than other religions. The parents might begin to feel as if their culture and holidays were being lost and that they had little control over their children's religious upbringing. The children could feel unwanted and persecuted at their school, and they might be ostracized and ridiculed for being a different faith. This is an unintentional result of a school environment dominated by a single religion, and children who practice other faiths can be made to feel like outsiders simply because they practice a different religion. This might sound like conjecture, but this frequently happens to American children who practice minority religions.

You may ask, "but how can we teach ethics without teaching religion?" Ethics are a central part of every religion, and the ethics of most religions are essentially the same: respect for other people's lives, feelings, and property. Removing the religious context and teaching children those ethics common to all faiths would allow children to learn ethics without the unique culture and traditions of minority religions being lost or compromised. In an effort to give an understanding of how Wiccans relate to others, I give you typical Wiccan family values:

Wiccans have a great respect for all people because no matter what form they wear on the outside or how much we dislike their persona, the piece of Deity that is their soul deserves respect. External traits, like race or appearance, don't matter because our souls come from the same source, and therefore, we are all related. The body is simply a vehicle that carries us as we travel the Earth. Wiccans believe we have had other bodies before the ones we have now, and we will have other bodies in the future. Hating people for the color of their skin makes as much sense as hating people for the type of car they drive.

Love of the Earth is a value Wiccans share. We believe Mother Earth gave birth to our bodies, and our bodies return to Her after we die. Wiccans see ourselves as caretakers of our Mother. We believe the Earth is a living thing, which nurtures us, not a lifeless planet to be dominated and subdued. Ecology and environmental issues hold great importance to most Wiccans. All creatures born from the Earth must share the Earth, and we all depend on one another to survive. We are all part of the same living organism, and we believe that whatever is done to the least of the plants or animals is done to us all. Poisons poured on the ground end up in our drinking water, and cigarette butts thrown on the ground take twenty years to biodegrade. Humans produce more trash and cause more damage to the Earth's ecosystem than any other animal on the planet. We kill more animals than cobras and destroy more forests than locusts. We trash the planet, destroy resources, and drive animals to extinction for profit, all the while seeming to think someone else will clean up the mess.

Wiccans view ourselves as one with the Earth. We are a part of it, connected to everything else on the planet. The Earth is our home, and we shouldn't trash it any more than we would trash our own homes. Life, all life, is a gift to be nurtured and cherished.

Equality between men and women is a value Wicca teaches. Wicca doesn't have teachings that place women in subordinate or submissive positions to men. Women are not only equal to men but also lead most groups. Women are viewed as the vessel of the Goddess just as men are viewed as the vessel of the God, and both are part of the One Power. Discriminating against people because of gender is as unconscionable to us as discriminating on the basis of race. Placing women in a subordinate role devalues their contributions to society and teaches girls not to strive toward their full potential.

Personal responsibility is a value most Wiccans share. People are responsible for their own actions and for the choices they make. Choices are more important than ability; the choices we make are the building blocks of our character. Ultimately, there are no winners or losers in life. All that matters is how we live. Wiccans ask people to make fair and honest choices even when they perceive the choice is not in their best interest. This is the true test of a person's character. Do people meet their obligations and responsibilities even when it's inconvenient and causes personal problems, or do they consistently try to make up excuses to avoid their responsibilities and try to justify irresponsible or harmful actions? Also, making amends for decisions that cause harm can't be done simply by asking Deity for forgiveness. People must take responsibility for their actions and make amends to the person or thing harmed. The potential for compassion and harm are a part of everyone, and our choices tell the world which path we follow.

Wicca teaches that words have power; therefore, we should say what we mean and mean what we say. Many relationships are damaged or destroyed by hastily or poorly chosen words. The old children's rhyme says "sticks and stones may break my bones, but words can never hurt me," and maybe that's true physically. However, emotionally, words can cut through people like knives, dissecting their self-esteem and making them believe they are less than they are. Even if we know a person's words are untrue, that little doubt nags us, and sometimes those words sound in our ears like the screams of a banshee. Lies also damage the person being deceived, and they leave their own mark on the soul of the person who tells the untruth. Some people justify lying and believe it is necessary, but each lie makes the next one easier. Soon one begins to tell lies more and more often with less and less justification, until even the person telling the lies begins to have trouble telling the truth from the fiction. At this point, people can no longer trust the liar. Wiccans believe people are responsible for their own words, and the retribution the Universe takes upon us for harm done with words is the same as for harm done with actions.

Religious tolerance is a value Wicca teaches. We believe Deity is vast, and because of the differences in culture and needs, it would be difficult, if not impossible, for everyone to view Deity in the same way. Wicca teaches that all goddesses and gods are simply different perceptions of Deity and are all valid ways to worship. We don't teach dogmatic adherence to one perception of Deity, and so the odds of Wiccans starting a religious war with their neighbors is virtually zero. Everyone should be free to worship Deity in a way that feels right to them, without having to look over their shoulder for people throwing rocks.

Selflessness, the ability to think of others before yourself, is another Wiccan value. Selfishness comes from the belief we are all separate individuals who are trying to win in life. When someone views everything in the world connected to everything else, they start to see that what affects one of us affects all of us, and there is no individual anymore. Lying, stealing, and cheating are harmful to all people, because we are all connected to each other. This isn't to say people shouldn't take care of their needs and desires, but when someone tries to justify stealing or lying because she is looking out for herself in some "survival mode," she is not practicing this concept.

Empathy for others, the ability to put oneself into someone else's shoes and to see how one's actions affect others, is a trait most Wiccan parents try to instill in their children. Wiccans tend to use inductive disciplinary methods, where they teach their children to think about how their actions affect other people. Inductive discipline helps develop prosocial children, who grow to be more selfless no matter what religion they choose as adults. Empathetic behavior should extend not only to other people but to the Earth as well. A person who is truly empathetic feels sympathy for an old-growth forest destroyed by logging or for dolphins choking on the trash and poisons people dump into the oceans as well as for the person living next door.

Independent thought is valued and encouraged in Wicca. Very little information is given in a "because I say so" fashion. Wicca encourages people to make their own decisions about what is correct. Students are urged to study and ask questions; introspection is required. Wiccans encourage people to think for themselves, making it difficult for rigid dogma to develop or for would-be gurus to collect large followings. This is the reason why many Wiccans are solitary, practicing on their own, where they can make their own decisions about how they worship. Also, children are typically encouraged to study other religions so that when they are adults, they can make informed choices and have confidence in why they worship the way they do and not just follow their parent's way of worship, never having considered and not knowing about other ways to worship.

Wiccans try to live in harmony with their surroundings. Walking gently through life maintains peace not only in their surroundings but also in their own lives. For years Wiccans have been practicing natural relaxation techniques that are now coming into vogue. Although these practices are not in themselves Wiccan, they use natural energies and natural magick that make them conducive to Wiccan life. Many Wiccans may use candles, as well as aromatherapy, color therapy, herbal healing, Reiki, Tai Chi, water fountains and other sounds of nature, crystals and stones, meditation, or yoga, just to name a few techniques. All of these help maintain a calm serenity that allows movement through life without as readily succumbing to stress.

Wiccan values are what we try to instill in ourselves and in our children to help us live our lives as we feel they should be lived. Every religion has its own principles by which its followers live, and every religion has its own way of teaching these principles. People will naturally feel their own principles and ways of teaching them are the best. The trick is for all of us to learn to respect other people's values, even if we don't agree with them. By respecting others' values, we allow them the freedom to worship the way they feel is correct, and they, in return, should give others the same courtesy. Mutual respect of others' religions would stop more than a few wars and allow people to quit focusing on the differences dividing us and instead look at our common values and our common desire to be closer to Deity. We can work to build fences to separate or bridges to connect, and each of us must decide for ourselves into which social construction project we will put our efforts.

For a deeper understanding about Wiccan ethics, please read:

FOUR

Living a Wiccan Life

Dancing in a Circle

Darkness covers the park, and a warm breeze rustles the leaves of the trees and flutters the folds of the robes of a group of people standing in a circle. A swing creaks in the background, and shifting patterns of light play across a table in the center of the group as wispy clouds pass across a full moon, illuminating a chalice of wine and plate of bread flanking a bowl of wildflowers. Arranged around the edge of the table and aligned with the compass points (north, east, south, and west respectively) rest a vessel of salt, a bell, a candle, and a bowl of water. The fragrance of jasmine and frankincense are carried on the breeze, wafting out of a small cauldron of slowly smoldering herbs from which tendrils of smoke arise. The smoke drifts across a silver circlet depicting the phases of the moon, worn on the forehead of a woman standing next to the table. She smiles warmly at the group, and lines of wisdom crease her face. Her robes shift, and her sleeve passes over the chalice as she reaches for the bell on the altar. Facing east, she plants her feet in the dewy grass, and raising her arms, she strikes the bell three times, its clear tones passing in waves over the ring of people. The wind shifts, and the rustling leaves seem to be singing in a language long forgotten but almost familiar to our souls, and maybe if we could only listen closely enough, we could understand what it is saying. "Element of Air," the woman calls to the breeze, "we ask that you join us here in our Circle. Fill us with the clarity of mind and the vision to see within and know ourselves as we truly are. Blow away the illusions our ego shrouds us in, that we may see ourselves as others see us, for only by knowing ourselves may we accept the imperfections and change the parts of our lives that need to be altered. So mote it be." Echoing the woman, those circled around her intone, "So mote it be."

Since the furthest reaches of time, people have worshiped Deity in some form. People have prayed to, sacrificed to, and worked in the service of some form of Deity before we even knew how to record the time that was passing. In the early 1900s a series of caves found high in the Alps revealed ancient altars where cave bear skulls had been meticulously arranged with other objects showing what appears to be evidence of worship dating back to at least 75,000 BCE.[1] From caverns covered in sacred drawings and sacred groves of trees, through the temples of Greece, to modern cathedrals, people have had their sacred spaces, rituals, and prayers all designed to bring their people closer to Divinity as they perceive it. Each religion has its own way of honoring Deity and unique rites to do so. Different traditions seem to work in similar fashions, and all are sacred to their followers; every religion is magical in its own way.

Wiccans don't usually have buildings in which to worship. We view Divinity as part of everything. This is especially true of nature, so when possible we worship in nature, but we also worship in living rooms, apartment clubhouses, or wherever else we choose to gather. When we gather, we create a sacred space in which to worship; we call this space a *Circle,* and it's typically formed by everyone standing in a circle. There are ceremonies used to create a circle of sacred space, and performing one of these ceremonies is referred to as *casting Circle.* Every tradition of Wicca has its own method of casting Circle, and these methods vary greatly depending on the reason why the Circle is being cast. However, there are some things most Circles will have in common.

The people who come together to worship do so in love and trust: love for ourselves, love for each other, and love for the Divinity that resides in each of us. When entering Circle, we are entering a space where we open ourselves completely to the Goddess and the God. People can open themselves fully only if they trust those with whom they are circling. Circles are participatory; everyone chants, dances, and shares within its space. One cannot be free to participate wholly or share what is felt in the soul if one is self-conscious because of concerns that people will judge or gossip later. A circle has no top: everyone stands in Circle facing each other looking into each other's eyes; no one sits on the side and watches, and everyone is equal within its boundaries. This lets us know we are a part of the whole and are, therefore, accountable to everyone for our actions, just as in all of life; we are a part of the whole Earth and are accountable to all other beings for our actions.

Wicca is a nature-based religion, and in respect for the Earth and all of nature, one of the first things we do when casting Circle is to invite the elements to join us. We view the primal forces of nature to be Air, Fire, Water, Earth, and Spirit. In the macrocosm, these make up the winds, the heat of the sun, the rain, the trees around us, and the order of nature. The expressions of these forces in nature are endless. In the microcosm, the elements represent the breath in our lungs, the heat of our skin, the blood in our veins, our bodies themselves, and the spirit that gives us life. All of nature can be symbolically broken down into these five forces, so by inviting the elements to join in our ritual, we affirm our connection to the Earth, of which we are a part and ask nature to share in our worship.

Wicca also honors Deity and the duality of all life by inviting the Goddess and the God to join in the ritual and bless all who are present. We view the Goddess and the God as always present, a part of us and a part of all creation. We ask everyone to focus on knowing that Deity is present and for the spirit of Deity to be especially felt at this time. After calling upon the Goddess and the God, the main purpose of the ritual begins.

Circles may be held to honor the seasonal holidays, for full or new moons, to heal someone, or for any other reason the group might decide to gather. During this time participants may chant, sing, dance, meditate, reenact myths or other sacred stories, discuss the significance of a specific season or moon, or help resolve a problem for one of the members. Some groups have a specific format they follow, while others change each time and are limited only by the creativity of the person writing the ritual.

Food is a very important part of life; it sustains us and maintains our existence. Food is a gift from the Earth, and the sharing of food has always been associated with hospitality, companionship, and commitment. To give thanks for the gift of sustenance and to acknowledge our dependence on this gift, Wiccans share a "ritual feast" to show our connection to the Earth and our gratitude to Deity. During the feast, usually bread of some kind and a chalice of wine or other drink are offered around the circle, and everyone shares a small portion of the food and a sip from the chalice. Afterwards, we thank the Goddess and the God for being with us and say good-bye to the elements.

This is the basic format for Circle, and the variations around this theme are many. There are, however, things you will not find happening in Circle. There are no animal sacrifices in Circle. Nature is sacred to us, and the idea of killing or harming an animal is abhorrent to our way of life. Orgies do not happen in Circle. Contrary to propaganda, and a disappointment to a great number of lascivious men and teenage boys, orgies do not happen. Circles are performed for sacred, religious reasons, not as an excuse for debauchery. Drug and alcohol abuse are not found in Circles. Wine is passed during some Circles, but people take only a sip. If someone is in recovery from substance abuse they simply hold the chalice aloft, in gratitude, and pass it on. People are expected to come into Circle with their minds clear and unclouded by the influence of chemicals. Circle is an experience of closeness with the Universe, the Goddess and the God, and all of nature. It is something we do as worship, it is a joyous occasion, and we take it as seriously as any other religion takes its worship service.

Birth, death, and all things between

There are three big questions all religions must answer: Where did we come from? Why are we here? Where are we going? The funny thing about these questions is they are all unanswerable. Well, all religions answer them; it's just the answers the various religions give don't usually match one another. All answers to these questions are hypotheses, which cannot be proven or supported with evidence. Whether people believe an answer is right or not will ultimately come down to their own faith. Religions can postulate and debate these questions until the sun burns out, and still no one is going to be able to prove one answer is any more right than anyone else's answer, nor can anyone prove someone's answer wrong, so for all practical purposes, they are unanswerable. Most of the debates of this nature reduce to a "we have to be right; therefore, everyone else has to be wrong" kind of argument, and that kind of judgmental mentality doesn't get anyone anywhere. What I am going to present here is a Wiccan viewpoint of death, birth, and why we're here in the first place, and my answers may differ greatly from other people's answers to those questions. If people find themselves saying, "but that just can't be true," please remember I am not asking everyone to agree with me. I am just giving people an insight into how someone who is Wiccan might believe. This is a very personal issue, and everyone is entitled to their own unique viewpoint. The search for these answers is, I feel, an essential part of the spiritual experience of living in this world.

Death—the real final frontier—is the last passage of our life here in this plane. This is the time of learning to let go. We must say good-bye to all we have accumulated and to those we have loved in this life. We leave this body behind and travel to the other side of the veil that separates this plane of existence from the next. This journey is the great equalizer because no matter how much money one has and no matter how many friends one has, in the end, everyone makes this passage broke and alone. However, we don't need to worry about death; it will find us when our time comes. Worrying about death is like going on vacation and worrying so much about the trip home that one doesn't enjoy the vacation. It has been said man is the only animal that knows it's going to die. I wonder if this is true or if we're the only ones who obsess about it. The truth is, we don't know what happens to us after we die. Religions make a great show of telling people about the afterlife, but when the twilight falls, none of us knows for sure, and the unknown scares us.

When studying the world's religions, there seem to be more rituals and ceremonies associated with death than with any other passage in life. Almost all of these ceremonies occur after we die, so they would seem to do nothing for the dearly departed. Such ceremonies simply comfort those who are still alive, to try to console and assure them the deceased is in a better place because we want to believe the afterlife is so much better than life here on Earth. We create human fantasies about the afterlife, fantasies of wealth, power, youth, and great food. However, once freed from the body, the soul is also freed from the petty desires of humanity. Streets of gold and endless sex appeal would undoubtedly seem silly to the piece of the Divine that is the soul in each of us.

What happens to our soul after we die? Are we truly immortal, or do we simply crumble into nothingness? These are eternal questions, and every religion has its own way to answer them. Most Wiccans believe in reincarnation because we believe the soul is not a "one use" item that retires from Earth after the body dies. Wicca believes we may choose to return to Earth again and again. Death to us is viewed as only a transition from this dimension to another dimension. To us, no one is born and no one dies because the body is only a vessel that houses our spirit while we are in this dimension. Our true self is the spirit, which is eternal; bodies are created and used until they can no longer function and are cast off when we leave this dimension. Think of the body like a car: there are different types and styles, and while we own them, we keep them tuned up and clean, but when time has worn its parts out and the car can no longer function, we get rid of it and get a newer model. When we get a new car, we are free to choose whatever type suits our needs and in whatever color we desire. Our choice of car doesn't change the driver, and in the end, maybe we should celebrate the birth of someone's new vehicle more than we mourn the loss of the old one.

Now, exactly what happens in that other dimension? Well, that's anybody's guess. Everyone's idea of what happens after we die is faith-based, not knowledge-based. Some say we review our lives, evaluate how well we learned the lessons we were supposed to learn, and plan out our next life to fill in the lessons we missed, or we may become the guardian spirits of others until the time when we are reborn, or perhaps we rejoin with Deity after we die. Speculation on this issue is a debate no one can win, since by the time one gets to the place where that information is known for sure, it's too late to tell anyone. However, at some point, for whatever reason, we choose to enter the dimension of Earth, and the first thing we experience is . . .

Birth, the first passage a person goes through in this life. We are floating in a warm, dark place when we are abruptly squeezed into a very cold and bright environment. We look around. Things are moving and reaching for us. Sounds assault our ears. Everything seems to be in chaos. Then, wait—something is familiar. This thing that is holding us is warm and soft. It smells like home, and that sound—*Thump-thump, Thump-thump*—we know that sound. This is where we are supposed to be; we are now safe. Welcome to the world. The child has just passed its first test and learned its first lesson. The world can be bright and cold, but it is also full of amazing sights, wonderful smells, and the warm interaction with other souls who, like this child, are blundering along doing the best they can.

The Wiccan belief in reincarnation often comes along with the belief that we choose the life into which we are born. This viewpoint gives parents a great responsibility, because this soul has entrusted them with its upbringing. It also gives parents a great response when children get to be teenagers and say, "Well, I never asked to be born." Our job as parents is to protect and nurture that soul, give it nourishment, let it explore, and encourage it in the pursuit of its interests. A child's soul should be free to discover the reason it was born into the world and fulfill whatever it came here to do or learn. Wiccans usually don't try to mold our children into some image we have for them. By imposing our ideas of hobbies, careers, or religion upon this soul, we may be making its journey through this life more difficult than it has to be. Therefore, Wiccans try to give children the guidance and direction they need, teach them skills and ethics we hope will help in their journey, and learn from them as much as they ever learn from us.

Why are we here? That newborn baby could probably tell us. I personally feel babies have to be born with no way to communicate; it keeps them from revealing the secrets of the universe and ruining the ending for the rest of us. Maybe people are here to learn specific lessons, and we are destined to keep having the same problems until we finally learn the lesson and move on to a new set of lessons. Maybe people are reborn when there is a need, and we are given a mission, purpose, or destiny to fulfill while we are on Earth. Buddhists believe we are locked into an eternal cycle of suffering until our souls have developed to a point where they find a way to break the cycle and not be reborn. Perhaps we choose to come back to Earth as a vacation, where everyone picks a character to play in a giant, ongoing drama. Any of these could be the reason why we are here; perhaps all of them are, or maybe none of them are correct. No one can prove why we are born or if there is even a reason. Many people will say they have the answer to this question, and some of those answers are extremely complex while others are quite simple, but in the end, people are simply presenting their opinion, often with great conviction, while the actual truth will remain forever elusive. This is why Wicca tends to be very tolerant of people's ideas about where we come from and why we're here. We don't need validation, so other people having a different viewpoint doesn't threaten our own. Any idea could be correct, so if these beliefs help those people live their lives and be better people, it doesn't matter whether we agree with them or not. People are born because this dimension provides us with an opportunity to experience and learn things we cannot experience and learn on the other side of the veil. The challenge is to live our lives fully and take the chances that will make us feel more complete: paint, sing, write, play, and dance; enjoy the feeling of being; help others and be the best, most loving and compassionate person we can be; and try to live up to the full potential of that piece of Deity that is the soul of our being.

The quest for the Divine
and the role of clergy in Wicca

A man hiking through the Himalayas is in quest of the golden city of Shambala. After climbing higher and higher for days, he meets a man riding on a cart pulled by two yaks. The climber asks the man if he has seen Shambala, and he answers, "Yes, my child. I have been there and know the way to the fabled city." The man offers to give directions so the seeker may find the city himself. "No," replies the seeker, "Let me simply sit near you so that I might hear your experience of the city, and I will be content." At this point many of you are thinking this guy is nuts. He climbs and searches, but in the end, he is content with only hearing about the city when he could have gone there himself. This may sound like complete lunacy, but this is exactly what many people do in their quest for spiritual fulfillment.

There is an old Oriental proverb that says, "The finger points to the moon; don't confuse the finger for the moon." Frequently a person searching for the Divine will find someone who, for whatever reason, they think has touched the Divine, seen Its shadow, or has at least heard about it. The seeker then abandons their own personal search for the Divine, opting instead to listen as someone else relates what the Divine means to them. To me, one of the purposes of any clergy person is to point people toward the Divine without letting them stop to stare at your finger.

In Wicca the clergy has two functions. The first is the civil function. In this capacity the Wiccan High Priestess or High Priest will officiate over rites and ceremonies. In every religion, there are people whose responsibility it is to bless babies, officiate at weddings, and oversee funerals. Wiccan clergy are responsible for conducting these ceremonies as well as moon and Sabbat rituals for members of the Wiccan community.

The second function of the Wiccan clergy is that of teacher and counselor. In this capacity Wiccan clergy act as guides for students, pointing them in the direction of Divinity and sending them on their way. The goal of Wicca is to guide people to their own personal identification with the Divine. However, like our hiker in the mountains, most people don't know where to begin looking for that place. It is impossible to teach someone the experience of the Divine, as there are no words capable of relating the uniqueness of the encounter. One can only be shown the direction and given tools to help in their quest. As Wiccan students begin their journey, their feet walk a wide path, worn smooth by the tread of every Wiccan student who has ever preceded them. If we are alive, we haven't finished learning, so all Wiccan teachers are themselves students of the Divine. Each teacher becomes a mentor and friend who holds aloft their lamp to illuminate the path they have already trodden, thereby giving the student the directions, tools, and the guidance necessary to help keep their steps along their path from faltering.

The Moons and Sabbats become a map for seekers. The ethical teaching of the Wiccan Rede is like a compass helping to keep us on course. Meditation and spellwork become a tent, sheltering us from life's stormy moments, while divination is a travel guide, giving us forewarning of difficulties ahead. As a Wiccan progresses along their path, teachers may change as the student's path diverges from one teacher and encounters another. As students progress, their path will narrow, becoming rougher, because this more personal path has been trodden by fewer people. Finally, as the student nears their goal, Deity and Nature will be their only teacher because the mysteries they learn can't be taught with words. As they approach the Divine, there will be no worn path, as the places they step will have never felt the feet of another soul. This path toward Deity will be of their own making because ultimately each of us experiences the Divine in our own unique way.

The job of a Wiccan teacher is one of friend and counselor, to prepare the student for the path ahead and set them free to walk that path themselves. Wiccans are taught to listen for the voice of the Divine as It whispers to them, not to rely on others to tell them what It's saying. If a student lingers indefinitely with a teacher, both student and teacher have missed this point.

As with any religion, the majority of the clergy function from a place of Divine altruism and only want to help students as they journey through life. However, a few will abuse their place of trust and seek to gain power over those who have come to them for aid. To help students separate the gold from the pyrite, Charles Mars wrote "The Seeker's Bill of Rights" (Appendix A) to let Wiccan students know the kind of things that should not be asked of them. Any person who is pursuing the Wiccan religion should read this document so they will have a better idea of whether the High Priestess or High Priest they are trusting with their spiritual guidance is legitimately looking out for their best interests or abusing their position of authority.

Along my path I have worked with some teachers who, wanting disciples, greedily clung to students and other teachers who pushed the student from the nest to see if they could fly solo when the student began to use the teacher as a crutch. Asking questions and learning from teachers is how we gain the tools necessary to find and follow our own path. However, having the tools means nothing if we just watch someone else using them, never trying them out for ourselves. Self-reliance and personal responsibility are ultimately necessary to achieve an identification with whatever forms of the Goddess and God we choose to follow and then through them find our way to the One.

Wheel of the Year

Every religious tradition has its sacred holidays, and Wicca is no exception. Wiccan holidays are set around the changing of the seasons and the times of planting and harvest. These holidays, called Sabbats, are often referred to as solar festivals because they celebrate the changes of the sun within a year. The sun is viewed as a symbol of the God, and the changes that occur in the length of the days relate to the life cycle of the God. Although Wiccans usually view the Goddess as eternal, the God is viewed as sacrificial, giving His life every year so our lives can continue. The God is born, grows as the days get longer, reaches the height of His power on the longest day of the year, then declines, and finally dies as the days again get shorter and His life energy has been poured out to the Earth. He is like the grain of the fields that grows, is cut down for our nourishment, and rises again. Wiccans call this cycle of the seasons the "Wheel of the Year."

Most of the original Pagan holidays have traveled with us through the centuries and have been preserved in some way in our modern culture. The same seasonal changes our ancestors celebrated are still celebrated by most people today even if the names have been changed and the meanings have been altered. Therefore, if you see similarities between how we celebrate some of our holidays and how other holidays are celebrated, this is because similar seasonal celebrations have existed within numerous cultures around the world for thousands of years. As an area was conquered, the invading people usually brought with them a new religion that the native people were often forced to follow. The native people would begin to adapt their existing religious traditions and celebrations to the new religion by incorporating their seasonal practices into the new holidays. Over many generations, most people forgot why these traditions were part of the holiday. Occasionally some people point out that a few of these traditions seem a bit odd and wonder why no one seems to know why they are being practiced, but most people don't care why such traditions are part of the holiday. They just keep practicing the same religious traditions that date back to their Pagan ancestors and enjoy every minute of it. There are eight holidays in the Wheel of the Year, and since the Wheel of the Year is just that, a wheel, there is no definite place to start; however, I am going to start with Yule.

Yule (YOOL)

The Winter Solstice, also called Yule, is celebrated on the longest night of the year. Winter Solstice falls around December 21 but varies from year to year. In the months before the solstice, the days get progressively shorter and the weather gets colder. To ancient people, life around them seemed to be ending at this time of year. Then after the solstice, the days began to get longer again. It was as if the sun had been reborn, and there was hope that life would return to the Earth. Nowadays the Winter Solstice is usually viewed by Wiccans as the time when the God is reborn from the Goddess. The sun, a symbol of the God, is now new and growing, the days are short but getting longer, so the God is viewed metaphorically as being in His infancy.

There are many traditions associated with this season that originated long ago and have to do with the returning light or life surviving when everything looks dead. Evergreen trees are green and living when all the other trees have shed their leaves and appear dead. Evergreens were, and still are, set up in homes to remind people that no matter how dark and dead the world looks outside, life always returns in the spring. The trees are decorated with lights to celebrate the reborn Sun and with apples, nuts, or other food items as a way of thanking the Goddess for the food She has given and asking for the food supplies to last through the winter. Holly and mistletoe, also always green, are religious symbols in their own right and are used especially as decorations in celebration of the solstice. Yule logs are decorated and burned on Solstice Eve as a way of symbolically carrying the light of the sun through the darkest night of the year. The Romans gave presents to celebrate the Feast of the Unconquered Sun. In other nations, the Solstice was a time to give gifts of food to important people in one's life because in the winter, in ancient times, nothing was more valuable than food. Variations of Santa Claus exist in almost every culture, and the variations usually relate back to some ancient god, Winter King, or shaman who brings food and gifts or makes predictions for people in the coming year.[2] Solstice traditions date back thousands of years. Today most Wiccan families have their own traditions and celebrate Winter Solstice in some fashion.

My family watches the Sun set on Solstice Eve and lights a candle to symbolically carry its fire through the night. We use this candle to light the Yule log, which burns through the night. Santa comes on Solstice Eve, so we get up at sunrise to watch the new Sun's birth, open Santa's gifts, and exchange presents with each other. In the afternoon, we make ornaments using pinecones slathered with peanut butter and rolled in birdseed. We then take the pinecones outside, along with apples and strings of popcorn, to decorate a tree in the woods so the animals can share the solstice with us. On the way home, we cut new mistletoe and holly that will hang over the door until the next year, when it will be burned with the Yule log.

Imbolc (Em-bowel/k) *or Oimelc* (Oy-melk)

In most groups, Imbolc is celebrated on February 1 or 2. However, some groups celebrate this holiday at the exact midpoint between the Winter Solstice and the Spring Equinox when the sun reaches 15 degrees Aquarius or on the second full moon after the Winter Solstice. Sometimes called Brigid's Day after the Celtic Goddess Brigit, Imbolc celebrates the first signs of the coming spring. The days are getting longer, and the first plants are starting to green. People can see signs of winter's end, and this festival is meant to hasten spring's return. Spring brings new life, new opportunities, and new chances to grow. Therefore, people begin to examine the old possessions they are carrying around and start to clear away the unneeded clutter from their homes, as well as from their lives, in order to have a nice, clean space for new and better things.

In ancient times, fires were lit, and young girls wore crowns of candles to add heat to the frozen Earth. Weather divination (future telling) was performed to try to determine how much longer winter would hold the Earth in its icy grip. It was once said that if a lark was heard at Imbolc, then the God would be returning more quickly to the Goddess and spring would begin early. If no lark was heard, then winter would last longer. The tradition of performing weather divination has been handed down and still remains today, and every February second a form of weather divination is performed, not by Wiccans, but by the general public. Every year thousands of people gather around a rodent hole in Pennsylvania to determine if spring is going to come early, and if the groundhog doesn't see his shadow, spring just might be right around the corner.

Many Wiccan families invite friends over to celebrate Imbolc; everyone brings food, and we bake braided bread for the table. We build a fire in the hearth and make corn dolls and Brigit's crosses to be hung in the house until next year for luck and protection. Everyone also brings their favorite divination method, and we spend the evening seeing what we can divine from tarot cards, tea leaves, palms, runes, and the occasional wine spill.

Eostre (Es-tra) *or Ostara* (Oh-star-ah)

The Vernal or Spring Equinox, called Eostre after the Anglo-Saxon Goddess of Dawn, marks the beginning of spring and is celebrated around March 21. The word *Easter* comes from the Goddess Eostre, whose animal symbol, the white hare, later became the Easter bunny.

Chicks and spring flowers are used as symbols for this season. However, the most pervasive symbol of this holiday is the egg. Chickens, who under normal conditions don't lay eggs during the winter, begin to lay eggs again due to the increased amount of light, and the ancient people rejoiced at this renewed source of food and because the days were getting longer. The egg is a symbol of fertility, and after a long winter with food supplies running low, fertility of the flocks and fields was and is very important to agricultural people. Eostre is a planting festival, and people want those newly planted crops to grow. People used plant dyes to decorate eggs, dying them bright colors and drawing symbols of the goddesses and gods on them. These eggs were then used to decorate altars to bring prosperity and fertility in the coming season.

The story of the Easter bunny laying colored eggs may come from an Anglo-Saxon myth of the Goddess Eostre. She heard the pleas of a little girl who had found a bird, near death, lying in a late snowfall. The Goddess rescued the frozen bird from death by changing the bird into her sacred animal, a white hare. The hare, still being part bird, laid eggs in the colors of the Goddess's rainbow. This story shows the growth and changes symbolically represented in this season, and these changes are mirrored in equinox stories in many cultures around the world. Nowadays Wiccans continue these traditions handed down from our ancestors.

My family's celebration of Eostre begins first thing in the morning. Our children wake up to find that Eostre's bunny has visited and with her the beginning of spring. The kids spend the day looking for eggs hidden around the house, although eggs usually continue to pop up for weeks. We color and decorate eggs during the day, and each child takes her favorite to put on her own altar. Weather permitting, we go to the park for a picnic where we hide eggs, fly kites, and try to keep the kids from gorging themselves on the candy the bunny left.

Beltane (Bell-tayn)

Beltane, also known as May Day, is celebrated by most Wiccans on May 1; however, the date may vary slightly from tradition to tradition as some groups may celebrate it at the exact midpoint between the Spring Equinox and the Summer Solstice, when the sun reaches 15 degrees Taurus, or on the second full moon after the Spring Equinox. The Celts viewed Beltane as the beginning of the summer season.

Beltane falls about the time when all the crops have been planted in the fields and was viewed long ago as a fertility festival to help promote a bountiful harvest and fertile livestock. Many ancient fertility rituals are intended to symbolically increase the fertility of the Earth, but one of the more common ones still used today is the Maypole. Maypoles, an ancient fertility symbol, are erected, and dancers spiral around the pole, intertwining brightly colored ribbons, which are tied to the top of the pole, wrapping the pole in a cocoon of rainbow hues. Other fertility rituals include selecting a May queen or lighting two bonfires and then driving cattle between them to increase their fertility. Traditionally pieces of the Beltane fire were taken home to light the cook fires and bring summer blessings into the home. Couples who wish to conceive leap over the fire to receive the blessing of the Goddess. Flowers of all kinds decorate this festival, where modern Wiccans wear garlands and chains of flowers in celebration, especially the eligible maidens. As Beltane is viewed as the time of marriage between the Goddess and the God, this is also the traditional time for young men to propose to their sweethearts, who might then become June brides.

On our family picnics on Beltane, we attempt to resurrect the lost art of making garlands and bracelets from flowers we have bought; however, there always seems to be liberal amounts of wild flowers in the mix. My daughters wear these lopsided creations in their hair as they dance and play in the park, scattering wildflower seeds to replace the flowers they have taken. We talk about our hopes for the year and what we want to "grow" in our lives during this year. Each of us decides what "seeds" we want to plant in our lives, and we write down our goals, keeping them with us through the day. In the evening we light a small fire, and each of us drops our paper into the fire and then leaps over it (remember, it's a small fire). Burning the paper and leaping the fire is intended to symbolically energize our desires and help bring them to fruition.

Litha (LEE-thah)

Litha is celebrated on the Summer Solstice, which is around June 21. Often called Midsummer, because the Celts viewed Beltane as the beginning of summer, the Summer Solstice is the longest day of the year. Litha is viewed as the time when the God is at the height of His power. However, His power begins to wane from this time as the days grow shorter and the God's life force flows into the plants that will be harvested as He sacrifices His life to sustain ours.

Traditionally, fires built to honor the sun and processions of people carrying torches were Summer Solstice traditions in many cultures. Athletic events were held in many cultures, where contestants competed in events of strength and skill in honor of the God. Fairy lore says the fairies are especially active at Midsummer, and food is frequently left out to appease fairies, who, like in Shakespeare's *A Midsummer Night's Dream,* could be especially mischievous at this time of year.

The sun is also viewed as a symbol of protection, and the focus of Litha is one of protection. During the festival people seek protection, sometimes for themselves, but more importantly for the animals and crops. By Litha the crops are growing, and the animals that have conceived are very near the end of their pregnancy. Though the people rejoice in this, they also know things can still go wrong. Blights can destroy entire crops, and drought can cause the strong plants to wither before they are ready to harvest. Therefore, protection magick is performed at this time, especially magick to help ensure that the harvest, which was and is so necessary for everyone's survival, is spared from harm.

Our family designates Litha as the time when we spruce up or replace our fairy houses. Fairy houses are small nests or tiny houses, which are decorated with pretty shinies, like coins and crystals. Fairy houses are placed amongst the houseplants and in the garden to give the fairies a place to reside. We add new shiny things to the houses and leave food and drink for the fairies. (A person can believe in fairies or not, but this does seem to cut down on the number of things "lost" around the house, so I'm not taking any chances.) We also update and renew the protection charms and spells around the house. We also usually attend a large annual community solstice celebration by one of the lakes, where everyone celebrates the longest day of the year with picnics, drumming, and dancing until long after sunset.

Lammas (Lam-mahs)

Lammas, called Lughnasadh (Loo-nah-sahd) by some groups, is a celebration of the first harvest. Lammas is traditionally celebrated on August 1, but some groups may celebrate Lammas at the exact mid-point between the Summer Solstice and the Autumnal Equinox, when the sun reaches 15 degrees Leo, or on the second full moon after the Summer Solstice.

By the beginning of August, grains such as barley, wheat, oats, and corn are ready to be harvested. This celebration thanks the Goddess for providing the first fruits from Her womb and to ask for protection for the crops that are still in the field waiting for later harvests. Grain is offered back to the Goddess in thanks for what She has given us, and ceremonies are enacted to ensure the continued growth of the crops still in the field. In ancient times there was, and still is for farming communities, a lot of work to be done during the harvest. Reaping and thrashing take time, and time available to bring in the harvest is very limited, so there are few big parties during this Sabbat. People are simply thankful the first harvest is in from the fields because this means everyone will at least have some food for the winter.

My family celebrates Lammas with a family feast. Everyone gets to pick their favorite foods, and we even use some vegetable dishes to fill in the spaces between all the desserts the kids have chosen. We give thanks for the harvest and then talk about the things we are "harvesting" in our lives. We spend the rest of the evening playing games and spending the time as a family.

Mabon (May-bon)

Mabon, the Autumnal Equinox, is a festival celebrating the second harvest. The Autumnal or Fall Equinox happens around September 21. At this time of year, the early grains have been harvested, and now it's time to harvest the ripened fruits and nuts. Apples, berries, and nuts are picked and preserved as jams and jellies or made into wines so they will last through the winter. Traditionally, at either Lammas or Mabon, the last of the late grain stalks would be made into a corn dolly which was believed to contain the spiritual essence of the grain which retreated into the last stalk as the grain was cut. The corn dolly would be brought into the home for the winter and either plowed it back into the field during the next growing season, thereby ensuring the fertility of the soil and returning the spiritual essence of the grain to the Earth, or saved until a new one was made the next year.

To understand this Sabbat, picture Thanksgiving and add to it the fact all food was grown yourself and with that food came the security you would not starve over the winter. Then you will understand how important this celebration was.

Today food is usually plentiful, and feasts are held as community or family events. My family celebrates Mabon with a feast with our friends. Everyone gets together and brings food. We Circle, giving thanks for the harvest and the sacrifice of the God, whose life sustains us. Everyone eats together, sharing food and enjoying the fruits of the harvest and the friendships we share. We talk about the year, what it has brought us, and what our "harvest" has been. The children take a portion of the food and drink to the fields or backyard, where it is offered back to the Earth and the Mother's children in thanks for Her blessing us with sustenance.

Samhain (Sow-in)

Samhain is the festival of the final harvest and is celebrated on October 31, although some groups may celebrate at the exact midpoint between the Autumnal Equinox and the Winter Solstice, when the sun reaches 15 degrees Scorpio, or even on the second full moon after

Mabon. At Samhain we celebrate not only the harvest, but we also remember our ancestors and those who have passed on before us.

The word *Samhain* is derived from a Gaelic word meaning "summer's end." It's not, as some people claim, the name of a Deity or demon. A variation of this holiday has been celebrated for six thousand years, and modern Halloween celebrations have their origins in this Sabbat.[3] Samhain celebrations are similar to the North American Thanksgiving and the Latin American Day of the Dead celebrations. Even though Samhain is traditionally celebrated on October 31, it isn't Halloween. I'm not saying Wiccans won't go out and have fun on Halloween like everyone else, but Wiccans don't celebrate Halloween as a religious holiday. Halloween is a secular (nonreligious) holiday where everyone dresses up and kids go around their neighborhood attempting to scare people and begging for candy. Samhain isn't about demons or blood and gore; it isn't about violence or scary things that go bump in the night. The demonic aspects of Halloween were created by the medieval Church, which transformed traditional stories of fairies into tales of demons; and the spirits of our ancestors were reinterpreted as malevolent ghosts, zombies, and ghouls.

Samhain has none of these horrific elements. The Celts viewed Samhain as the time when the God, having exhausted Himself giving life energy to the crops, died and was mourned by the Goddess until Yule. For this reason Samhain has been viewed as the time when the veil between life and death was thinnest and the spirits of our ancestors could return to be close to those they had left behind.

Nowadays altars are set up with pictures of those who have passed on, and food is left out or places are set at the dinner table for them. Even though we know people never really die, because the spirits of those who have crossed over are always close to us, it is still nice to have a time of year set aside to remember those to whom we have been close, so the special memories about their time here will not be forgotten.

My family spends the day carving pumpkins and baking pies. We have an early dinner, where we spend time sharing stories about deceased family members and other people who have passed on. We let the kids go trick-or-treating and then go to a Samhain Circle and harvest carnival, where we play games, bob for apples, roast pumpkin seeds, and have a great deal of fun. I have been happy to see that in the last few years there has been an effort by the general public to return Samhain to its original Pagan roots and celebrate it as a fall or harvest festival rather than celebrate all the violence and horrific aspects that have become associated with Halloween.

Esbats (Es-bots)

Sabbats are the solar festivals celebrating the changing seasons and the harvests; they honor the God, who is represented by the sun. Esbats, also called Moons, usually honor the Goddess, who is represented by the moon. Esbats follow the lunar cycle and honor the full moon in all its glory and the new moon in its solitude. The three phases of the moon, waxing, full, and waning, represent the three faces of the Goddess as Maiden, Mother, and Crone respectively. The Sabbats are community events, holidays celebrated by everyone together. In contrast, Esbats are times of worship usually honored alone or in small groups rather than as community events. Most covens meet to worship as a group at the full and/or new moon. Moons are times of introspection and meditation. However, healing or some other type of magic, as needed, are sometimes performed during moon rituals.

There are thirteen moons during the year, each having different rituals and names that vary depending on the tradition. The names and rituals usually reflect changes in the Earth, Nature, or life related to personal changes and growth in the individual. The names of these moons could be related to agriculture (Seed Moon or Harvest Moon), animals (Wolf Moon or Turtle Moon), or trees (Oak Moon or Holly Moon). Numerous variations exist depending on which metaphors are most appropriate for the different traditions.

My coven celebrates Moons as family events, where all members bring their children and we Circle together. We discuss how the energy of that moon is affecting our lives. For example, during the Mother's Moon, we discuss those things in our lives that seem to need nurturing, and we honor the pregnant mothers. The kids are allowed to speak and participate in the rituals if they wish. Everyone brings food, and we eat and talk after the Circle.

The pentagram

Every religion has its sacred symbols. The most common sacred symbols within Wicca are the pentagram and the pentacle. According to the *Illustrated Oxford Dictionary,* pentacles and pentagrams are five-pointed stars.[4] The two terms are synonymous and may be used interchangeably. Some groups differentiate between the two, saying a pentagram is just the star and a circle around a pentagram makes it a pentacle. However, this may differ from group to group. Historically, the pentagram has represented magick, wisdom, protection, and perfection. Wiccans today also view the pentagram as a symbol of the elements: the upper point representing Spirit, and the other four points representing Earth, Air, Fire, and Water. Wiccans almost always wear their pentagram with the Spirit point up; this symbolizes the spirit above the physical aspects of life, guiding day-to-day decisions.

The pentagram is a star sometimes surrounded by a circle. However, never has one little star struck so much fear into some people's hearts. I find it a little surprising that pentagrams sometimes elicit such a negative response. By definition a pentagram is merely a five-pointed star. There are fifty of them on the American flag; I live in Texas, where there is one big pentagram on the Texas flag, and many of the highways have a huge pentagram, complete with a circle around it, on bridge supports. I have heard people protest that stars aren't pentagrams because pentagrams are open and stars are filled in. However, a triangle doesn't cease to be a triangle if it's colored in, and a colored-in pentagram is still nonetheless a pentagram. Most of the time, people either don't see the one I wear or they don't react to it. However, there are some people who react as if I were going to eat their children. This reaction may be caused by Hollywood's unfortunate tendency to feature pentagrams prominently, and incorrectly, in many of the horror movies they produce. When combined with all the negative propaganda Witches have been subjected to over the centuries, this reaction is regrettable but not surprising.

The pentagram is an ancient symbol that has been used for thousands of years by many different cultures. Some say it originated from the star found in the middle of an apple when cut across the center;[5] however, its true origin will probably always be a point of speculation. The pentagram is also called the "endless knot" and was used by the Pythagoreans as a symbol of perfection. Until the medieval period, the pentagram was a lesser-used symbol by Christians, where it was said to represent the five wounds of Christ. Evidence of this can be found in the fourteenth-century story of Sir Gawain and the Green Knight, where Sir Gawain's shield is emblazoned with a golden pentagram representing the five knightly virtues. As a symbol of protection, the pentagram has historically been worn by many law enforcement officers as their badge. Today, it is worn by Wiccans as a symbol of their faith and should not be regarded with fear or apprehension.

Spells

Many people are drawn to Wicca with visions of spell-casting dancing in their heads. They envision themselves as Prospero standing on the rocks, controlling the weather as lightning flashes around them. They want to use magick to have fairies pick up their laundry, make money pour from the sky, clear up their acne, and make their breath smell like roses. These people are sorely disappointed when they learn this is not the way magick works and find either different reasons for being Wiccan or some other path to follow.

I make my living as a professional magician, and people often ask me if I'm going to perform "real" magick. My usual answer is that real magick takes a lot longer and doesn't have as much entertainment value. What they really want to know is if magick is real or not, and the answer is yes; it is real, but just not the way they think of it. Hollywood has led people to believe magick is accompanied by eerie lights, colored smoke, and a symphonic score to emphasize the climax of the incantation. While this all makes a really nice effect in a movie, it's not the way magick actually happens.

Magick works because there is spiritual energy in the universe that, when directed toward a specific goal, can cause something to happen. Spiritual energy is all around us; it flows through us, and we use it unconsciously every day of our lives. It is a gift from Deity and is freely given for all to use. Spiritual energy is accessed unconsciously by people when they have a strong desire or need. It is accessed through prayer, and it is also accessed with spells. This energy is used to heal sickness, help resolve problems, and aid people in need.

When someone wishes to cast a spell, they gather some of this spiritual energy and direct it toward a goal they wish to accomplish. The more energy gathered, the greater the effect, and the effect is cumulative. For example, if a person is sick, the more people casting spells or praying, the more healing energy is directed toward that person, and the more it can help them get well.

Think of the spiritual energy available to us as if it were an ocean and the goal to be accomplished were a fire to be extinguished. Now, I don't care how big that fire is, the ocean can quench it; the problem is getting the water to the fire. Water is moved in buckets; spiritual energy is moved by the mind with will and intention. If someone were trying to put out a fire with water from the ocean, they could run to the ocean with anything from a thimble to a bucket and scoop out water and throw it on the fire. Even a thimble full of water would have some effect on the fire, even it if wasn't noticeable, and if a million people each threw a thimble of water on the fire, it might even go out; however, a bucket full of water will prove more effective. In the physical world, a person's strength and size limit the size of water bucket they can carry; however, in the spiritual world, we are limited only by our belief and will. With magick a person can dump a "bucket" of spiritual energy the size of a water tower on that fire and never strain a muscle.

The key to using magick is will and intent. Will controls how much energy is accessed and when it is going to move; intent tells the energy where to go and what to do when it arrives. One has to be specific and focus clearly on what is to be accomplished to get the best results. I think of it like working with my kids. If I tell them to take their laundry to their room, I will most likely come back later to find the laundry still sitting there and them saying, "I didn't know you wanted me to do it now," or I will find the clean laundry stacked on the floor in their room and them saying, "But you didn't tell me I had to put it away, too." To be most effective, spells have to clearly direct spiritual energy so the energy goes exactly where and does exactly what the person wants because the energy will work to put out whatever fire it's sent to, even if it's not quite what the person had in mind.

Spiritual energy must also be gathered effectively so that large buckets full of energy are being dumped on the problem rather than little thimbles full. To aid in gathering energy, spells use a variety of natural methods to increase the amount of energy directed toward a problem. In an effort to increase the energy gathered, and thereby the effectiveness of the spell, Circles may be cast, chants used, candles lit, and incense burned. Various herbs, oils, or colors may also be used because they resonate with energy similar to the desired goal and will, therefore, make the spell stronger.

Real magick is someone carrying mint leaves in her purse to attract money. Someone lighting a blue candle and envisioning their sick mother getting well is also magick. Likewise, someone putting on lipstick and perfume with the intent of drawing romantic attention to herself would be casting a simple love spell. Real magick does not have the Hollywood special effects, but the results are powerful, although rarely instantaneous.

When casting spells, Witches harness some of the universal spiritual energy, focus it toward a specific goal they wish to accomplish, and turn it loose. Magick is like prayer with props and is extremely effective when used properly. However, it's not going to give a person all the money they desire or make someone do another person's bidding. There are ethical considerations, and spells that seek to bend someone else's free will, harm others, or have greedy intentions will probably not work and may even have serious repercussions upon the caster, as stated in the Rule of Three. Therefore, magick, like prayer, is a tool to help in times of need or to help bring a person closer to Divinity. It is not a substitute for hard work, study, or the use of wisdom in everyday life.

For a deeper understanding about Wiccan life, please read:

FIVE

Misconceptions about Wicca

IN ORDER TO discuss how misconceptions have arisen regarding Wiccans, one has to open a discussion of one of the most regrettable periods in the history of humanity. The Renaissance period (14th to 17th century) brought many wonders of art and science into the world, but the birth of the Renaissance period was accompanied by the type of pain and suffering that has, fortunately, rarely been seen in history. The birth pains of the Renaissance period involved the Inquisition. Sometimes referred to as the Burning Times, this period of history was so detestable that on March 12, 2000, Pope John Paul II issued an apology for the Catholic Church's actions during this time. Pope John Paul II said, "We are asking pardon for the divisions among Christians, for the use of violence that some have committed in service of truth, and for attitudes of mistrust and hostility assumed toward followers of other religions."[1] This general apology was accompanied by a specific apology to women by Cardinal Francis Arinze, who said women are "all too often humiliated and marginalized."[2]

I don't intend to imply that my comments in this chapter about the Church are in any way directed at or attacking the current Roman Catholic Church or its members. It can be inferred from Pope John Paul II's comments that the current Catholic Church wouldn't condone the horrific acts of its Renaissance incarnation. The only reason I am compelled to discuss this vile period of history is that a portion of both the Inquisition's efforts and the efforts of the local courts who enforced the laws of the Church were focused on hunting down and executing witches. Now remember, the word *Witch* means a person who uses some form of natural magick, but the ways people claimed witches used magick were so ghastly and fantastical that the only similarity modern Witches have to those who were hunted down during the Renaissance is the term itself. Within this chapter, I will usually use the word *witch* to refer to the fantasy version of witchcraft and *Wicca* or *Witch* to refer to the modern practice of witchcraft. The majority of the victims of the witch hunts were women. They were widows, midwives, and anyone else who found themselves afoul of the Church or society, and most of them were, like their tormenters, Catholics. Few of the victims of the Inquisition were practitioners of a pre-Christian Pagan religion. Even though the witches who were hunted during this time existed only as illusions in the minds of the witchhunters, and never actually existed, most of the ugly stereotypes about Wiccans came from this time period. People seem reluctant to relinquish their view of this fantasy idea of the witch, possibly because some believe as John Wesley did in 1768 that "giving up on witchcraft is, in effect, giving up on the Bible."[3] I don't think this is true, but others might retain this viewpoint; however, for whatever reason, Wiccans today are still stigmatized by these fictional creations from the Renaissance.

Changes in society

People are often told Witches are evil people who form pacts with the Devil, eat babies, and stomp flowers. This image descends to us from the fear and propaganda of the Renaissance, where almost every human woe was blamed on witches. Supposedly witches caused hailstorms, destroyed crops, changed people into animals, and killed children. No wonder people became so afraid of them. However, these accusations were motivated by the Church's fear that it was losing control of a rapidly changing society.

During the Dark Ages, the Catholic Church had gained a firm hold on Europe and brought with it a dualistic view of the Universe. Everything was divided into good and evil. Whatever was good, its opposite had to be evil. God was good; the Devil was evil. White was good; black was evil. Day was good; night was evil. Medieval society was held together by the feudal hierarchy, with the Church controlling all aspects of life.

However, between the thirteenth and seventeenth centuries, European society changed. Society turned toward industry, trade, education, and economic development, which led to more jobs in the cities. Merchants flourished, and a middle class formed. Men worked in an attempt to be successful, and this frequently led them to delay marriage, which left women in a position of either living with their families, who may not be able to support them, or seeking employment of their own.[4] Copernicus refuted the Ptolemaic view of the universe by telling people the sun did not revolve around the Earth, and humanity, therefore, ceased to be the center of the universe. Skeptics began to turn the magnifying glass of Aristotle's rules of logic on the Church, questioning its ideals and the very existence of God. These changes in society alarmed the Church greatly. The Church had little power over the emerging middle class. Women who were not subjected to the authority of a man could not be controlled as easily, and anything challenging people's belief in God or the Church's position that man was the center of God's creation would be vigorously opposed, as Galileo found out. These views were all threats to the Church's power.

One of the ways the Church chose to combat this change in society involved transforming the perception of the Witch from a healer and magical technician into a puppet of Satan. Witchcraft became "theological damage control," not only by answering the skeptics' doubts but also by assigning blame and designating a scapegoat for all of society's woes.[5] Witchcraft was portrayed as the antithesis of the "true faith," and witches were said to do everything exactly opposite of the Church.[6] Thus, the Church became everything light and good; witches became everything dark and evil. The dualistic viewpoint of the Universe taught by the Church made it easy to convince people that witches were the soldiers of Satan. As Satan's minions, witches could be blamed for all the problems in the world, and any sociological changes the Church deemed inappropriate could be quelled by labeling them a plot of Satan.

It was more advantageous for the Church to use witches as scapegoats because witches looked like everyone else, so one could never tell who might be a witch. These fantasy witches were, as James Connor says, "the terrorists of the seventeenth century—unseen, moving about society disguised as ordinary citizens, with malevolent wills hidden behind smiling faces."[7] Witches could be a person's neighbor or even his wife, and one would never know it. This left those in charge free to grab people they felt threatened the Church's control of society and torture them until obtaining a confession. Each new confession resulted in more fantastic stories and made the case stronger in the minds of the people whose prayers for protection were carried toward heaven, on the smoke from the bodies of the innocent women and men who had become human sacrifices, burnt offerings to the gods of greed, power, and control.

Witch spotting

"How do you know she's a witch?" This question was asked in the movie *Monty Python and the Holy Grail,* and the crowd answers, "Because she's dressed like one." They then respond she has turned someone into a newt, but he got better. Finally it's decided she is a witch because she has a wart. As silly as it sounds, for centuries no more proof than this was needed to have someone arrested as a witch. However, what do Witches really look like? Can you spot them as they walk down the street? Is there some kind of ritual to perform or test to determine whether or not they're Witches?

Ask kids what Witches look like, and they'll probably say to stay on the lookout for an old woman with warts, who wears a black pointy hat, talks to her cats, and quite possibly has green skin. This image of the crone as witch has always been the most common stereotype, although I think the green skin was added because of the movie *The Wizard of Oz*. In ancient times, the crone was thought to be an image of power: she was knowledge, wisdom, and experience all wrapped into one. The crone became a threat to the powers that be because she could not be controlled easily and people looked up to her, seeking her advice instead of the advice of the Church.[8] Therefore, because of the Church's influence, the crone was transformed into an image of evil; her image became spiteful, vindictive, and mean. If a woman kept to herself, she was said to be working evil and consorting with the Devil. If she went out, she could be viewed as looking for people and things to destroy. If she happened to talk to herself sometimes, that could be used as proof she was cursing the neighborhood children. This belief developed into many of the geriatric prejudices that now pervade Western society, where older men tend to be viewed as knowledgeable and capable, while older women are often seen as senile and bitter. However, not only the old could be identified as witches; the ugly, the deformed, the bewitchingly beautiful, and any woman who was considered too smart, too clever, or too wealthy were also included in the prejudicial listing. Witches included anyone people wanted to label a witch.

Now, if you want to know what a Wiccan looks like, simply look around, and you will find that Wiccans look the same as everyone else. Wiccans look like teachers, doctors, artists, and shopkeepers; they are women and men of every occupation, race, and social class. Wiccans have the same goals, dreams, and feelings as everyone else, and above all, they are people: mothers, daughters, fathers, sons, sisters, brothers, and cousins.

Is there a test to tell if someone is a Witch? In the days of the Inquisition, people believed that telltale signs would appear on someone's body if they were practicing witchcraft. If a person was accused of witchcraft, no proof was necessary; the accusation alone sufficed for the accused to be handed over for trial. The Inquisition would strip the individuals, shave off all their body hair, tie them down, and examine their nude body very closely, searching them for a Devil's mark that was erroneously believed to have been left by Satan. Any irregularity on the skin could be interpreted as a mark of the Devil. Moles, birthmarks, and dark freckles were enough to convict someone, and protruding moles that could be construed as an extra nipple were viewed as proof positive of someone's guilt. Any physical characteristic contrary to the norm could be seen as a sign of being a witch; blue eyes or red hair were considered to be dead giveaways.[9] Most people could not pass such physical scrutiny without being found guilty.

Sometimes needles were used to poke and prod the accused persons skin and eyes as interrogators looked for a spot where the Devil's touch had removed all feeling from the skin. If the person was found to have a spot that, when prodded, didn't cause them to scream in pain, they were guilty of witchcraft. Suspected witches were sometimes tied up and thrown into the water, reasoning that water, which was used for baptism, would reject anyone in league with the Devil. If the suspected witch floated to the surface, they were considered guilty and hanged. If they drowned, they were innocent—dead but innocent. Sometimes accused people were forced to carry a hot iron and endure many other near-impossible tortures in attempts to prove their innocence. Once accused, nearly all "suspects" were found to have some characteristic that, to the court, proved they were a witch.

During the Renaissance, the Catholic Church created most of the witch stereotypes that have now been reinforced and added to by Hollywood. Wicca is a religion, and no distinguishing marks or tests prove someone is Wiccan. Witchcraft is not hereditary, so a person can't be one-sixteenth Wiccan on their mother's side. Wicca doesn't require its followers to receive tattoos or brands; we don't even have a secret handshake. One can no more tell that people are Wiccan by looking at them than one can tell someone is Catholic, Protestant, or even Buddhist. The only thing Wiccans all share is a common respect of nature and a reverence for Deity as both a God and a Goddess.

Are you a good Witch or a bad Witch?

People have an unfortunate tendency to try to divide all things into good and bad: good dogs and bad dogs, good books and bad books, good calories and bad calories. We tend to judge things and label them according to our perceptions, and that judgment may forever color our viewpoint because "it" now has a label. Once something has been labeled, it's very difficult to get someone to change that label because people seem to think this would be admitting they had been wrong the first time, that they had erred and were, therefore, less than perfect. So people cling to their labels with a tenacity that would make a pit bull proud. Unfortunately, not everyone labels things the same way; what one person has labeled as bad, another person may label as good. This breeds conflict because people have an unfortunate tendency to view their own label as the definitive one, and people tend to view as wrong any opinions that differ from their own. Often if the "offending" people don't change their view, they will also be labeled bad. This is the source of most disagreements in the world, not to mention quite a few wars.

In reality both good and bad labels are a matter of perspective. Good and bad are value judgments, and neither is accurate, except in an individual's own mind. From where we stand on Earth, we lack the Divine perspective and can't always see the reason why something happens. I have to trust that there is a reason for every action and that in time I might understand why an event occurred. Let's imagine for a moment that life and all its events are being painted by Deity and that each event fits together to create a giant mural. Now imagine that we are ants crawling on that mural. From our perspective, the whole of the mural is impossible to see; we can only see the point where we now stand. We might perceive that point to be the blackest, most depressing spot in the entire painting; however, if we could back up and see everything as the Divine views the world, that black spot could be the shadow that offsets and helps create the most beautiful part of the scene. Even events most people would consider terrible may set in motion a chain of events leading to something those same people would view as good.

There is an old story I frequently use to illustrate this point. A man and his son lived in a mountainous region of China, and all they had was each other and a horse they used to plow their fields. One day the horse ran away into the mountains, and the nearby villagers began to talk about how awful this was because without the horse the man and his son could not plow their fields to grow their food. The old man, however, remained calm and simply said that he couldn't judge whether the horse leaving was bad or good. Two days later, the horse returned and brought with him four wild mares. The villagers rejoiced at the man's good fortune, as he now had more prosperity than most people in the village, but the old man responded that he didn't know whether this event was good or bad. The following day the man's son was attempting to break one of the mares so she could be ridden, and she threw him from her back, breaking his arm. The villagers moaned that this was terrible because without his son in good health, it would be difficult for a man of his age to plow the fields. The old man shrugged and went on about his business without deciding whether his son's arm being broken was good or bad. A week later the army came through the village and took all the young men away to fight in a far-off war, but the old man's son, being injured, was left behind. Now, can you judge whether the horse running away was a good thing or a bad thing?—No. If a bad thing causes something good to happen, was the original event good or bad? It could be argued both ways, and in the end, each person will have to decide for themselves or trust in the Divine that all will work out for the best.

"Are you a good witch or a bad witch?" This was the first question Glenda asked Dorothy in *The Wizard of Oz,* and indeed, this is often one of the first questions people ask when they find out someone is Wiccan. Unless they have reason to know better, many people's first reaction is to think Witches are evil, but they may have heard there can also be good Witches, so they want to know to which Witch they are speaking. Unfortunately, the whole question is meaningless and inappropriate. It always sounds to me like the person is referring to a disobedient dog: "Bad witch, you spilled candle wax on the carpet, bad witch!"

Using "white Witch" and "black Witch" is no more appropriate because a value judgment is still made and the color black is traditionally assigned to represent evil. People started using the term "white witch" in the seventeenth century as a way to distinguish actual Witches from the fantasy witches the Puritan preachers railed about from the pulpit. These fantasy "bad witches" go about the country trying to destroy beauty and goodness; they stomp flowers, drown kittens, eat children, and cause male-pattern baldness. They also don't really exist.

Wiccans are Witches, and they are people, and like all people they make choices. Some of these choices are beneficial, and some of these choices may be rather unfortunate. Wiccans should be judged by their actions, just as all people should be judged by their actions as individuals. If a person who is Wiccan lives by the principles of Wicca, then that person is a Witch. No qualifier is placed before "Witch," and none should be added.

What if someone asked, "Are you a good Christian or a bad one? a good Buddhist or a bad one?" I've heard people refer to "lapsed Catholics," but that's not the same as saying they're "bad." If a man goes to religious services every week with his family but spends the rest of the week beating his wife, hanging out in bars, getting drunk, and starting fights while trying to pick up coeds, do we start referring to him as a bad Buddhist, Christian, Jew, or Muslim? Of course not. People think of him as a person who is making some really bad choices. The man would probably not even be viewed as a true follower of his religion at all because he is not following the tenets of that religion and living his life as he should; he just wears a religious mask in an attempt to give himself legitimacy.

The same is true with Wiccans. If people continuously make choices in violation of the Rede, they are either Wiccans who are making some very poor choices, or they are not truly Wiccan because they are not living according to the principles Wicca sets forth any more than the drunken adulterer is truly following his religion. People could take the drunken adulterer, parade him through the streets, hold him up as an example of his religion, and proclaim loudly that people of his faith are wife beaters and drunkards. People could cry that to preserve decency, people of this faith should be hunted down before they corrupt our children. A mob could be whipped into a pitchfork-wielding frenzy and begin dragging people from their beds. However, judging everyone in the religion by the actions of this one person would not be fair to the majority of peaceful, loving people who practice that religion.

This exact same thing has been done to suspected witches for many centuries and is still done to Wiccans now. During the Renaissance, people accused as witches would be tortured until they falsely confessed to some heinous crime, after which they were held out as an example of what witches do, even though they were neither actually a witch nor guilty of the crime for which they were condemned. However, even if a person *was* a Witch and guilty of criminal actions, it's not fair to judge all Witch by the actions of a single person. Just because someone calls themselves Wiccan and has chosen to wear a Wiccan mask because it makes them feel powerful, different, or scary does not make them truly Wiccan. Everyone is judged by the choices they make, and if a person makes selfish or harmful choices, they may be a selfish or harmful person, but they should not be labeled a "bad Witch."

Pointy hats, black cats, and brooms, oh my!

One of the greatest campaigns of misinformation and propaganda ever waged against any group has been blasted at Witches. Before the fourteenth century the Roman Catholic Church in the Canon *Episcopi* considered it heresy even to believe in witches, and the Church officially regarded witchcraft as mere illusion.[10] However, in the fourteenth century Pope John XXII, convinced that witchcraft was spreading across Europe, authorized the full use of the Inquisition against witches, and it became heresy not to believe in witches.[11] Prior to this time, people who were thought of as witches were people who simply lived their lives the way their ancestors had for centuries before. They were people the community believed to have special powers and abilities given to them by the gods, and through the correct use of spells, they could help people by altering the natural world in certain ways. However, during the fourteenth to seventeenth centuries, witchcraft was transformed by the Church and became perceived as a force for evil that created problems instead of solved them.[12] Since then, witches have been maligned from pulpits and public squares, subjected to the most fantastic and ridiculous claims, and tortured in some of the most horrible and inhumane ways known to man. Throughout the Renaissance and continuing on into the seventeenth century, there have been outbreaks of witch hysteria where people dragged their neighbors from their beds with very little, if any, real evidence and tortured, burned, hanged, or beat them to death as witches.[13]

This kind of insane mob mentality doesn't get started by saying someone practices a different religion. If someone went around saying, "Mary down the street worships a Goddess," the reaction from the uninformed might be "Oh, my!" or "That's awful!" but no one is going to drag people out the door of their homes and beat them to death. To get a real raving fanatical frenzy going, one can't simply tell people that witches worship other deities; someone would have to tell people that witches sacrifice children to these gods, drink blood, fornicate with the Devil, and cause impotency. These are classic charges that have been leveled against many different groups. The Romans falsely claimed the early Christians committed almost the same list of crimes, and Christians, during the Renaissance, then used an almost identical, and equally false, list of crimes against Jews and witches.

Beginning in the fourteenth century, the Church went to great lengths, including misquoting biblical passages, to convince people that witches were participating in a great number of fictional heresies.[14] Some religious leaders actively tried to convince people that if they didn't get rid of anyone who might be a witch, the crops would fail, their children would disappear, the rivers would turn to blood, and Satan would appear in the town square dancing a little jig. Now, with the proper motivation and after being whipped into a fervor rivaling that of Super Bowl Sunday, the angry mobs would take to the streets waving torches, looking for the supposed enemies of society. A host of fictional heresies were "confirmed" by the confessions of torture victims, who were never witches to begin with, so many of these imagined evils stuck and became the "facts" about Witches that many people still believe to this day.

Devil worship and sacrifice

The most pervasive lie about Witches is that they worship the Devil. According to the medieval viewpoint, all things good come from God and all things evil come from the Devil. Therefore, if witches had power over nature, it must be from Satan, and the only way to obtain that power was for people to sell their souls to him. This belief was reinforced when a large number of victims of the Inquisition confessed under duress to worshiping the Devil. Unfortunately, these confessions were obtained only after people had been tortured enough to make them confess to worshiping chocolate milk if that's what the inquisitors wanted to hear—anything to stop the pain.

The truth is, Wiccans do not worship the Devil. Wicca is a religion not in any way based on, shaped by, or reliant on Christianity. The Devil, or an ultimate incarnation of evil, is a belief unique to Zoroastrianism and the Abrahamic religions: Judaism, Christianity, and Islam. Other religions, including Wicca, do not have this entity, and therefore the adherents of those religions can't worship something that doesn't exist from the viewpoint of their religion. Saying Wiccans worship the Christian Devil is as ludicrous as saying Buddhists or Hindus worship Satan; it would be an improper mixing of religious pantheons.

Another falsehood about Wiccans is that we sacrifice animals or children. Wiccans do not sacrifice any living thing in any shape, form, or fashion. Nature is sacred to Wiccans, and we would not harm any living entity. I know Wiccans who are animal rights activists, who are vegetarians, and who will walk a bug outside rather than step on it. Now, not all Wiccans are this protective of every living thing, but no Wiccan should ever sacrifice an animal.

The stories of witches sacrificing children to the Devil possibly began as a way to get rid of midwives. The *Malleus Maleficarum* says, "No one does more harm to the Catholic faith than midwives."[15] Midwives did more than just deliver babies. They were the village healers who used both magick and herbs to heal and provided women with birth control. They were the village counselors and advisors; they removed curses, predicted the future, and arbitrated disputes. The work of the village midwife was one of both healer and psychologist, and this trod on the toes of the male doctors and priests.[16] Midwives were powerful women in a now male-dominated society that viewed ambition as a vice that ruled "wicked women."[17]

Sex and Wicca

Sexual issues have always played a big role in anti-witch propaganda; in fact, the description of sexual acts with demons is one of the most consistent elements found in witchcraft confessions. Witches were said to have fornicated with the Devil, demons, and animals; had wild orgies; incited men to lustful thoughts; made men impotent; and stolen men's penises, which they hid in birds nests.[18] The Renaissance was a very sexually repressed time. Women were always to be completely covered. Sex was viewed as Original Sin. Sex was to be indulged in only for purposes of reproduction, and even then, it was probably better not to enjoy it. What better way to make society hate and fear a group of people than to invent grotesque, perverted sexual stories about witches that were guaranteed to be abhorrent to the population as a whole.

Another possible motivation for the sexual mania of the witch-hunters is expressed by Walter Stephens in his book *Demon Lovers: Witchcraft, Sex, and the Crisis of Belief.* Stephens theorizes that the sexual perversions of witches became the cornerstone of the witches' confessions, because the inquisitors themselves were wrestling with their inability to logically prove the existence of God. The inquisitors seemed convinced that if they could prove people had intimate physical contact with the Devil or demons, then that would logically prove the Devil and demons were physically real and active in the world. This was important because if one could prove the Devil existed, then it could be logically concluded that God also existed and was active in the world. This "desire to be convinced of the reality of spirit was the psychic glue that held the witch myth together."[19]

The reason for women's many carnal abominations, as stated in the *Malleus Maleficarum,* an approved document of the Roman Catholic Church in the fifteenth century, was that women are feebler both in mind and body than men and are intellectually more like children because there was a defect in the first woman; she was formed from a bent rib and was therefore "an imperfect animal."[20] Witches were said to incite men to passion. This is where the description of a woman as "bewitching" originates. The *Malleus* tells us how to tell if a man is under the lustful spell of a witch.[21] First, if he is lusting after a woman in spite of the fact he has a beautiful wife, then the woman he is lusting after is a witch. Second, if he is lusting after the woman so much he can't be talked out of it, then she's a witch. Third, if he wants to be with the woman day and night and travels to see her unexpectedly, she's a witch. Men were said to be always in control of their emotions; therefore, it couldn't be his fault if he follows a woman around with lustful intentions. The doctrine of the Church at that time insisted that men were in control of their passions and that women's carnal lust was insatiable.[22] These are only some of the reasons the Church considered women to be evil temptresses who were constantly trying to pervert men's souls.

Just to set the record straight, the sexual stories about Wicca are not true. Granted, Wiccans as a whole have a more liberal view of sexuality than perhaps some other religions do, but the religion is not based on nor does it prescribe guidelines for sex. While listening to a radio program, I heard an "occult expert" ask a Wiccan caller about the Great Rite. The caller explained that this ritual honors the creative energies of nature by using a chalice and a blade to symbolically portray the mating of the God and Goddess and that this ritual is performed by some groups at certain times of the year but has no actual sexual content. Our "expert" then, putting on his best "I've got you now" voice, said, "But it's symbolic sex," as if Wicca revolves around sex.

I have never understood why some people have huge problems with even the thought of sex. Everyone, please raise your hand if sex is *not* responsible for you getting into this life. What, no hands? That's what I thought. Almost every living thing on the Earth reproduces itself through some form of sexual reproduction. Sex is an essential part of nature, and the symbolic Great Rite used as a part of some Wiccan Circles acknowledges this in a fashion that is not, by any stretch of the imagination, lewd or erotic. There's nothing wrong with sex as long as it's an individual's choice. However, no one ever has the right to use anything, especially religion, to try to coerce people, telling them when, where, or with whom they should have sex. If someone is told by a High Priest or High

Priestess that people must have sex with them in order to join a coven or become a Priest or Priestess, they should turn the other way and run. Sex should be the choice of consenting adults, and just because a religion recognizes that all nature propagates itself through some form of sexual union does not mean the followers of that religion are hedonists whose entire world revolves around sex. People who come to Wicca looking for wild orgies and sexual promiscuity end up leaving with their egos deflated.

Flying on brooms

What Halloween witch's costume would be complete without her broom? The image of a witch flying through the air on her broom is a very pervasive image that first appeared in 1280.[23] But how were witches supposed to have flown? Older versions of this story have the witches being carried not by brooms but by animals or demons. The *Malleus Maleficarum* says witches make an ointment from the limbs of unbaptized children (yuck!) and anoint a chair or broom with it. The witch is then immediately carried through the air either visibly or invisibly.[24] Every witch from the Wicked Witch of the West to Harry Potter is pictured flying on a broom. Witches were said to be able to fly up their chimneys and out of their locked houses, traveling long distances at great rates of speed and returning the same way.

The truth of the matter is that Witches use their brooms for the same purpose everyone else does: cleaning. As magical tools, brooms are used ceremonially in preparation for casting Circle to clean the area of negative energy, but no one uses them as transport. Though no one is sure how this particular flight of fantasy began, one of the popular explanations supposedly comes from an ancient fertility rite where people rode brooms and pitchforks around a field, leaping into the air and encouraging the crops to grow high.[25] Regardless of how this story began, it gave the Inquisition a way to explain how witches could get from their homes and travel a great distance to meet with the Devil, even though no one saw them coming or going.

Familiar spirits

Witches were said to have familiars, animals given to them by the Devil to do their bidding. These animals, supposedly, were not actually animals at all but were minor demons given the form of animals to aid the witch in her evil deeds. The list of animals accused of being familiars includes almost all of the animals one would commonly run into in Europe: dogs, cats, toads, rats, bats, goats, chickens, and rabbits. Any animal could be suspected of being a spawn of Satan. Familiars were a useful aid in helping explain a witch's power. Most people had pets or farm animals, and if someone could recall seeing a person talking to their animals, that could be used to prove the animal was the person's familiar. If an animal was seen in the vicinity of a person who later was injured or became ill, then this could be used as proof the owner was a witch, who sent the animal to cause harm. This expanded the number of ways to implicate someone of witchcraft. Even if the suspected witch had never had contact with the "victim" or had a dozen people who could provide alibis, the suspect could still be convicted if the inquisitors claimed the "witch" sent her familiar to cause the damage.

Wiccans usually love animals and tend to have many pets (that cat lady on the block could very well be a Witch), but all this is because of our connection to nature and love of life. All our pets are of the normal animal variety, but don't tell someone their pet is "normal" unless you want to hear about how smart Fluffy is and how she does the cutest thing. Wiccans tend to talk about our animals as if they were our children, but none of them are cloaked demons or imps in disguise. How many people today have a pet they talk to and love very much? How easy would it have been for any of us to have been convicted of witchcraft because we love our animals too much?

Witch's hat

The witch's hat is an essential part of the ensemble for the stereotypical witch. If the witch costume didn't have a hat, people could mistake the person wearing it for a vampire or someone who lost their way to a Cure concert, but why has this conical hat become a ubiquitous image of witchdom? No one knows for sure, but the Church might have said witches wore pointed hats to represent Devil horns, since the Church made the same accusation when tall conical hats were all the rage for ladies of the court in the fifteenth century.[26] The witch's hat could be an ancient tradition, or it might be the invention of eighteenth-century illustrators of early children's fairy tale books.

Many Witches say the hat represents a *cone of power* that was believed to channel energy from the cosmos into the head of the wearer, which would also explain why wizards are pictured wearing a similar pointed hat and why the class dunce was crowned with this kind of hat in an attempt to increase intelligence. Maybe the hat was added by illustrators to suggest that witches were backward, antisocial people who continued to wear pointed hats long after they were out of fashion. Whatever the reason, the hat stuck, but only as a Halloween getup. Most Wiccans don't wear these or any other hats while worshiping.

The image of the Witch

The images the average person associates with Witches were creations of the Church in the fifteenth century, which transformed the image of Witches from magickal healers and diviners into servants of the Devil. However, this should not come as a surprise to anyone because during this time period, the Church attacked, killed, or maligned anyone who did not share its worldview.

For example, the Cathers in southern France were an ascetic sect who had a dualistic view of the world that differed from official Catholic doctrine and rejected some of the sacraments. This made them heretical in the eyes of the Church. When they would not return to the Church, Pope Innocent III called for a crusade against them. During the twenty years of warfare that followed, southern France was decimated. In 1209, the inhabitants of the city of Beziers were massacred. One leader, before the massacre, was asked how to distinguish the true believers from heretics; he is said to have replied: "Slay them all. God knows his own."[27]

Jews and Moors were hunted by the Spanish Inquisition. The Crusades pounded the Muslims. Missionaries forced native peoples in the Americas and other countries to convert, and the Dominicans were busy ferreting out witches, Protestants, and anyone else they thought was undesirable. Therefore, witches were not the only victims of the Church's religious cleansing campaign.

All the things that happened during the Crusades and the Inquisition happened because the Church controlled all aspects of life at the time. The Church controlled the courts, education, and social life. Everything had to fall in line with Church doctrine and was subject to its approval. This left the Church open to abuse or kill those who had differing viewpoints, making it impossible for these people to do business, receive an education, or be a functional part of society.

This is why many Wiccans oppose religious doctrine intruding into public forums. Issues like school prayer or the posting of the Ten Commandments may seem benign, but they can lead people to perceive that the United States has an officially recognized religion, leaving all other religions in a second-class position. This begins to set up the same situation that caused the persecution of so many people in the past. Wiccans want to make sure people have learned from history because we don't want to repeat the mistakes that once led to the deaths of tens of thousands of people.

For a deeper understanding of misconceptions about Wicca, please read:

Are Wiccans discriminated against? Page 205
Do you have to be special to do magick? Page 208
Is there an official Wiccan dress code? Page 211
Are Wiccans psychic? Page 214
Can Wiccans tell the future? Page 215
Aren't male Witches called warlocks? Page 217
Is Wicca Satanic? Page 218

SIX

The Personal Experience of Spirit

YOU NOW HAVE had an introduction to the concepts and ideas that make up Wicca. Thank you for taking the time to try to understand the Wiccan religion. I realize that for some of you this was a difficult thing to do, and I applaud you for making the effort to understand religious beliefs and ideas that may be very different from your own. Even if you continue to disagree with your friend or family member's religious choice, you have made an effort to learn something about their beliefs, and that is more than many people are willing to do. Wiccan beliefs and many of the concepts that form the foundation of Wicca may seem foreign or strange to many people. Even after understanding *WHAT* Wiccans believe, some people might still be struggling with understanding *WHY* Wiccans believe some of the things we do. Unfortunately, there's no way to communicate all the different reasons why someone might be Wiccan or how each individual Wiccan might experience Deity.

Wicca is an experiential religion. Therefore, some parts can't be taught or explained. One has to live the Wiccan path to truly understand it, and everyone experiences Wicca in their own way. No two people are the same; all of us see the world from our own perspective. We each have our own priorities, and each of us experience Divinity in our own unique fashion. People who are more emotional about religion may experience Divinity as a feeling that lifts them up and fills them with a calm serenity, while people who approach religion from an intellectual standpoint may experience Divinity as a satori, that divine epiphany that brings understanding and clarity. Because everyone is different, no two Wiccans will experience Divinity in exactly the same way, and no two Wiccans will practice Wicca in exactly the same fashion.

When one really thinks about it, no two people of any religion will practice their religion exactly the same, whether they are Christian, Buddhist, Muslim, or any other of the world's diverse religious paths. Each religious devotee will practice their religion in their own unique way and for their own reasons. Wicca acknowledges this fact and allows individual Wiccans the freedom to follow their own path within the framework of Wicca.

Flexibility in understanding Divinity is at the heart of Wicca and is perceived by Wiccans to be a great strength. Each person's freedom to perceive Deity in their own unique way is what makes Wicca a personal and individual religious experience. Wiccans believe that however one experiences Divinity is the correct way for that person.

Even though a formalized structure works fine for many religions, if someday, hundreds of years from now, some group were to standardize the Wiccan religion into a rigid list of beliefs and dogmas and tell Wiccans they must all experience Divinity in the same way, I believe the loss of flexibility would be a fatal wound to the heart of Wicca. I think that on that day Wicca would cease to live and grow and would begin to die. Like an ancient and glorious tree that begins to rot from the center, dying by degrees until only the lifeless shape of its former self remains, Wicca would start to decay until all that was left was the rotted shell of something once vibrant and growing.

People can no more be forced into a different religious experience than they can be forced into being right-handed. You can be told all people should write with their right hand, and you can even go through the motions of using your right hand, but if you're actually left-handed, it's not going to truly work for you. Allowing people to experience the Divine in their own way means Wicca is like nature, always living, growing, and changing.

For people to completely understand Wicca, they would have to live it. They would have to experience a year not as a collection of months and quarters but as a dynamic changing set of seasons that flow gracefully into each other. People would have to let themselves change along with those seasons, feeling how each one affects them in a different way. They would have to see how the changing seasons relate to their life and the changes they go through as they age. They would have to be able to look out at a meadow and see grass and flowers, and even the ragweed and pollen, as living entities connected to every other entity on the planet. They would have to begin to see the web of life as it attaches to each plant, animal, and insect; then they would have to see themselves not as the spider who sits on the web separate from everything else, but rather see the web running through them. Everything they do pulls on the web, affecting every other thing. Only then could someone start to see why others might choose to be Wiccan.

I would like to conclude the first part of this book with a story in prose I have adapted from the poem "The Blind Men and the Elephant" by John Godfrey Saxe, which is about several blind men who wanted to experience an elephant.[1] Four blind men who, having heard the elephant was the greatest and most powerful of creatures, wanted very much to experience the elephant firsthand. These men traveled a great distance and suffered many hardships in their attempt to find the elephant. When at last the blind seekers discovered the elephant, they asked it if they may be allowed to touch its greatness because they would not be able to experience him any other way. The elephant, being a noble and gracious beast, allowed the men to approach so they might experience him directly. The first blind man stretched forth his hand and touched the elephant's broad side and declared that he now understood that the elephant is great and strong because it is like a wall. The second blind man reached out and, encountering the elephant's tusk, proclaimed that the elephant is mighty and fierce because it is like a spear. The third blind man stumbled and, reaching out, grabbed the elephant's tail. From this he understood the elephant could save them and give them hope because it is like a rope. The last man bumped into the elephant's enormous leg and determined that the elephant is supportive and nurturing because it is like a tree. The four walked away arguing and fighting, each trying to convince the others that his experience alone was correct and true. The elephant simply shook its head and sighed, knowing that each man's understanding of him was correct based on his own experience but that each of them only understood the tiniest fragment of what an elephant truly is.

For those of you who still want more, please read:

What if I don't agree with my friend or loved one's religious choice? Page 221

How do I find a Wiccan Circle? Page 224

What do I need to know before attending a Wiccan Circle? Page 226

PART TWO

Deeper Understanding

QUESTIONS, QUERIES, METAPHYSICAL
CONUNDRUMS, AND THINGS THAT
KEEP A PERSON UP AT NIGHT

A Deeper Understanding of Wicca

Why did they have to tell me they were Wiccan?

If you are reading this book, someone has probably shared with you that they are following the Wiccan religion. Sometimes people wonder why their friend or loved one decided to tell them. Such people probably subscribe to the "ignorance is bliss" school of thought and were very happy not knowing, or at least actively pretending that they didn't know, that their child or coworker followed a different religious path. If that friend or loved one is like most of us who have informed our families that our religion is different from the one in which we grew up, the most likely reason is that they trust you on a deep level and want to be able to share with you something very personal about their life.

Religion is one of the most intimate aspects of a person's life. Religion has been defined as the ultimate concern of a person; therefore, what is most important in a person's life is their religion. People who follow Wicca are usually very committed to living their life and walking the Wiccan path; therefore, their religion is what is most important to them. When someone is close to another person, they want to be able to share things that are important to them; if they keep their religion secret, they are cutting other people off from the essence of their life.

If someone has shared with you they are Wiccan, they risked the very real possibility you would react to propaganda you may have heard and reject them based on a stereotype that has no basis in truth. That friend or loved one has taken the risk that you will discount the good person they have always been and judge them because they are "different." What that person wants you to understand is that they are the same wonderful person you have always known; now you just know a bit more information about what makes them wonderful.

In sharing their religious beliefs with you, they are not trying to convert you or tell you your beliefs are any less valid; they are simply sharing with you an intimate detail of their own life. They are still the same person they were yesterday and the day before. Their children are still the same ones your kids played with yesterday, and their house is the same one you have always visited. Nothing has become dangerous or grown fangs overnight.

When they share their chosen religious path with you, they are saying they respect you enough to not keep secrets from you. They are giving you the option to tell them you love them, not because they conform to some perceived social norm, but because you love the person they are and know them well enough to understand nothing they are a part of could possibly be harmful or evil.

Why did they hide the fact they were Wiccan from us?

Many times people wait a great deal of time before they reveal to anyone the fact they are Wiccan. The time they spend hiding their religion from others is sometimes referred to as being in the "broom closet." People who decide to hide their religion may feel unsure of how others in their family, at work, or in their community will react. Some people wonder why someone would hide their religion and think this indicates something must be wrong with Wicca. They may think the only reason a Wiccan would have for hiding their religion from the world would be if there were something sinister or shameful about their beliefs. Usually, if a person hides the fact they are Wiccan, it's because that person fears others will have a bad reaction to the information based on the negative propaganda surrounding Wicca. Fearing a possible negative reaction, some Wiccans feel it is easier to keep their religious choice private than risk an unwanted confrontation. Let's face it—the two subjects people typically don't talk about are politics and religion. Discussion of these subjects tends to raise people's blood pressure and has led to more than a few deaths.

Therefore, when people decide to reveal that they are Wiccan to someone, they may drop hints or ask people what they think about a concept or idea related to Wicca. People do this in an effort to "test the waters" and see how others react in an effort to gauge people's reaction to what they really want to reveal. Finally, sometimes after many false starts, the closeted Wiccan will either tell their friend they are Wiccan or that friend will somehow find out. After revealing their religious affiliation, they will wait, holding their breath, for their friend's reaction, which could range from "that's great" to "get away from me; I never want to see you again!" How the answer affects the Wiccan depends on their relationship to the person they told. Family, friends, coworkers, and neighbors who find out someone is Wiccan can all create their own set of problems.

Family is a strong bond, and no one wants to risk severing the connection between themselves and one's parents or siblings. Therefore, people often agonize more over telling family than they do with any other group. Often family members say they disagree with someone's choice to be Wiccan but love them enough to let them make their own decisions. However, in some people's minds, the person ceases to be their son or daughter and instead becomes someone who has turned away from their upbringing and betrayed their religion. Others are told their parents don't want to see any evidence of their religion or hear about Wicca at all. Rather than make an effort to learn about what their child believes, these parents pass their child's religious choice off as a phase and immerse themselves in the comfortable waters of denial. A parent who can't acknowledge their child's religious choice may leave that child with the feeling that their parent can't accept them for who they are and thinks of them as a deviant or social pariah because their choice of religion is different from the majority.

When a coworker finds out someone is Wiccan, often the news quickly spreads through the office grapevine. Depending on the religious climate in that office, the reactions may range from apathy to horror. For some people, finding out a coworker is Wiccan, in their mind, transforms him from Bob, account supervisor, into Bob, that "evil witch person." They just know Bob's greatest joy is ruining their lives. In fact, he must have cast some evil spell that kept them from getting their last promotion, and that time they were unprepared for their presentation was "Bob's fault." People's reactions can sometimes border on the ludicrous. However, all joking aside, people sometimes lose their jobs after people find out they are Wiccan. Firing someone because of their religion is illegal. Therefore, what frequently happens is that after their boss learns they are Wiccan, their once glowing evaluations suddenly become substandard, and they are fired or otherwise forced to leave. Another tactic is to make their workload suddenly increases to a point where they are forced to quit. This does not happen in all work environments. Many employers couldn't care less what religion people are as long as their work is done. However, the fact that Wiccans do sometimes lose their jobs because of their religion is enough to make people pause before they reveal their religion at work.

Unfortunately, Wiccans are not the only people who can be made to suffer because of their religious choice. When people are members of a minority religion, especially when they have switched from the majority religion, they are hesitant to tell others. Unfortunately, prejudice runs rampant in our society, and while racial prejudice is frowned upon, religious prejudice is often not only condoned but also frequently encouraged. When members of a community are mostly one religion, people are often told not to associate with a person of another religion because that person could give them different ideas, which could endanger their souls. Sometimes people are told that if other religions are allowed to exist, it will endanger the well-being of the community and their children. So with a sanctioned prejudice born of misplaced religious fervor, some people have sought to cleanse the world of what they perceive to be foreign and dangerous religious ideas.

In order to accomplish this, attempts have been made to convert or shun those who practice other religions. In some extreme cases, houses of worship have been burned, and people have even been killed in attempts to suppress religious diversity. Some religious groups have written books and given seminars to teach their followers methods of targeting members of specific minority religious groups for conversion. School boards pass dress codes that exclude minority religious symbols, and people refuse to let their kids play with children whose families practice different religions. I have known people whose car windows have been smashed because their bumper stickers expressed an alternative religious viewpoint. People have been taken to court because someone felt their being Wiccan made them an unfit parent. Stores that sell religious supplies for minority religions have been picketed out of business. Also, neighborhood children have been told not to play with my daughters because of our family's religious beliefs. I never thought I would have to explain to a crying nine-year-old that a bigot is someone who judges people they don't know based solely on race or religion.

Stories are told of how early Christians kept their religion secret from their friends and neighbors. Their need for secrecy was because, being a minority religion, they were discriminated against. The fish symbol, according to popular reports, is said to have originated as a code used by Christians to identify one another at this time. Were they hiding their beliefs to conceal sinister aspects of their religion? Prejudice and discrimination are real risks for someone who practices any minority religion. Jews, Muslims, Buddhists, Hindus, and other minority religions all face the possibility of discrimination in the United States. However, the possibility of discrimination for Wiccans is even higher, because the only thing many people know about Wicca involves misinformation and lies. Some people are very comfortable not knowing and don't want to accept that what they have always believed about Wicca may be inaccurate. It's often easier to believe the lies about Wicca than to learn the truth and easier to hate those who are different than to learn they are people just like everyone else.

When minorities no longer fear discrimination and people with different views are perceived as individuals rather than dangerous, when people no longer have to fear for their life, livelihood, or happiness because their view of Deity is different, then all people can share their religions openly. However, until then, there will be some who feel it's necessary to hide their religious views.

Here is a true story. A friend of mine was going to be visiting her parents and, because she didn't want to have to hide who she was, told her parents about her Wiccan religious beliefs. This is the letter she received from her father in response to her sharing this information:

> Step-mom discussed with me, the conversation the two of you had Wednesday concerning your "spiritual" journey. I must say I was taken back by your revelation and have spent considerable time in prayer and discernment over this issue.
>
> There are a few things that I am going to say that cover how I feel and requirements for your conduct concerning e-mails, phone calls and other communications with us. I want to also lay down the ground rules that must be followed while you are visiting with us.
>
> I feel you have not been willing to tell us about your new search and discovery because you knew that we would not give you full, free approval of this type of activity. While I realize you are an adult, I have to question any activity that has to be done in secret and kept from your family and those who love you. As I understand it, you feel you have some "divine" calling into this life style. Again, I have to say anything done in secret and on the sly is questionable. During our conversations and conversations you had with your grandmother, you continuously referred to the place you were visiting as a "Community Center," in essence whitewashing and giving a socially acceptable name to something that may not in reality be socially acceptable. One has to wonder why the secrecy and deceit, if in fact this is a true "spiritual calling." I have to wonder if this "calling" is in fact just a personal need for acceptance and approval during a time of emotional stress and self doubt and low self worth.
>
> I do not approve of the road you have chosen to take at this point in your life. I do love you and will continue to do so, but I

can not accept the new life style you are choosing. I will pray that your eyes are opened and you are shown the false way and dark path you have chosen to follow. When you are sending e-mail or calling on the telephone and communicating with us do not send items or jokes that are based on pagan ideas or life style. We found your recent "joke" about a pagan going to heaven offensive and blasphemous in nature. Also nothing on Satan or devil worship. We do not desire any pornography or similar items, jokes, URL's or articles from anyone that are of this nature.

When you come to visit the following are the basic rules which we have given to the others to follow in our house. You will not bring any books, music, clothing, jewelry, relics, artifacts or other items which are part of your current "religion." You are not to perform any of your rites, rituals, training or practices while in our home. You will not use foul, dirty or degrading language or comments. Nor discuss things that are objectionable to others.[1]

In many ways, this response is nice compared with how other parents have disowned their child completely. In the first few paragraphs, the father questioned why his daughter felt the need to hide her religion,, and in the last few paragraphs, he made it clear he didn't want to hear, see, or know anything about her religion. The fact the daughter attempted to share her choice of religion doesn't change the father's perception that she was hiding her beliefs. Also, since her dad doesn't want any information to help him make an informed decision, one would wonder why a person in this situation would try at all. Combine this with the fact that the father tells her not to send pornographic or Satanic information, even though there is no indication she ever sent her dad anything like this before. Apparently it's the dad's belief that Paganism, Satanism, and pornography are all linked together. So after revealing to her parents she is Wiccan, the daughter has become, in their minds, a Satanic pornographer who makes bad religious decisions because she has low self-worth, and the parents want to hear nothing that might change this viewpoint. Gee, I can't imagine why people hesitate to tell others they are Wiccan.

I generally don't go out of my way to let people know I'm Wiccan. If they ask me, I will tell them because I won't lie about it, but I'm not going to introduce myself by saying, "Hi, I'm Bryan, and I'm a Wiccan." The people who are close to me know my religious beliefs, and the others will find out if they need to know.

I let my actions be a testament to who I am, and people can judge me by those actions. There have been many times after meeting me that people have told me what a wonderful Christian example I set. I smile and say thank-you because there is no reason to correct their perception of my religion. Besides, most of these occasions are neither the time nor the place for religious discussions. However, I sometimes wonder if their perception of my life would be as glowing if they knew my true religious path. Conversely, people whom I've never met have accused me of practicing the basest of human depravities simply because they know my religion. Perception is everything, and many people would prefer to judge people based on fear and ignorance rather than learn about who they are and judge them as an individual.

What does the word *Wicca* mean?

When I began attending interfaith events many years ago, everyone always curiously asked what religion each person represented. When I would answer "Wicca," a curious sequence of events frequently occurred. Their faces would go blank, and I could almost see the tiny electrical flashes and smell the ozone as the synapses fired in rapid succession, searching through every dusty file squirreled away in the darkest recesses of their brain as they attempted to find some reference for the word *Wicca*. Then suddenly their faces would light with an epiphany, and they would say, "So what does that stand for?" The decision they would invariably arrive at is that since they had no reference for the word *Wicca*, it must be an acronym, like PETA, MADD, or NATO. They just need to know what it stands for, and all would be made clear. Unfortunately for them, answering that question isn't as easy as rattling off a string of words because the individual letters don't stand for anything. What Wicca stands for is the hearts and minds of the people who follow the Wiccan spiritual path.

The word *Wicca* is actually the masculine form of an Anglo-Saxon word for sorcerers or men who practice magick. The word for sorceress or women who practice magick was *Wicce* (WIK-shuh). By the Middle Ages, when Old English had progressed to Middle English, the word *Wicca* had ceased to be used, and *Wicce* had been transformed to *Wiche,* which through the years morphed into the modern word *Witch.*[2] When witchcraft started to become public in the 1950s, it's said that Gerald Gardner, who became convinced that using the word *Witch* would cause a great deal of misunderstanding and negative publicity, chose to go back to the Old English word *Wicca,* perhaps choosing the masculine form because it sounded less like the word *Witch* even though it meant the same thing. Gardner's use of Wicca instead of *Witch,* for magical traditions, transferred to other groups who were probably equally concerned about public reaction to the word *Witch.*

Today Wicca has become the collective term for a diverse group of religious traditions that use the Wiccan Rede—*an it harm none, do what you will*—as their central ethical code. Wiccan is the term used to describe a practitioner of Wicca, one who follows any of Wicca's spiritual paths. Using the word *Wicca* today helps distinguish Witches who live by this ethical code from those who may not.

The word *Wicca* may be unfamiliar to many, but with the exponential growth in the numbers of Wiccans worldwide, more and more people are encountering it. When I began representing Wicca in the public forum, the word was usually met with confusion. Now it is typically recognized for what it is. Many people now know Wicca doesn't stand for anything except the followers of a specific type of nature-based religion whose practitioners have great reverence for life and a joy in living it.

Is Wicca a real religion?

In order to determine if Wicca is a real religion, one must first determine what makes *any* religion a real religion. Is the reality of a religion found in its tax-exempt status? No, the tax-exempt status just means the government has determined them to be a nonprofit organization. Housing programs and public schools are also tax-exempt, and I don't think anyone is confusing them with a religion.

Is a religion real because it has big buildings? At one time the church was always the tallest building in town; now financial institutions often have the tallest buildings. I'm not going to comment on what that says about religion in America, but the buildings wouldn't seem to define religion.

Is religion found in the robes and props? Candles, chalices, religious symbols, and sculptures are all pretty and can create an atmosphere of religion. However, every theater company has robes and props plus some cool lighting effects and a fog machine. I have met a few people who swear the theater is their religion, but I don't think the robes and props are the defining point of any religion.

Does one judge a religion by the number of people who follow that religious path? Numbers are no guarantee of correctness because, as Galileo showed when he proved the Earth revolved around the Sun, even ten million people can be wrong. If a person is devoted to a religion, they don't care if there are millions of people backing them up or if they're marching that path solo. Religion is very personal, and if a person is following a religion only because everyone else seems to be, I would think there is a problem.

Is religion in its sacred texts? Some might say yes, but I think sacred texts are more of a guide to the religion, telling a person what the rules and theology are, not the religion itself. Besides, Buddhists don't have a sacred text, and neither do Shintos, so some religions rely on them and others don't.

Is religion found in the rituals and ceremonies? The rituals and ceremonies are a big part of all religions, but other people also have rituals. The Masons and the Boy Scouts have rituals and ceremonies, and neither of these is a religion. Therefore, religion isn't found just in the rituals.

Do deities make the religion? Well, I think we're getting closer here. I mean there can't be a religion without at least one deity—or can there? Buddhism doesn't have deities, at least not in the way most people think of deities. So while a belief in deities may be closer to what makes a religion, they're still not the totality of the religion.

The essence of religion isn't any of the things one can see or talk about or even express adequately in words. If a person can see it, it's not the essence of religion; if a person can touch it, it's not the essence of religion. The tax-exempt status does nothing except help keep the doors open if one has a building on which to pay rent. The buildings, robes, and props put one in the mind-set for a religious experience. The number of followers helps give energy to one's convictions. The sacred texts are the roadmap to religion guiding us in symbols and metaphors. The rituals bring us closer to the deities, and there we have a defining point of religion. Does the practice of one's faith bring the person to a closer relationship or identification with the Divine? If the answer is yes, then it's a religion. When people leave a religious ceremony, they should feel more in touch with the Divine, more connected to Deity; in short, they should feel better when they come out than when they went in.

Wicca gives people a system of beliefs and guidelines by which to live. People come to Wiccan rituals and leave feeling better, more connected with Deity than when they arrived. Wicca helps them deal with the crises life throws at them. It helps comfort them when they're sad and raises them up in their triumph. Wicca sees people through from birth, through life, and out through death's door. Wicca helps people identify with Deity and is, therefore, a real religion.

This is the essence of popular religion, and I say *popular* because it's what most people are seeking in religion. People come in once a week, month, year, or moon cycle to recharge themselves. They leave feeling connected to Deity and may not think about it again until they begin to run down and need to recharge again or until tragedy strikes and they need comfort. That's how many, probably most, people use religion, and there's nothing wrong with using religion this way.

Rather than end at this point, I want to take the idea of religion one step further. Beyond the practice of religion is the experience of spirit. Spirituality is a oneness with the Divine that transcends religion. To me, this is the reason why interfaith groups can function in harmony; even though their members may represent twenty different religions, they all speak the same language—that of the spirit. The spiritual experience isn't an emotional response to one's surroundings or the situation. This experience is when the energy of the Divine reaches out and fills a person so completely that the experience transforms them so they are no longer the person they were a few minutes ago and will never be that person again. This is an epiphany where even for a second a person seems to have a greater understanding of the Divine and knows two things simultaneously. First, they have a clearer understanding of the Divine and one's place in the world; they feel connected to Deity and all living things. Second, there is no possible way they can explain it to anyone else. There is no way to clearly explain with words something that can be experienced only through the spirit. The touch of the spirit is what Wiccans, and people of any faith, are usually striving toward. It's a personal, spiritual experience, an encounter with Divinity so unique that, even though the person may continue to go to religious services, the person no longer needs to recharge because they are directly plugged into the Divine.

From the moment of that epiphany, they are practicing a new religion and they are the sole practitioner. This new religion may have all of the practices and exactly resemble their original religion, but it's different in one crucial way. It's not based on what the person has been taught about Deity; it's based on what they have personally experienced of Deity. Once a person has experienced Divinity, there will no longer be doubts, as one can't be made to doubt something they have seen. No one can convince them they're practicing their religion wrong because they know it's right for them. It's unexplainable because every experience is unique, and communicating that event in a way that will make sense to others is impossible. One can't be taught the experience. One can only be pointed in the direction, and it's up to the seeker to find this philosopher's stone that pours forth the pure essence of spirit, giving one the truest form of religion—their own.

Can anyone be a Wiccan?

One of the popular beliefs about Wicca is that it is passed down through family lines. Television shows like *Charmed,* books like *Harry*

Potter, and movies like *Scooby-Doo and the Witch's Ghost* give people the impression that being a Witch is something genetic. In *Charmed,* the sisters inherit their powers from their mother. In the Harry Potter books, most of the witches are born into magical families, and in *Scooby-Doo and the Witch's Ghost,* a character is able to defeat the villain because she is half Wiccan on her mother's side. Such stories give people the false impression that being Wiccan is something passed down from generation to generation in certain magical families.

There are two broad categories of religions: hereditary and creedal. To be a member of a hereditary religion, one must be born into that religion. Hinduism and Judaism are hereditary religions; therefore, to be a Jew or a Hindu, one must usually be born into those religions. It's possible for someone to convert, but it's difficult and often frowned upon. Creedal religions are religions that have a creed, some statement of faith adhered to by people who wish to practice that religion. In a creedal religion a person simply says, "I am now this religion," and it becomes so. Christianity and Buddhism are both creedal religions because anyone can convert to either of these religions regardless of their birth or background.

Wicca would fall under the heading of a creedal religion. Wicca isn't something into which one is born; in fact, most of the people who are currently Wiccan converted from another religious tradition. Wicca teaches that magick is a natural force and is available to anyone who wishes to use it, no matter what their genetic pedigree. No one can claim to be a full-blooded Wiccan, half Wiccan, or three-eighths Wiccan twice removed. People become Wiccan because that is the religious path they choose to follow. Anyone who wishes to become Wiccan can do so regardless of ancestry.

Why do people change religions?

According to the Web site *ReligiousTolerance.org,* Wicca is the fastest-growing religion in the United States, with the number of Wiccans increasing by tens of thousands every year. This is amazing considering Wicca doesn't proselytize (seek converts) or have large churches. Given the public relations problems, the distinct possibility of discrimination, and the chance of creating grinding friction with family and friends, why would someone want to be Wiccan?

Admittedly, some people claim to be Wiccan for exactly these reasons. Some people are looking for the attention. They not only want to be different—they thrive on appearing weird. These converts will talk loudly about spells, use the word *witch* for its shock value and, taking fashion tips from Elvira, wear clothing that looks like it came from an Addam's family garage sale. These shock witches frequently have little actual information about Wicca, but at any event they will almost always be the first ones the media interviews. Before someone points this out, there are many devout Wiccans who like to dress in black, and I am not referring to them, as they have every right to dress as they wish. I am referring to the people who wear Wicca as a fashion accessory but cease to be witches when a new trend blows through town. With the exception of those who come to Wicca for the shock value, most people seek out Wicca for the same reasons people come to any religion. They are trying to make sense of the world, their life, and Deity and are seeking a place where they feel they belong.

Most people change religions because they feel something is missing from their current religion. They may be unfulfilled and unhappy and seek a new religion to find the happiness, understanding, and sense of belonging they feel is lacking from their life. They seek their fulfillment from without, wanting something else to complete them, and think that by following the tenets of a new religion and attending whatever rituals or services are held by that faith the fulfillment they desire will find them. These people trust that if they follow the rules and perform the rituals of their chosen religion, something outside of them will fill them with the peace and happiness they seek.

If someone is trying to find happiness, they can fill that void, at least temporarily, with any new religion. When entering a new religion, one gains new friends and a great deal of attention because of their "conversion," and such attention can be very gratifying. Many times new converts begin zealously condemning their former path. This happens, first, because converts to anything, from religions to Amway, are a little overly gung-ho, and, second, people want to prove to everyone, including themselves, that the choice they made was wise and correct. With time, the attention dwindles, the luster fades from their conversion experience, and the seeker is likely to be off to find the next "true path."

The problem is, what most people seeking happiness are looking for is something outside themselves to bring happiness. Money, attention, sex, and even religion only create an adrenaline-powered illusion of happiness that is more mania than real happiness. Wicca tries to teach people that true happiness must be found within oneself. Until people begin to look within for their answers, no "Hail Mary" or Moon Circle will ever bring lasting joy. When one is truly happy, the joy arises from touching the spirit of Divinity, which resides within each of us. When we are in contact with Divinity, the peace is evident regardless of which religion we practice. This is not manic elation but the calm contentment of the stream which is constantly fed from its spring and loves life no matter how many rocks around which it must flow. When people are happy with who they are, there is no need to either defend their current religion or vilify their former one; they are simply happy and content with who they are.

Those who come to Wicca for spiritual reasons have heard the voice of Divinity calling from within them. They seek a spiritual path that can help guide them toward a greater identification with that Divinity. Finding a new religion in the quest for spirit is profoundly different from people who try to use religion to fill the holes in their lives. The quest for spirit requires we ask questions and search for those answers within ourselves. The answers will be somewhat different for each of us because we are different souls with different reasons for being. Even if Deity is one, It is so vast that It can be perceived in an infinite number of ways, all of which are valid.

The Wiccan quest is a spiritual one and is the proverbial road less traveled because, even though we may begin our journey with guides, eventually we must find our way alone, carving our own path in the wilderness of spirit. The path of the spirit can be found within every religion; however, some people feel more comfortable in one religious context than they do in another. People worship in the way best suited for them, and Wiccans are happy when someone finds their true path, no matter in which religion they find it. Wiccans can rejoice when people find within themselves the fulfillment they were seeking and not become distressed when someone else's religious path is different from their own.

Is Wicca a cult?

The word *cult* has become a pejorative buzzword that is used by individuals wishing to cast a shroud of suspicion over a religious group. Knowing that the term conjures up images of poisoned Kool-Aid and heavily armored encampments, alarmists often try to scare families into forcefully restraining any family member who shows an interest in any religious group that may be considered outside the norm. The problem with defining whether a group is a cult or not lies in the fact that no universally accepted definition of the word exists. Different groups often make up their own definition or find one that best fits their agenda; until nowadays the word *cult* seems to have come to mean any religious group the person doesn't like.

However, some definitions of *cult* are frequently used, so let's take a look at a few of them and see how they apply. The *American Heritage Dictionary* defines *cult* as "a system or community of religious worship." By this definition Wicca would be a cult, but then so is the local Baptist church. In fact, by this definition every religion in the world is a cult, so we're in good company. *Cult* has been defined by some as a religious tradition that differs from the predominant religion of the community. This would make Wicca a cult in the United States, along with Buddhism, Islam, and Judaism. However, by this definition, Christianity would be a cult in India or Iraq. If you define *cult* as a religious group that is not Christian, again Wicca would qualify, but so would Buddhism, Hinduism, and several other religions that have been around a lot longer than Christianity.

The definition I usually use is "a religious group headed by a charismatic leader who is the source of, or interprets, all spiritual information for his or her followers, who are absolutely devoted to him or her." This definition would include Jim Jones and David

Koresh, along with many televangelists. Wicca, however, does not now nor has it ever fit this definition.

The anti-cult writer Marcia Rudin, MA, believes cults have the following fourteen characteristics:[3]

1. Members swear total allegiance to an all-powerful leader who they believe to be the Messiah.
2. Rational thought is discouraged or forbidden.
3. The cult's recruitment techniques are often deceptive.
4. The cult weakens the follower psychologically by making him or her depend upon the group to solve his or her problems.
5. The cults manipulate guilt to their advantage.
6. The cult leader makes all the career and life decision of the members.
7. Cults exist only for their own material survival and make false promises to work to improve society.
8. Cult members often work full-time for the group for little or no pay.
9. Cult members are isolated from the outside world and any reality testing it could provide.
10. Cults are antiwoman, antichild, and antifamily.
11. Cults are apocalyptic and believe themselves to be the remnant who will survive the soon-approaching end of the world.
12. Many cults follow an "ends justify the means" philosophy.
13. Cults, particularly in regard to their finances, are shrouded in secrecy.
14. There is frequently an aura of or potential for violence around cults.

Rudin's first point is that cults "follow an all-powerful leader." Wicca is not a religion of gurus; there are no great teachers whom everyone follows around, waiting for pearls of wisdom to fall from their mouths. There are small groups, often referred to as *covens*, usually consisting of less than fifteen people, who have a High Priestess and/or High Priest in charge of the group. The person in charge of the group will usually have studied for many years in another group before being allowed to start their own group. However, each High Priestess or High Priest is only in charge of that one group. There is no great hierarchy, no one above them to whom they must report, no bishops, no lamas, and no pope to give the final ruling. A group's leader might turn to the High Priestess with whom they studied for advice, but the final decision belongs to the individual. I am not saying people have never let their position go to their head and set out on their own little ego trip—it happens, but rarely. The system is set up to prevent one individual from gaining too much power.

What bonds Wiccans together are our common beliefs. We honor both the Goddess and the God, we revere the Earth, and we celebrate the cycles of nature. Wicca is a religion of individuals who tend to be very strongly opinionated about their religion, and individual opinions may differ from one to another. However, Wiccans are not usually dogmatic about our beliefs, and even though convictions are very strong, Wiccans can typically discuss beliefs in a civil manner and allow others to have differing views. This makes it very difficult for people to gain much power or try to set themselves up as an icon. The rule for Wiccans when dealing with any situation is "use your brain." Wiccans are usually taught to question authority because ultimately, final authority, and responsibility, comes down to just one person—yourself.

A High Priestess or High Priest in charge of a group leads the rituals, performs weddings and funerals, and helps guide the people in their group. Unless they are asked for help or advice, the they usually lets people live their own lives. There are strong ethics of behavior to which a High Priestess and High Priest should adhere, and those who abuse their position or act unethically may be ostracized by the rest of the community.

Rudin's second point is that in cults "all rational thought is discouraged." Wicca, in contrast, requires people to question and explore their religious beliefs. In fact, most people come to Wicca because they were questioning their previous religion and did not find the answers they needed. If someone studying Wicca is given information that seems to make no sense, they are encouraged to ask questions and discover answers for themselves.

The third characteristic of cults that Rudin lists is "deceptive recruitment techniques." Wicca does not recruit or proselytize in any way. If someone starts studying Wicca, it is because they picked up a book on their own or tracked down a teacher themselves. We don't go out seeking students. In fact, some priestesses require a potential student to ask three separate times before taking them on as a student. Wicca also routinely requires students to complete a one-year basic course in Wicca, which often requires research and individual study, before the student can join a coven to ensure the student fully understands their religious choice.

A fourth characteristic of cults is that "a cult weakens the follower psychologically by making him or her depend upon the group to solve his or her problems." In sharp contrast, Wicca seeks to empower individuals, helping them gain the ability to be strong and find answers for themselves. This isn't to say a priestess or priest will refuse to help someone who is in trouble; we all get our share of distress calls at four in the morning, as I am sure clergy of every faith receive. However, as people grow in Wicca and learn to handle their own difficulties, those calls should become much less frequent. There is a saying in Wicca that unless you can find what you are seeking within yourself, you will never find it outside of yourself. Wiccans are taught just that: to find their answers within themselves, be responsible for their own actions, and clean up their own messes.

Rudin also points out that "cults manipulate guilt to their advantage." In *Illusions,* Richard Bach says, "Your conscience is the measure of the honesty of your selfishness." Guilt tells us we have done something that violates our own moral code of ethics. We messed up and now need to fix the situation. Guilt, as an extension of the conscience, is something that should be listened to because it keeps us honest with ourselves and helps prevent us from hurting others. However, guilt for guilt's sake is counterproductive. If a person feels guilty because of something they have done, they should seek to fix the problem they created or make amends for their mistake. If those are not options, the person should at least use the feeling as a reminder not to let the situation ever occur again. Carrying guilt when there is no solution or when the person was not responsible for the problem wears on the soul and is counterproductive to spiritual growth.

The sixth characteristic Rudin lists is "the cult leader makes all the career and life decisions of the members." A Wiccan coven operates in many ways like a family, except the members of my coven are not my children; they're my friends. I respect each member for their own individual talents and for what they bring to the group. However, if a person wishes to leave the coven, they can do so at any time. Their jobs and personal decisions are their own, and the only time I would ever try to interfere in a person's life is if they were doing something I thought was self-destructive, like abusing drugs or alcohol. People's lives are their own, and a Wiccan clergy member's job is to aid and advise them for as long as they seek our help but to allow them to make their own choices and find their own path, even if that path veers away from ours.

Rudin also says, "cults exist only for their own material survival and make false promises to work to improve society." There is usually no monetary input from the members of a Wiccan coven to the group beyond helping to pay for supplies used by the group for rituals, and even then the priestess often foots most of the bill. Wiccans often work to help further religious tolerance, environmental concerns, gender equality, and animal rights, but they do so following their own conscience and donate their money to nonprofit organizations as they see fit. Sometimes an individual coven might choose an issue they feel strongly about and donate their time as a group. I have known covens that worked in soup kitchens, collected food for the AIDS food pantry, and collected clothing for women's shelters. Whether these activities truly help society or not isn't mine to judge, but I do know Wiccans are encouraged to give of themselves to help others whenever they can.

The eighth characteristic on Rudin's list is that "cult members often work full-time for the group for little or no pay." The Seeker's Bill of Rights (Appendix A) states that everyone has "the right to compensation for professional goods and services." Simply put, if you do work for someone, you have the right to be paid. No one should be required to work to put cash in the pocket of the group or its leaders. This document was put together specifically to protect people who are new to Wicca ("seekers") from being preyed upon by unscrupulous people who might use the trappings of Wicca to prey on the unsuspecting.

According to Rudin, "cult members are isolated from the outside world and any reality testing it could provide." Wicca is just the opposite; students are never isolated from society. They work with everyone else, go to school with a variety of students, and are encouraged to read about not only Wicca but also other world religions. Ironically, many larger religions often encourage members not to work or socialize with people who are outside their religion and even send their children to special schools where they will encounter only members of their own faith. Wiccans can't and shouldn't isolate themselves from society. For practical reasons, it is impossible for Wiccans to segregate themselves. We don't build compounds, and everyone chooses their own job and friends, many of whom will be members of other faiths. I have never told one of my students not to associate with someone who was of a different faith, but people have told my friends they shouldn't associate with me because of mine. I require my students to study other religions so they will gain a working knowledge of how other people worship, and I don't worry they might be "lost" to some other faith. If they find a religion to which they feel better suited, then I am happy for them because their well-being is my primary concern.

Tenth on Rudin's list is that "cults are antiwoman, antichild, and antifamily." Women's issues are very important to Wicca. Women lead the majority of Wiccan covens, and many rituals and ceremonies honor the birth and growth of children as part of a whole family. Children are integral to life, and as a life-affirming religion, Wicca honors each new birth as a wonderful addition to the world. Even the covens that don't allow children at their rituals still view children as gifts from Deity and could not be referred to as antichild.

The eleventh characteristic on Rudin's list is that "cults are apocalyptic and believe themselves to be the remnant who will survive the soon-approaching end of the world." Wicca is a religion centered on living and learning while we are on the Earth, so there is a connection to the cycles of nature and the growing seasons as well as a focus on natural remedies to health problems. While this kind of mind-set could be applied to some post cataclysmic event scenario, and while I can't speak for every Wiccan, I am not aware of any large movement in this direction. While many Wiccans will say the Earth is being destroyed by war, pollution, industrialization, or a host of other factors, most Wiccans apply their efforts into educating the public about the dangers of such problems in an attempt to slow or stop the problem. Effort put into trying to prevent the destruction of the Earth, which we hold sacred, seems a more profitable use of time than preparing to survive on a burnt and broken planet.

Rudin says, "many cults follow an 'ends justify the means' philosophy." Wiccan ethics are specific: Wiccans are to harm nothing. If an action would result in harming someone or something, it shouldn't be done. Even if one thinks the world would be a better place without so-and-so or that a certain company is polluting the planet, it is still not acceptable to act in a harmful manner to fix the situation. The old adage that two wrongs don't make a right applies here. The means used to reach the end are just as important as the final outcome.

Another characteristic on the list is that "cults, particularly in regard to their finances, are shrouded in secrecy." Profiting from spirituality is unethical in Wicca. Wiccan clergy usually have regular jobs or other means of supporting themselves. High Priestesses and High Priests do not charge for their duties as leader of a group. All rituals, counseling, and other work they do for their group and the community is usually done free of charge. Coven members are rarely asked to contribute money to the coven, and when a request *is* made, it is usually only a small amount to cover supplies or coven membership dues in an organization. Therefore, there are usually no finances to abuse and nothing to hide or keep secret.

The final cult characteristic Rudin lists is that "there is frequently an aura of or potential for violence around cults." Living in peaceful harmony with nature and those in the world around us is important to Wicca. There is no coercion to remain in a group, nor is there encouragement toward violence. Problems are solved by discussing the issues, and frequently a consensus is reached. Violence can be a problem in any religion where individuals might resort to unfortunate means to solve perceived problems. However, Wicca teaches that violence is not the answer to a problem and frequently causes more problems than it solves.

The bottom line is that all religions have people who abuse that religion for their own gain. Followers of these religions are as mortified by the unethical actions of these individuals as is the rest of the public. However, an unethical person who professes to practice a religion should not be used as the standard by which all members of that religion are judged. It's an unfortunate fact that every religion may eventually have its David Koresh or Jim Jones, but one should not judge the whole religion by the few bad apples in it.

Is the Wiccan religion safe?

When lecturing about Wicca to the general public, I almost always come across at least one person who wants to know if Wicca is safe. This person is usually a very nervous mother who has recently learned her grown child is Wiccan. She has seen movies where witches summon spirits that possess people and conjure demons that break free from control, eating everyone present. Given the number of dangerous and demonic forces she imagines her child surrounded by, I'm surprised this poor lady has been able to sleep due to the nightmares she's given herself. If one writes down everything Hollywood portrays witches to be and then lists everything Wiccans actually are, they'll find few items common to both lists. The problem is actual facts about Wicca aren't very exciting and don't make good film footage, so movie producers usually opt for the flashy, scary, and fictitious version. Unfortunately, not everyone realizes how little truth is in the movies, and we end up with our unfortunate, insomniac mom.

Wiccan rituals are completely safe. No one is possessed by evil entities or summons flesh-eating, pan-dimensional demons. No one is sliced, sacrificed, poisoned, or even levitated. The only injuries I have ever seen are a few burnt fingers while attempting to light candles and an ankle twisted during a circle dance. On the whole, the most dangerous part of a Wiccan ritual is driving a car to get there. Wicca is a life-affirming religion that encourages its members to take personal responsibilities for their actions. The only physical or psychological dangers in Wicca are those common to all religious practices. These involve the physical dangers of tripping over objects or dropping something on one's foot and the psychological dangers of becoming overly fanatical about one's beliefs.

Being Wiccan is no more dangerous than being any other religion, and depending on one's perspective, it's safer than some. If one uses a bit of common sense and pays attention to one's surroundings, a person needn't suffer so much as a scratch as a result of being Wiccan.

Why would people call themselves a Witch?

In popular use, the word *witch* has come to mean someone who spitefully tries to harm people or someone who is remorselessly evil. It has become a vile expletive hurled at characters in soap operas because the rhyming "B-word" won't make it past the censors, but *Witch* wasn't always used this way. Witch comes from the Old English word *Wicce*, which was the feminine form for someone who performs magick.[4] There was nothing evil about the original use of the word. The Inquisition is largely responsible for adding the evil connotations because the medieval Church believed witches gained their power from the Devil, and thus began the downhill slide to where the word *witch* is today. Along the way the word has also meant anyone who practices magick, an ugly old woman, an exceptionally beautiful girl, a medium, and a certain type of fish.

The meanings of many words in the English language have changed over time, and the current definition of a word may have little to do with the original meaning. Originally, the word *witch* didn't have all the nasty connotations currently attached to it. So how does one combat the rather nasty downslide the word has taken over the centuries? The only way a word shifts meaning is through its use, so if a word is never used except in unflattering ways, the definition of that word will always be less than desirable. By using the word *Witch* with its original meaning, people are attempting to strip away the layers of green-faced overcoat that have been applied over the centuries, restoring the word *Witch* to its original magical finish.

Granted this seems a daunting task, considering the original definition of *Witch* has been on life support in some hospital in Salem for the last few hundred years and the nastier definitions aren't going to give up their inheritance easily. However, just in the last ten years we have seen color return to its cheeks. It's beginning to breathe on its own again, and I swear I saw its toes wiggle the other day. Seriously though, Witches know changing the public perception of the word *Witch* isn't easy and has caused more than a few public relations difficulties. However, the definition will not change itself, and changing the public perception of the word is the correct thing to do. Besides, we really have no choice. If we go around saying we worship the Goddess and practice natural magick, people are probably going to call us Witches whether we want them to or not. So, rather than go around denying we are Witches and giving the word negative power over us, we accept the word *Witch* but offer people the correct definition to replace the unflattering one they might have intended.

The nasty definitions are hanging on from a time when anyone who used magick was viewed as being in league with evil forces. Fortunately, many people no longer have that view, so it's time to slay the evil definitions that have usurped the power of the word *Witch*. Wiccans are trying to restore the word *Witch* to the definition "someone who uses magick," but I would suspect many Witches wouldn't mind keeping the definition "an exceptionally beautiful and beguiling woman" hanging around a bit longer. The word *Witch* when used by Wiccans refers to someone who sees the world as a magical place and who uses this natural magick to help themselves and the world around them.

A Deeper Understanding
of the Wiccan View of Deity

Why do Wiccans worship a Goddess?

In the beginning of our lives, we knew only our mother. She was the whole world to us: she bore us from her womb, she gave us her breast to nourish us, and she comforted us when we slept. Joseph Campbell wrote, "When one can feel oneself in relation to the universe in the same complete and natural way as that of the child with the mother, one is in complete harmony and tune with the universe."[1] Naturally, one of the most ancient concepts of Deity was of an all-caring Mother with child who gave birth to people, fed them from Her body, and took them back to Her when they died. Mother Goddesses, in one form or another, are found in the mythologies of almost every culture around the world. The Goddess is the archetype of the feminine in all of us; all at once She is our mother, our grandmother, and our daughters. The Goddess is the anima, which Jung defined as:

> Not only the mother but the daughter, the sister, the beloved, the heavenly goddess, and the chthonic Baubo. Every mother

and every beloved is forced to become the carrier and embodiment of this omnipresent and ageless image, which corresponds to the deepest reality in a man. It belongs to him this perilous image of woman.[2]

The image of the Goddess is frequently divided into three aspects corresponding to the life stages of women: the Maiden, the Mother, and the Crone. These three faces of the Goddess are archetypes of womanhood found throughout mythology in almost every culture of the world. The Greeks embodied all three forms as one in the Fates, where the Goddess is the maiden Clothos, who spins the thread of life; the mother Lachesis, who measures it out; and the crone Atropos, who cuts it, making way for rebirth. The energy of the Goddess is nurturing and caring, whereas the energy of the God tends to be dominating and aggressive.

One of the first religious mysteries involved women bleeding every month without dying, and if she held her blood for approximately ten cycles of the moon, her belly grew round and she gave birth to new life. Figures carved around 18,000 BCE show an understanding of this relationship between women's fertility and the moon.[3] Women, who created life through childbirth, were once viewed as extensions of the Goddess and directed the daily lives of the people. It is possible that it was once common for women to decide how the village was going to be run, when the food was planted, and what herbs to use for healing. The men would have typically been the hunters, who did the dangerous job of finding meat for the clan, and the warriors, who defended the clan from outside attacks. Men and women would have each had their jobs, their roles in society balancing each other, as they worked together for the good of all the people. However, land and possessions were passed down matrilineally, through the mother's line, because everyone knew who the mother of a child was, but many people didn't know why a woman got pregnant. Nowadays we take this for granted, but remember, Antoni Van Leeuwenhoek didn't discover sperm cells until the seventeenth century.

Somewhere in prehistory, there seems to have been a change in the perception of the world. This may have occurred partly when men discovered that through sexual intercourse they were necessary to the reproductive process. In some cultures men then reasoned they alone were responsible for children and women were simply an incubator for their seed, a vessel for men to use as they wished. In these cultures men controlled society through violence and owned the women who bore their children. Without the women's power in society to balance male aggression, nomadic herders from the Syro-Arabian deserts in the south and Indo-Europeans from the north moved out and attacked the more peaceful agricultural villages, annihilating these villages to extend their power.[4]

As nations formed through domination of people, these patriarchal conquerors began to change the goddess-centered mythologies of the existing matrilineal cultures.[5] The various Mother Goddesses who brought forth all life were typically replaced with Father gods, warrior deities who were often viewed as ruling over the goddesses and subjecting the people to their will.[6] The goddesses of the indigenous people were replaced with the gods of the conquerors or relegated to secondary roles, and gods of war were elevated to supreme rulers of heaven and Earth. For example, Persephone, who was previously both Goddess of Growth in spring and the Goddess of the Underworld in winter, was changed from being Queen of the Underworld to the kidnapped consort of the new God of the Underworld, Hades, who forced her to stay in the Underworld for half the year. To justify women's subservient role, the mythology of the conquerors frequently blamed women for all the evil in the world. Woman became the one who ate the forbidden fruit that caused man's suffering or who opened the box allowing pestilence and disease into the world.

The crone aspect of woman was the one most affected by the reduction in status of woman. In ancient times the crone had been valued for her wisdom. She gathered a lifetime of wisdom and shared this with the tribe. The crone was closest to death, and her menstrual blood had stopped flowing, which meant her reproductive magick was now retained inside of her, so she had great power. The crone scared men because, even if they could rape the maiden and enslave the mother, the crone had power and magick; therefore, she presented a greater threat to male dominance. The crone became vilified, and her power became regarded as coming from an evil source. In stories she became the one who stole babies, cursed fields, and made women barren. When the world started to judge the value of a woman by her ability to please men and a woman's appearance became her primary attribute, the crone was deemed useless, an image to be feared, scorned, and destroyed.

Women were pushed down into a subservient role where they were to be submissive to their husbands. However, from time to time, women have tried to rise up from this role of servitude only to be slapped back by a society where men were in control. The ways women have been put into servitude are numerous. In some cultures, they are forced to wear veils and not speak in men's presence. During the witchhunts, hundreds of thousands of people were murdered over a four-hundred-year period, and the majority of those killed were women. If a woman was too old, she might be a witch; if she was too pretty, she was beguiling men's minds, giving them impure thoughts; if she used herbs, she was healing with magic; if she had too much money, she was in league with the Devil. Women became the root of all evil, and if a woman did anything that seemed to give her power, pride, or confidence, she could be declared a witch, tortured, and killed. Women are still often perceived to be in subservient roles, and when they push beyond their perceived place, they are labeled "pushy," "lesbian," or simply "bitch." Throughout history women have been killed, raped, beaten, and verbally debased when they tried to assert themselves. Society places glass ceilings over women's corporate advancement and keeps them out of "men's" jobs. Women are perceived to be cooks but not chefs, secretaries but not bosses, nurses but not doctors, teachers but not principals. Whenever women assert more power, people often try to put them back in "their place."

Women are now rising in status and influence, moving into politics, owning companies, and rising to positions of authority in all areas of life. The bookshelves are filled with books teaching assertiveness, independence, and power to women. The Goddess is returning, and Her light is helping women to blossom like the flowers in spring. Many Unitarians openly embrace the Goddess, mainstream religions have women's groups that discuss Divinity as female, and Goddess-based religions are becoming the fastest-growing religious groups in the world.[7] The Mother is coming back home, but how will Her sons receive Her? Will they open their arms and welcome Her back to their lives, making them whole, or will they take up arms against Her and try to destroy Her as She approaches the door?

Studying Goddess-based spirituality has shown me people's perceptions of the world are colored not only by their belief in Deity but also by which form of Deity they choose. The belief in a female Goddess helps one see the world as nurturing and compassionate, where things are soft and loving like a mother. The view of Deity as strictly male can say to women they are less important and reinforces a patriarchal worldview. When we view Deity as strictly male, women have no Deity who looks like them, and their psyche often cries for one. Many women wonder how a male Deity could understand the problems women face in their lives when they know men don't. Many women want a Goddess who looks like them, who gives birth, bleeds, and feeds Her children from Her breast, however metaphorical that may be. Belief in a Goddess can give women more confidence and lead them to become more self-assured, making them a part of the cosmic forces and a conscious creation of the Universe.

Studying the aspects of the Goddess, in Wicca, has given me a great respect and reverence for women. I can look at not only where women are now but also where they could be. I have learned the only way the situation can get better is not only by women banding together to stand up for what they know is right, but also by men joining them in trying to end the inequitable treatment and restoring true balance to society.

Men also benefit from having a female aspect of Deity in their reality. Men may not wish to pray to a Goddess, but simply believing Deity can be manifested as female changes the male's worldview. The perception that men have the divine right to rule over women ends when men start to see women as the spiritual equals of men. With the viewpoint that women are part of the Divine, eventually an end could come to glass ceilings, job discrimination, and sexual harassment. Women would be given their rightful position of equality in the world and no longer be relegated to second-class citizenship.

I have two daughters who will grow up in this world and deal with its prejudices and inequalities. My daughters are very important to me, and so is the quality of life they will live. I don't want them to marry someone who mistreats or belittles them. I want them to have the courage to walk out on someone who is abusing them rather than stay because they feel they either deserve the abuse or have no other place to go. I want the world to be a place of opportunity for them. They are being taught that they are an extension of the Goddess, who gives life to the world. They view women as being blessed with the ability to bring life into the world and will not go through life believing they are cursed to endure the pains of childbirth. Worshiping Deity in a female form gives them the opportunity to grow up with a vision of Deity who looks like them, rather than having a male form as their only choice for Deity. These teachings will hopefully give them the confidence to interact with people on an even level. They will be able to challenge people who still feel women are second to men and show them women are leaders who can use compassion and nurturing influences to solve problems. I want my daughters to grow up knowing a woman's true value is in her intelligence, not in her beauty. They are taught to be strong and independent, relying on their own accomplishments, not defining their existence in terms of a man. Only through righteous outrage did women get the right to vote, better pay, and property rights, and only through continued effort will women change society's perception and become equal. I want my daughters to understand the differences between men and women and to realize that the world will grow only when all of us start to cooperate and work together as two halves of a whole. This is the kind of world mind-set I would like to see, and it has to be built one mind at a time.

Isn't the Wiccan view of Deity impersonal?

Life can be scary. Apocalyptic visions of Death, Hunger, War, and Disease ride out from our televisions, and twenty-four-hour coverage of every horrific event worldwide pours into our CNN-infested brains. People have begun to think the violence in the world has dramatically increased when the truth is it only seems that way because we are now directly exposed to almost every destructive act on the planet. We crave news about our neighborhood, and our neighborhood has become the entire planet. The unfortunate consequence of this is that many people react to a shooting in Bombay as if the gunman were on their very street. If we expect the world to be violent, violence will be what we find. I think the miracle of the modern world is that people aren't too scared to risk getting out of bed in the morning to go to work. The only way many people accomplish the act of living their day-to-day lives is through turning to spirituality and religion.

Central to people's spiritual and religious beliefs is their perception of Deity. Many people are comforted by a perception of Deity that holds and protects them, comforting them when they're grieving or afraid. The perception of Deity as a Universal Order or transcendent entity is a tad impersonal for their liking.

Someone once asked me why I would want to worship a transcendent Deity when to him Deity was his friend, knew his name, and cared if he was happy or not. It took me a second to respond because I don't like playing "my Deity's better than yours" games, as they are pointless and only lead to arguments without solving anything. Wiccans don't usually care how a person perceives Deity because to us Deity accommodates whatever perception one is comfortable with. To Wiccans, Deity is ultimately the Universe and can be all things to all people, so if one group wants to see Deity as personal, Deity will say, "I can be that." If another group chooses to perceive Deity in a different way, It will respond, "I can be that, too." Therefore, to Wiccans it doesn't matter which perception, personal or impersonal, one chooses because Deity can be both or neither.

Pondering my answer for a moment, I posed this question. "Which is more personal to you, your best friend or your blood?"

He opened his mouth to answer, thought about it, closed his mouth again, then said, "Why?"

"Well," I said, "you perceive Deity as a close friend, one who knows all about you, all your faults, and loves you in spite of them, correct?"

"Yes," he replied.

"I view the Universe as a living thing," I explained. "Deity is not only around everything but also a part of everything. We are not separate from that Universe; we are a functioning part of it."

The difference between these two perceptions is that in the first, people see themselves in a relationship with a Deity that is external to them, and in the second they identify with a Deity that is a part of them. Wiccans usually see Deity as a part of everything, including other people. Deity is a part of our being. It infuses us, gives us life. We have consciousness and reasoning ability because of that Divine spark within. Therefore, to me, Deity is my soul; it's like my blood or bone, part of that which is me. So the answer to the question "Isn't the Wiccan view of Deity impersonal?" would depend entirely on whether one considers the blood coursing through their body as personal. If one considers blood, muscle, and bone personal, then the Wiccan view of Deity wouldn't be impersonal. I consider these parts of the body very personal, as one would cease to live if any one of them were missing. The choice to view Deity as either personal or impersonal is an individual one with both viewpoints being valid.

Since Deity can be all things, Wiccans may choose to perceive Deity as an internal piece of them, as an external force, or as both at the same time. Many Wiccans will prefer to view Deity as any of a myriad of goddesses or gods, external forces each separate and distinct from each other. In these forms Deity can be related to and walked with. Deity can comfort and speak to people as an external separate entity, while simultaneously being part of their very being. This may sound odd to some people, but remember Wicca isn't an either/or type of religion; more often than not the Wiccan viewpoint is one of "yes/and." Deity, to Wiccans, doesn't have to be either personal or impersonal; Deity can be both.

Wiccans have complete freedom to perceive Deity however they wish to perceive It. Ultimately no one's perceptions of Deity can be proven. Each of us has our own individual image of what Deity is to us, and we have faith that our perception of Deity is correct for us. People's visions of Deity are based on their own personal experience of spirit. It's what we know in our souls to be correct. It's not dependent on anyone else agreeing with us and doesn't preclude someone else having a different perception. The universe is a big place, and to Wiccans, Deity being the guiding force for the universe is even bigger and can literally be all things to all people.

How can people be Divine beings when they are flawed?

Too many of us view ourselves as imperfect, flawed individuals who live in a sinful world and are more than deserving of the punishments heaped upon us. With attitudes like this, it's no wonder people have trouble feeling close to Deity. Deity, holding out a cup, offers us a drink, saying, "You are parched. Take this and cool your throat." Too often people reply, "I'm not worthy," and cringe, thirsty, in the corner. Deity offers us a feast, saying, "You are famished. Come sit at my table and eat," to which many people reply, "I'm not worthy," and hide, hungry, under the table. Worse than this, anyone who says to Deity, "Thanks, I'll eat and drink with you," other people tend to look at with an expression of "Who do they think they are?" and start trying to drag them from the table. Deity starves no one. There are blessings enough for everyone, but people have to accept what is being offered to them.

Deity forces blessings on none. Each of us is perfect just the way we are. "Wait a minute," you say, "I wear glasses and braces, I have acne, halitosis, sweat like a pig, and have a really weird mole on my butt; how can I be perfect?" The Divine responds, "Yes, you are all those things, but you were given them because they make you perfectly suited for the lessons you are here to learn." Therefore, people need to quit spending so much time worrying about how they missed out because they don't measure up to someone else's standards for the ideal person and start using the talents and skills they do have. People tend to be very good at recognizing all the things they think are wrong with them; our culture seems to have taught people that to even acknowledge they have good qualities is arrogant and prideful. As such, people deny their positive qualities to everybody else until they succeed in convincing themselves that they are worthless. One problem with this self-degradation is that thoughts are things, and whatever we direct our thoughts toward is where our energy goes. If people tell the Universe they are worthless, ugly, incompetent, or unworthy of happiness, the Universe will tend to accommodate our beliefs; whatever people believe about their life is usually what they will find.

Most Wiccan traditions empower their practitioners with the knowledge that people are magical beings and part of the Divine, who are on this planet to learn, achieve, and grow spiritually. Everyone has the potential to be great, but people tend to squander their days making excuses for why they don't accomplish more. "If only I were older, younger, taller, shorter, blonder, smarter, assertive, richer, . . ." People can come up with excuses forever as to why they haven't done more with their lives. However, the real reason most people don't do more is that they're afraid to try. The "what if" demons creep into their head and keep them from following their dreams. "What if no one likes it, what if I fail, what if people laugh at me?" These demons creep into the mind, filling it with a myriad of imagined horrors that people believe will happen if they step off that wide, well-trodden path and chase their dreams.

Wicca teaches that everyone is part of Deity and people are on Earth for their spirits to learn and grow. People have the opportunity to learn from their mistakes and grow from how they relate to the challenges of life. Each of us is born with something to do, and I think people spend most of their lives trying to figure out what that thing is. Then, once they've found it, they're too afraid to actually try to achieve that goal. Most people don't seem to trust the Divine enough to take a chance; instead, they feel they're unworthy of achieving their dreams.

The only way people can swim in the waters of their Divine potential is to let go of the side of the pool and trust in Divinity. Wicca strives to drive away those demons of doubt, challenging people to live up to their Divine potential and find their bliss. Everyone is perfectly suited for the life they are living, and those flaws people perceive in their lives are tools of creativity and opportunities to learn. Yes, following your dreams can be dangerous, but to achieve, one has to take a few risks. Myths aren't written about people capturing fireflies in their backyard. People must face, fight, and triumph over their own personal dragons to reach their full potential.

Don't Pagans worship idols?

Idolatry, the worship of idols, is often misunderstood and usually misrepresented in Western culture. The popular image that springs to the minds of many people is one where a group of people bow and scrape around a large, grim-faced stone image. Everyone chants in some unrecognizable language as a young, half-naked girl is dragged to the base of the image. In movies, idols glow, speak, track down blasphemers, and dance little jigs when someone plays a lively tune. Since people see idols portrayed as having supernatural powers, why shouldn't they think people who worship idols believe the images possess the same powers? This idea is more than a bit ridiculous, but I have often heard people derisively scoff at idols, saying things like, "Can you believe she thinks that rock is going to help her?" or "I wouldn't worship something I could carry around in my pocket." Idols are made from stone, clay, metal, paper mache, or anything else someone can draw, sculpt, or cast, but Wiccans don't believe these objects have supernatural powers.

Idols are images created by artists to represent a deity. Idols may have characteristics and symbols associated with the deity represented, but these objects are viewed neither as being the deity nor as an exact portrait. They are intended to put a person in touch with the spirit of that deity and give a person a physical image that connects them mentally and emotionally to that deity, but those images are not believed to actually be the deity.

Wiccans don't worship the image; they honor the Deity represented by that image. While, to some, the two may seem the same, there is a significant difference. Wiccans don't believe the statue itself has any power; it is the Deity the statue represents that has the power. A Wiccan honors and worships Deity through the idol's physical representation of that Deity. It's human nature to try to put a face on Deity; most people have created a mental image of Deity, if not a physical one. We will hue our idols from the mental ether, forming images in our minds if we don't carve them with our hands. Most Wiccans do not believe their image is the only form possible for Deity. Since the Divine is part of everything, any image of Deity is possible because everything is part of the Divine. Therefore, Wiccans usually see each idol as a single image of the Divine, not the only one.

If a Wiccan uses an image of Deity (and many don't), they usually find some representation, either concrete or abstract, that seems to speak to some part of them and use that as their personal image of the Divine. Personally, I like the Buddhist images of Tara and Kuan-Yin, while others may prefer images of Greek, Egyptian, or Celtic origin. Each person has something inside of them that says, "That's it," and know they have found the image that resonates with their being. Wiccans also know it doesn't matter if others use the same image, or if they're the only one who sees Deity in this way, or even if someone else uses a different image for the same Deity. Remember, Wiccans honor the Deity represented by the image; they don't worship the image itself.

All physical images are the artists' attempts to capture the essence of their vision of the ultimate mystery, and therefore, each is valid and meaningful to the person using it. All images used are personifications of the Divine. Therefore, some people might argue that true idolatry would be the belief that one image of Deity, whether carved in stone or described on paper, should be worshiped as the only true and correct form of Deity. People use these images because it is easier to comprehend an image of Deity that has features we understand rather than try to comprehend an incomprehensible, transcendent power. Images are more comforting to the human psyche and easier to identify with.

Why would a person use myths in religion when myths aren't true?

I have heard recordings of lectures by Joseph Campbell in which he has claimed one of his favorite definitions of mythology is "Other people's religions," and a popular definition of *mythology* is "stories that aren't true." There's a human tendency to view our own religious stories as true and brand everyone else's religious stories as "mythology." Some people disregard the spiritual significance of myths because such stories can easily be shown to be untrue. Everyone knows the world isn't swimming through space on the back of a giant sea turtle and fire probably wasn't given to humanity by a coyote, so what good are myths? What many people fail to realize is that myths aren't supposed to be true. If they were, they would lose their power, becoming no more interesting than yesterday's news blowing down the street as discarded papers.

Myths are religious stories meant to speak to the soul; they are intended to teach us about life, the Divine, and our place in the world. Campbell said myths are "The song of the Universe, the music of the spheres."[8] History may be interesting to many, and history can be learned from, but history is a factual, often biased account of events that happened long ago and in other places. Myths speak in symbols and metaphors that resonate to the core of our being, eliciting a deep psychological response. When myths are interpreted and applied to modern times, the myths become timeless, and their lessons can be as applicable to our lives today as they were to people thousands of years ago. Yes, Wiccans use myths, and we know those myths aren't factual or historical because if they were it would destroy much of their usefulness and relevance to our lives.

Myths are religious stories intended to teach us about life through the use of metaphor. According to Joseph Campbell, myths serve four functions: mystical, cosmological, sociological, and pedagogical.[9] The mystical function identifies us with the transcendent mystery that is Deity and the Universe and connects us to the mystery that is intellectually unknowable.

Using metaphor, the cosmological function describes the creation and function of the universe and the Earth. This is the concrete, scientific aspect. Myths might have been thought to be factual during the time they were in wide use, but a four-thousand-year-old view of the universe is no longer going to be scientifically relevant, and no attempt should be made to try to make myths factually conform to modern science. Trying to scientifically prove a metaphor is preposterous. Remember, myths aren't intended to be factual or scientific accounts, and no one should try to pretend they are.

The sociological function of myths explains our purpose for being here and how we are supposed to behave while incarnated on the planet. The mythological stories model how we are to treat others and how we are to relate to or identify with the gods.

The last function of mythology is the pedagogical function. This function of a myth teaches people how to live life, find their own identity, and understand their identity within Deity. The myth teaches what is expected of children, how to be an adult, how to deal with old age, and how to approach and go through death's door. Mythology in this role is intended to take the fear out of life and comfort us in times of hardship.[10]

However, people will still wonder how myths can do all this for someone when that person knows myths are not true. As an example, think about those sappy Internet stories that perpetually circulate involving a teacher, coach, or other mentor who believes and encourages someone at a critical time in their life. This turns the person's life around, causing this once floundering individual to grow up and become a doctor, scientist, or religious figure. The now successful individual gives the credit for their life turning around to that mentor from their youth, who attends the person's graduation, wedding, or Nobel Prize ceremony. These stories are all heart wrenching and guaranteed to leave mascara-stained droplets on the reader's page.

If we view this story on a factual level, a person may feel the teacher was a wonderful person, and isn't it great the child's life turned out so nice? However, if we view this story on a mythological level, metaphorically *we* are each the teacher and the student. We are supposed to see that everything we do affects others and that for good or ill, we are affected by the actions of those around us. We are intended to apply the story to our lives and make an effort to do as that mentor did by using our actions to bring about a positive change in the lives of those we touch. On the factual level, if the story is later found to be untrue, a person feels cheated and deceived. Thinking that no one really does such nice things for others, they may begin to doubt the goodness of people. If a person views this story on the mythological level though, it doesn't matter if the story is true or not because it's the application of the story to one's life that is important. Whether the story is factual or not is irrelevant.

Myths are poetry that touches the very core of our being, striking resonant chords deep within our psyches. They teach us of Divinity, give us clues about how to relate to others, and teach us how to deal with the changes that are a part of living. They are intended to be metaphors for life, not eyewitness accounts. If one tries to read myths as true stories, the myths will eventually crumble into dust, but if myths are viewed as lessons, they become the soil, sun, and rain that help a person's spirit grow and burst into flower.

Why is there evil in the world?

The short answer is there's not evil in the world. We only perceive things as evil; however, my wife pointed out that this answer would leave lots of room for misunderstanding and I might want to elaborate a bit. Therefore, I want to use an analogy.

On any night, if you ask a child to go outside, the child will probably hesitate, telling you it's dark and scary; however, if you repeat the request during the day, they will charge through the door, never hesitating or thinking of the outdoors as scary. We are raised viewing the world as a set of opposites: light and dark, good and evil, hot and cold. Everything is viewed as a struggle between two opposing forces with humanity caught in the middle attempting to exist in this maelstrom of polarity. We view the world with two minds, dividing people and actions into separate camps, deciding whether everything is right or wrong, black or white, good or bad, guilty or innocent. We identify ourselves with one camp and tend to view everyone else with fear and suspicion. This is the reason behind most of the conflict in the world: Some people view their own race as good, so others are bad. Some people feel their religion is right, so other religions are viewed as wrong. If they are wrong, their followers probably have some dire motive for following such religions, and that would mean those who believe in those religions are evil and must be stopped. One can see how this line of reasoning can quickly get out of hand. People are certain light and dark, good and evil, and hot and cold are opposing forces in the universe, which just goes to show how concepts about which we are positive can sometimes be wrong.

Light is a force of nature; it moves at a rate of 299,792,458 meters per second, will bend in response to gravity, and is reflected by objects. If one begins taking away light, our surroundings become dimmer and dimmer until there is no light, which we define as dark. Darkness is not a force of nature; it is simply the absence of light. Darkness doesn't move. A person can't shine a beam of dark on the wall. They can cast a shadow, but that's blocking the light, not projecting darkness. Darkness doesn't reflect or refract. If you open the door to a dark room, light pours in; the darkness doesn't pour out. If we light a candle, its energy shines forth, driving back the darkness.

Again, darkness has no energy of its own. People only perceive that it does. Any power darkness has is only in our minds. We know light is energy, and in our minds we have given power and energy to its opposite until we have mentally created a force of nature that doesn't really exist. We could easily eliminate the word *dark* from our vocabulary and just refer to the luminescence of a room in terms of how much light is present. For instance, we could say, "Honey, could you turn on the lamp; the ambient light is beginning to fade," but somehow I don't think this would catch on. Areas we call dark are simply places hidden or closed off from the light. If we add light to these hidden places, the dark instantly vanishes because there was never really anything there to begin with; it was simply an area devoid of light, waiting for illumination to find it. Remember, light and dark are being used here as an analogy for the Divine radiance in our lives, which, like light, is available to all.

It's the Wiccan perspective that Deity reveals itself through nature and that there is no evil in nature. Animals will hunt and kill but only to survive. Earthquakes and volcanoes may wreak havoc, but there is no malice or intent to harm in them, and the tornado that destroys a city is reacting to natural laws with no underlying fiendish purpose. From a Wiccan perspective, Deity, like light or heat, has no opposite. We simply are allowed to choose our level of exposure. Now, it is my viewpoint that Divinity sends forth energy, and since there is nothing that is not part of Divinity, everything radiates this energy unless we choose to disconnect or shade ourselves from it. The energy of the Divine is love, peace, joy, contentment, and happiness, and as with light, there is no opposite power—only the absence of Divine energy. We perceive the absence of love to be anger and hatred; without peace we worry; a lack of joy we define as sorrow. Divine energy flows freely through all who want it; however, there are people who choose to separate themselves from the Divine, and like a cloud passing overhead, a shadow falls on them. As the light of peace and love diminish, we experience fear or anger. Just as one can choose to live their life hidden away from the sun, emerging only during the depths of the night and fleeing to the darkest cellars during the day, someone's soul can choose to eschew the Divine spiritual light, hiding in the darkest recesses of the spirit until all the brightness of compassion, mercy, and kindness have been extinguished, leaving only cruelty and bitterness in the void. This person has not been filled with evil; they have been made devoid of goodness. As a room without light is perceived as dark, a soul without Divine radiance is perceived to be evil.

Divinity is at the center of our being, and it radiates love and compassion, which we are envisioning metaphorically here as light. As we move away from our center, this radiance dims, becoming shadowy and getting progressively darker until somewhere on the edge we would reach blackness, a separation from the Divine. This point is so blocked or so far removed from Divine energy that no joy or happiness can reach it. Such a separation can become so great that our souls become dark, and violence, fear, and sorrow become the only things we know.

This dark place completely removed from Divine love and compassion would be the only place, in my thinking, that deserves the title *Hell*. However, it's not a place we are sent to as punishment or even after we die. To me, Hell is where those who keep moving away from the Divine eventually arrive on their own. It is a place of anger and despair without any hope because those who dwell in this dark place have turned their backs on their center, the source of all hope. We begin to feel that Deity has abandoned us, which can't happen; we can, however, abandon It. The problem is compounded because as we move away from the Divine, we seek shelter in the ego, which shadows us further by telling us we are the only ones who are important and everyone else doesn't matter. The ego tells us our pain is greater than that of others, who can't possibly understand our life. The ego locks us away in a castle called "me and mine." We indulge our baser instincts, blocking more light from our being.

Moving toward our center will place us once again in touch with the Divine and with love and hope. However, to do that, one must first escape from the castle and stop wailing about one's miseries long enough to listen for the voice of the Divine and see that point of Hope, shining like the North Star, that will guide us home.

One might wonder, if all we have to do to be happy is open ourselves back up to the Deity, which is already a part of each of us, why doesn't everyone walk around in a state of unbridled bliss? I know there are those out there who are saying, "All right, I'm ready. Come on and whack me upside the head with some magic wand and make me happy." Unfortunately, no one can do that. People have to find their own joy and happiness. To obtain joy and happiness, we have to give up anger, insecurity, and sorrow; for most people, this is not an easy thing to do. To achieve joy we must give up anger: no more cussing out other drivers, ranting about politicians, or screaming at sales clerks. People have a tendency to identify themselves with their pain; they define themselves in terms of their sorrow, anger, or greed.

How many people do you know who, when they run into someone, begin the conversation by telling all about their problems? Some people call others to let them know when something bad occurs. Couples play the "I've had a worse day than you" game, complaining about politics, the weather, their job, or their kids. These people seemingly define themselves in terms of their problems, and if they were given the option of trading their complaints for blissful happiness, it would be a difficult decision. We bond to our miseries, waving them in front of us like a flag, comparing our problems to other people's problems with the victor scoring some kind of martyrdom brownie points.

Sometimes people don't want to step into the light because they see their shadow emotions as beneficial, even helpful, to their lives. We refuse to give up anger because we feel it keeps us from being a victim. We won't give up our fear because we think fear will keep us safe, and we value aggression because we feel it will give us a competitive edge in life. We hide in the shadows because, like the wolf, we feel the shadows provide us with cover, obscuring our faults from others, making us look better because of the low light. Most people avoid the fullness of the Divine light because, like trying on a bathing suit under florescent lighting, all the things we view as flaws are exposed, and most people would rather deny they have faults than face their imperfections. It is easier to live in the shadows, hiding away from Divinity, than to admit we have done things we know were wrong.

This aspect of human nature is illustrated in Genesis where Adam and Eve hide from God after eating the fruit from the tree of the knowledge of good and evil. God asks, "What have you done?" Does Adam confess to what he did and say, "I ate the fruit, and I am sorry for my mistake"? No. Instead, pointing to Eve, he says, "She made me do it." Then does Eve admit she was wrong? No. Pointing to the serpent, she says, "It made me do it." The snake is the only one who doesn't blame someone else. We have all done things that have harmed others, even if the harm was unintentional at the time. So we hide in the shadows, away from the light of the Divine, pretending we have no faults, blaming everyone else for our missteps.

If we step into the light, we are faced with our choices and have to take personal responsibility for our actions by admitting to ourselves without excuses that we stole someone else's work, lied to get promotions, and even were a real jerk to Sandy in the tenth grade. All the thousands of regrettable things we have done in our lives glare at us with no possibility of doing them over and fixing the situation, but that's the point: we must learn from the mistakes in our life or we will continue to repeat them over and over. By admitting our faults and taking responsibility for our actions, we break the cycle, coming further out of the shadow and drawing ourselves a bit closer to the Divine.

However, because of the way the world works, we need the shadows. People learn from pain, and choosing to walk in shadow gives us the opportunity to grow and develop as people. The state of perpetual bliss might be great for helping others aspire to enlightenment, but it doesn't teach them much. They seem to have already learned the lessons the rest of us struggle with day after day. Their existence seems to be a signpost pointing the way for those who still struggle.

Their lives seem to shine as beacons while our lives cast shadows. However, if one is here to learn lessons, the shadows are where those lessons are learned. When walking in the shadows, we are partially shielded from the Divine light and, therefore, experience such emotions as fear, anger, greed, and selfishness.

We then have the opportunity to face those shadowy demons, and we have several options open to us when confronting them. We may choose to hide, ignoring or denying the demons, pretending they aren't there, all the while fearfully cowering on the inside, hoping they won't find us. We may be terrified some "evil" part of us will assert itself and people will see the darkness within us. We can also choose to run, retreating further into those emotions and, therefore, deeper into the darkness, separating ourselves even more from the Divinity within. Risking the possibility of getting lost in the shadows, we flee even deeper into the dark forest we are told of in myth and end up getting consumed by the demons from which we flee. Lost in a maelstrom of violence, hatred, or despair, we may become, by degrees, the evil we fear.

Seeing nothing around but the deepest of shadows and not knowing which way to turn, people frequently blame Divinity for the problems they have created, causing even further retreat from the light out of misplaced anger or resentment. This further separation elicits even more fear, anger, and anxiety, and people may begin to revel in the "evil" by lashing out violently at others or turning to drugs or alcohol in their attempt to cope with the self-destructive spiral into the demonic darkness their life has taken.

Believing they are contemptible and filled with sin, some people see the darkness as a punishment for their transgressions. These people fear the shadow but refuse to move further into the light because they think they deserve the darkness and are unworthy of the Divine light.

The last option is to face our fears and see the shadow demons for what they are: illusions that have no form or substance of their own. The darkness can't hurt the eternal part of us that is a piece of the Divine. The shadow is a testing ground for our souls, and each of us has the choice to either move away from the light, becoming by degrees more "evil" as we move into darkness, or face our shadows and strive toward the light. Facing one's shadow is knowing we have the potential to do harm and doing good anyway. It's acknowledging that we are not perfect and have harmed others. Rather than denying that part of ourselves, we embrace it. We rectify harms when possible and deal with the world as a unified being. The potential to harm is with each of us, but we choose whether or not to act on those impulses.

I think the difference between someone who has faced their shadow doing good and someone who has not is that the one who *hasn't* faced their shadow does good because they desire a reward or fear punishment, and the one who *has* faced their shadow does good because that's what is right. We should do good because we acknowledge that those we help are also a part of the Divine and, on that level, we are the same. We all share that Divine spark, and we honor it by trying to refrain from damaging another or harming by thought, word, or deed. Most people are so repulsed by their shadow side that they refuse to acknowledge it and frequently deny its existence.

Looking within ourselves and embracing our shadow is what makes us whole and is essential to moving toward the light or experiencing the Divine in our lives. Once we have faced our shadows, we learn from them, growing and becoming better as individuals. In this way we gradually move out of the twilight of the Divine and let the morning light spill over the horizon of our life, gradually driving away the darkness and filling our souls from within.

How does Wicca feel about science?

Science and religion have often been perceived as being opposing forces locked in Olympian combat with the hearts and minds of humanity being the prize of the victor. Religion is frequently depicted as a moral edifice with science attempting to chip away at its foundations. I have often heard people protest that science only seeks to disprove religion so that spirituality will be removed from people's lives. Drama not withstanding, scientists are usually more interested in proving the truth than in dismantling religious edifices. Unfortunately, when scientific exploration bumps into religious sacred cows, the scientific equivalent of the running of the bulls occurs. Religion marshals its forces and strikes out at the scientific trespassing onto sacred ground, seeking to defend their citadels of tradition against anyone who might question their dogma. Throughout the centuries there have been many instances of titanic clashes between religious teachings and scientific advancement where religion achieved temporary victories. Eventually, when the tide of evidence swelled to the point that the discovery could no longer be ignored, religion had to modify its beliefs to accommodate the new information.

Galileo was tried as a heretic and almost burned at the stake for proposing the theory that the Earth revolved around the sun at a time when religious teachings held that it was the other way around. "Experts" were lined up to debunk that "round Earth" theory. Leeches were used for centuries to suck the ill humors from patients but were eventually replaced by more scientific medical treatments. Even today, some people seem to believe there is a scientific conspiracy to falsify evidence with the intent of destroying religion. Despite overwhelming evidence to the contrary, some people still argue that the world is only a few thousand years old. When I was in junior high, my science teacher explained to our class that dinosaurs never actually existed; she said fossils were placed in the Earth by God to test our faith. "Experts" are now lined up to debunk evolutionary theory, and cutting-edge scientific thought like negative time and multiple dimensions are simply scoffed at.

More often than not, these clashes are not the result of science attacking religion but of religious institutions being unable or unwilling to adapt to new scientific findings. With all the history of friction between scientific and religious institutions, it's only reasonable that some people might wonder how the Wiccan religion relates to the scientific community and its understanding of the world.

The Wiccan perception of the cosmos and the formation of the world are completely compatible with current scientific thought. Wicca looks out at a universe formed from Deity, but since we don't have dogma indicating a timetable or specific mechanism for the creation of the universe, we are able to work with current research as to when and how the universe began. So the big bang theory and the idea of an expanding universe don't cause Wiccans any doctrinal difficulties. Wicca sees their creation myths as stories meant to teach lessons or spiritual truths; we don't typically view our creation stories as historical truths. So the evolutionary theory of progressive development of plants and animals is also compatible with Wiccan beliefs. Therefore, Wiccans tend to look at evolution as the incredible way Deity chose to weave the fabric of the world, seeing the evolution of differing species as the Divinely guided flow of the Universe rather than as something that happened purely by chance.

Scientists frequently mock some Wiccan beliefs because most Wiccans believe in some form of psychic abilities and magick. Scientists scoff because most psychic phenomena have never been proven in repeatable laboratory experiments. To counter this, some Wiccans point out that not being able to prove something is different than disproving it and that the adage "some things must be believed to be seen" may hold true. Many Wiccans believe that psychic and magical energy are of a different form than electromagnetic energy and that science simply has yet to discover a proper method to measure this form of energy. After all, five hundred years ago electricity was scoffed at, two hundred years ago the idea of radio waves was mocked, and only a hundred years ago the idea of atomic energy was considered ludicrous. Today valid research is being conducted in the area of paranormal events, but the research is still early and sparse. Few scientists want to conduct serious research into the paranormal because funding is limited and they have a fear of being ridiculed. When it comes to psychic occurrences, I believe this is a case where religion is starting to poke at a few scientific sacred cows.

Wiccans not only approve of the scientific study of nature, but many Wiccans also actively study scientific principles and the latest research in biology, paleontology, and quantum physics. A saying frequently used by Wiccans and others is "as above, so below." This indicates a belief that the Divine has ordered this earthly dimension to reflect the spiritual dimension. Most Wiccans regard nature as a part of Deity and strive for a deeper understanding of the natural world because that understanding helps us delve deeper into the mysteries of the Divine and of the spiritual realm. Many of Wicca's spiritual lessons are expressed as metaphors from the world around us. Light, heat, seasons, conservation of energy, atomic theory, evolution, and quantum physics may all be seen as metaphors for spiritual truths given to us by the Divine to aid us in unlocking those mysteries. When asked if Wicca has a holy text, a Wiccan standing in a park might spread their arms wide to encompass the trees, grass, and all of nature. The universe is our sacred text, and most Wiccans believe the Divine is written into the very fabric of that universe. So, far from shunning scientific investigation, Wiccans usually welcome scientific discoveries about the universe that can lead us to a deeper understanding of the Divine.

While Wicca sees the scientific exploration of the natural world as an asset to our understanding of the Divine, Wiccans do often oppose what we see as the irresponsible use of science to damage the world around us. Applications of scientific discoveries that produce copious amounts of nonrecyclable, nonbiodegradable waste or consume large quantities of nonrenewable resources are seen as harmful to the planet and to future generations. Wiccans are typically environmentally conscious and usually oppose technologies that pollute the air or water, produce biological or nuclear weapons, lead to deforestation, continue the extinction of species of plants or animals, or otherwise rape the Earth. Just because people can do something doesn't mean it's morally or ethically right to do it, and today's profits can't be purchased at the expense of our future generations. If a scientific advancement comes with a long-term ecological price tag, it shouldn't be pursued no matter what short-term convenience it provides. The lifeblood of our children is too high a price to pay for convenience or profit.

Can someone be Wiccan and practice another religion?

People often want to place walls between religious traditions, compartmentalizing them into neat little cubicles. Each religion is in a separate cubicle, and no one is allowed to be in more than one at the same time. If someone decides to leave a cubicle, they are expected to either jump into a new one, wander the hallways in indecision, or refuse to step into any cubicle by choosing to leave the building.

However, can one mix these cubicles and be a Hindu-Muslim, or a Buddhist-Baha'i? Well, with Wicca this is hypothetically possible.

Wicca has sometimes been described as a sort of unified field theory for religion. That is to say, many Wiccans believe there is one creative power and that Divinity can be perceived in a multitude of ways. There are Wiccans who use an Egyptian pantheon of deities and those who use Greek or Roman, while others may prefer Celtic, Scandinavian, African, or a mixture from many pantheons. If all these different pantheons of deities can be used, why couldn't one use the deities of a contemporary religious tradition? Now, I'm not advocating the practice of mixing religious traditions; I'm just pointing out that some people have proposed this possibility.

If a person followed the Wiccan Rede, celebrated the Moons and Sabbats, but chose to honor the teachings of Buddha and view the Bodhisattvas as their deities, that person might be described as a Buddhist-Wiccan. Likewise, if a person chose to follow a Hindu pantheon of deities, that person might want to describe themselves as a Hindu-Wiccan. There are a number of Wiccans who blend their Jewish heritage and religious teachings into their worship, and I have frequently heard them refer to themselves as Jewitches. There is also a group of people who follow the Wiccan Rede and celebrate the Sabbats but choose to use the Christian deity structure and call themselves Christian-Wiccans.[11] This particular group believes in a Christian trinity of God, Goddess, and Jesus as the sacrificial solar Deity. So at least this one group believes the two religions can be mixed and that it's possible to follow both simultaneously.

However, some people believe that if a person tries to devote himself to more than one religious tradition, that person runs the risk of watering down both, producing a mush that is devoid of much of the spirituality of both traditions. Many Wiccans might object to blending faiths in this manner, but I would suspect the greater uproar would come from whatever religion is being combined with Wicca because while Wicca views all religions as valid for those who follow them, followers of some religious traditions refuse to recognize the possibility that other religions have any spiritual value. These people would probably be greatly offended by someone attempting to blend their religious tradition with Wicca. One has to admit that a person shouldn't start combining religions in this fashion without expecting to catch at least a little flack from both their chosen traditions.

Wicca is very open to allowing people to find their own spiritual path. Many Wiccans blend elements of Buddhism, Hinduism, or even Christianity into their spiritual practice, but most stop far short of hyphenating their religion. If a person follows the Wiccan Rede, honors the God and Goddess in some form, and celebrates the Sabbats, that person could legitimately call themselves Wiccan. If that person also believes they are simultaneously honoring the deities and practicing the tenets of another religion, that is their choice. Combining religious traditions isn't something for everyone, and those who do so should expect to raise at least a few hackles on both sides of the hyphen.

A Deeper Understanding about Wiccan Ethics

Don't Witches curse people?

Hexes, curses, the ability to make someone pay for something they have done—this is a popular idea, and some people fall prey to the pretty illusion of power as it dangles before their nose. Certainly there is a potential to harm with magick, but a potential also exists to harm people by physical means such as slashing tires, throwing rocks through windows, or even picking up a gun and shooting those who anger us. Not retaliating against those who we feel deserve it, whether by physical or magickal means, requires a cool head and a sound ethical structure. A woman once asked me if Wiccans are able to curse people. I asked her if a person can pray for someone to get hit by a truck. She was visibly affronted and snapped, "Not in my religion." I said, "No, you do have the ability to pray for someone to get hit by a truck, but your religion teaches that praying for harm to befall a person is an unethical use of prayer, so you wouldn't *choose* to do that." In the same way, a Wiccan wouldn't choose to curse a person because we understand that curses are an unethical use of magick.

Unfortunately, the reality of the situation is that people are cursed and hexed all the time, but it's not Wiccans who are responsible for most of the cursing. In a 1994 Gallup poll, one in twenty Americans said they have prayed for harm to come to others, and those are just the ones who admit to doing it.[1] People unintentionally curse others all the time: people will damn others by wishing harmful things will happen to them, hoping someone won't show up for work, or wishing a person would just go away. People view these as just thoughts, which can't hurt anyone, but thoughts are things and have their own energy. They are the basis of all magick, and all previous examples are unintentional curses.

There is a substantial amount of research into the effects of negative prayer and unintentional curses that proves such effects to be very real. This research is documented in the book *Be Careful What You Pray For . . . You Just Might Get It* by Larry Dossey, MD. Dossey discusses "prayer muggings," which are instances when a person prays for someone else to lose so they can win, and manipulative prayers, where people pray for someone to think or act the way they wish them to or pray for the person to perform some action that will somehow benefit the person or persons who are praying. Prayers of both types happen all the time, and both are curses that are controlling, manipulative, and highly unethical by Wiccan standards.

People sometimes believe they're not cursing someone because they don't feel they are using "negative energy." This thought may help ease a person's conscience, but there is no such thing as negative energy. Energy simply is. Whether it's used in ways viewed as positive or negative depends completely on how one employs the energy. Applying the terms *positive* and *negative* to energy is simply a convenient way to think about how that energy is being used.

Consider a knife. A knife is neutral; it is simply a tool that everyone is free to use. In the hands of a surgeon, it becomes a tool for healing. In the hands of an artist, it creates beauty. However, in the hands of a killer, it becomes an instrument of fear and destruction. The knife itself is not positive or negative; it is the use we make of the knife that may be assigned those terms.

Magick is a tool that can heal, inspire, bring people back from the brink of despair, or be used to curse and harm. The user of the tool governs the way it is used. Also, whether something is a curse or not depends greatly on the viewpoint of the observer. One person may view an action as a blessing, while another views it as a curse. If a group of people don't want a liquor store in their area, they would consider it a blessing if the store closed, while the people whose families relied on the income would consider its closing a curse.

Magick requires the focus of a considerable amount of energy. When dealing with any kind of energy, one must remember that like attracts like. Energy directed toward healing, compassion, and love attracts the same. However, if energy is directed with anger, hatred, or violent intent, the energy focused in that way will return to the person. As discussed in chapter three, Wiccans believe that the energy sent out not only returns to the person who sent it but that it will also return stronger. This is the "Rule of Three," which states that all energy one puts out returns to the caster threefold.

The Rule of Three is great when one is performing beneficial spells where the returning energy adds to the caster's general health and good fortune. However, if someone is trying to curse others, the energy that flows back to the caster will be filled with hatred and anger flowing through them like snake venom poisoning their soul. The person begins to sink deeper into spiritual darkness that they are creating by drawing away from Deity. Any damage the person may be doing to their adversary is nothing compared to the damage they are doing to their own life. The lives of people who have tried to walk this path can be consumed by their own hatred. They attempt to destroy someone else's life and wonder why their family, social life, finances, and health crumble around them. The energetic forces they direct toward themselves are brutal, and the sad thing is they usually blame the person whom they are trying to curse for the problems befalling them, even though the harm is a result of their own actions.

Therefore, while the temptation to curse that annoying person might be strong, as might be the temptation to punch them in the face, both should be resisted. Attacking another by physical or magickal means violates Wiccan ethics and would not be done by someone who is truly following the Wiccan path.

How can a person live without harming anything? Even vegetarians can't live without harming plants.

Walking hand in hand across a fragrant meadow, two young lovers seek the perfect picnic spot. Finding the ideal picturesque location, they spread a blanket on the ground, unpack their basket, munch ham sandwiches, share cheese, and sip wine. After dinner they hold each other while watching the sunset. As they pack to leave, let's look at this scene again to see the path of devastation carved by this simple and innocent act.

As the couple left their car, a bee flew into it and, becoming trapped, perished as the temperature rose. As our loving couple strode toward their picturesque spot, they trod on two beetles, a centipede, and a host of meadow vegetation. Their blanket covered a sapling oak that had just begun to reach skyward, and their picnic basket sheared off the young giant at the ground, assuring it will never reach the heights to which it aspired. Our picnickers squashed three ants just before they reached the potato salad, and the young man swatted and killed a mosquito as it attempted to have its own picnic on his date. The sandwiches cost the life of one pig, a tomato, and a head of lettuce. Potatoes were killed for the salad, and cows were raised on a factory farm to produce the cheese.

Life feeds on life. Everything from bacteria to mammals feed on something that was once a living thing. This has been represented as the cycle of life, where the herbivores eat the plants, the predators eat the herbivores, the predators die, and what's not consumed by the scavengers becomes fertilizer for the plants. When one thinks about it, life is a horrific cycle of carnage with everything living a sort of vampiric existence off the life force of some other living thing. A portion of the mythology of every religion is devoted to the psychological justification of living off death. Whether it's a god decreeing the plants and animals to be our food or the buffalo dance, which is a ritual to ensure the rebirth of the slain animal's spirit, such stories help us to mentally deal with the fact that our continued existence comes at the cost of the living essence of the plants and animals with which we share the planet. Into this slaughterhouse of vegetable and animal species comes Wicca saying people can do whatever they want as long as it doesn't hurt anything. When hearing this, one might ask how this can be accomplished, and the answer is, it can't. There is no possible way a person can continue to live without harming something. We accidentally tread on countless critters, we consume animals and plants for nourishment, we pollute the planet, and I haven't even started to address what we're capable of doing to each other. So is the Wiccan Rede an impossible standard? Yes. Does that invalidate its usefulness as a religious ethical measure? No.

The ethical standards of most of the world's religions are ultimately impossible for us to achieve. The Wiccan Rede, like all ethical guidelines, is a standard to which we aspire. We can't live without harming something, but we can strive to do as little harm as possible. We can make a concerted effort to inflict no intentional physical or emotional injury on another person and make amends for the unintentional ones. We can be kind to the animals we encounter and respectful of the Earth. I'm not saying everyone should be a vegetarian because everyone is free to draw their own lines in regard to the food they eat and shouldn't be condemned for their decision. However, as long as those animals intended for consumption are still alive, they should be treated with the respect due all living things and should be killed with as little suffering as possible. Their sacrifice should be acknowledged, and no one should receive pleasure from the death of another living thing. We can honor the Earth from which the plants we eat grow while we use as few of its resources as are necessary for us to survive. We can reduce pollution by generating as little trash as possible and recycling as much as we are able.

It's impossible to live on this planet without harming something every day of our lives, but keeping the fact in mind that we are doing so helps assure we do as little damage as possible. We can be careful of our resources and not overconsume or take more than we intend to use—not be wasteful. We can strive for our lives to have as little harmful impact on the world around us as possible, even if harming nothing is an impossible goal.

How can words harm someone?

The children's nursery rhyme goes, "Sticks and stones may break my bones, but words will never hurt me." While this nice little chant is filled with good intentions, it is not entirely true. Thoughts are things, and words have power, but they only have power over us if we allow them to affect us. The only defense against people's jeers is found in our self-esteem. A person who completely knows and accepts who they are will neither be decimated by the criticism of others nor inflated by their praise. A completely self-assured person lets the poisonous verbal barbs bounce off the armor of their self-knowledge.

Unfortunately, not many of us are at this level of self-assurance. We are neither faster than a speeding sarcasm nor can we leap tall praises in a single bound. We get angry when someone blows their horn at us on the freeway, flush when someone smiles at us, and may throw out a new outfit because we overhear a stranger in the elevator say, "Can you believe what she was wearing?" The opinions of complete strangers can cause an emotional roller coaster ride on which our self-esteem is pitched from side to side even though the comments come from people who know nothing about us. If the views of strangers can cause such turmoil, how much more damage is done when the comments come from friends or family members?

One never knows when someone else will take a callous or ill-chosen word to heart. Another person's words can't harm us if we don't allow them to harm us. However, that fact doesn't absolve us from blame when we verbally lash out at someone. If we are having a bad day, that does not give us the right to take our emotions out on someone else and start ripples that may contribute to major changes in a person's life.

My grandfather was always an active man. He was always healthy and looked years younger than he actually was. After he retired he served on the boards of several national organizations as well as his local school board. He also loved to play golf and played several times a week, competing in tournaments and winning many of them. The club he played at held tournaments in which the foursomes were randomly assigned, which gave people the opportunity to meet others. At one of these tournaments, a twenty-something-year-old man in my grandfather's group snipped, "Old people should not be allowed to play in these tournaments. They slow the rest of us down." I have no idea why he said this: maybe my grandfather's game was a bit off that day, maybe he wanted to walk faster than a man in his late seventies could manage, or maybe he just had a bad day. Whatever the reason, the effects of that one comment were devastating. When my grandfather got home, he put away his clubs and never touched them again. He sold his club membership, and on that day he quit living and started dying. His health deteriorated, and the years seemed to catch up with him rapidly, aging him many years in only a few months. He continued to get sicker and weaker until death became a kinder option than life.

My grandfather's downslide resulted from two mistakes: one person made a callous comment, and another person accepted that comment into his reality. I am sure the person who said "old people shouldn't be allowed to play" didn't intend for his words to have a far-reaching effect, but they did. How many of us have behaviors whose origins date back to some snide comment someone made when we were young? Many people may not smile because someone, maybe in junior high, said they had ugly teeth, or they may never wear shorts because someone said they had funny knees. Remarks like these, even by strangers, still affect our lives thirty or more years after they were spoken. Every statement we make is a stone thrown into the waters of people's lives, and we never know how big a splash we make or how far the ripples may travel.

People might feel the consequences of our words long after we have forgotten uttering them. Words can have the soothing power of a healing salve or the destructive force of a cannonball, so we should always choose our words wisely and with the intent to heal, comfort, and build up people, never with the intent to lash out or harm. This takes self-discipline and a certain amount of empathy for the feelings of others. Considering the ramifications of one's words before speaking ultimately makes one a better person, and the real struggle in life is to be a better person today than we were the day before.

On the other side of this discussion, we have to armor ourselves against the slings and arrows of outrageous comments by not taking other people's words automatically to heart. We have to learn to separate the occasional bit of constructive advice from the barrage of drivel we are assaulted with daily. When people don't know us, can we really believe their assessment of our life or personality is valid? If a mechanic walked out to our parked car and, without turning it on, began to tell us everything he thought needed to be fixed, we would probably find a different mechanic. However, if a complete stranger calls us an idiotic jerk, we may begin to fret for days wondering what we did, trying to decide how we can fix ourselves. The truth is, comments hurled at us by near strangers usually have more to do with them than with us. Such people may be having marital problems, or their boss may have just berated them. They are lashing out at the first person who crosses their path.

We never know the motivation behind the words, but we can choose to accept their assessment of our life and personality or we can let their comments roll off our backs. We know ourselves far better than anyone else could ever understand us. If we learn to be honest with ourselves, we can use that honesty as a shield, defending our fragile ego from the random gravel kicked up by the unthinking masses as they pass.

What does Wicca teach about social issues such as abortion, euthanasia, and homosexuality?

Many social issues bleed into religious issues when religious institutions weigh in with their opinions and expect all their members to fall obediently in step with religious dogma. Religious groups have told their members what to believe on controversial issues ranging from slavery to card playing. Disagreement with the official stance on a perceived pernicious issue is sometimes seen as high treason against the deities of the religion. Disagreements have led to angry splits within religious groups where members on both sides of the argument believe they are on the moral high ground and have Divine sanction for their stance. The two groups set up camps and fling verbal volleys at the erring party. Sanctimonious bickering continues until some critical mass is reached. One side either gives in or a sort of religious mitosis occurs where a sect divides into two groups, one of which moves down the street and tacks *reformed, new, true,* or *enlightened* on the front of the old name. Scenes such as this occur far too often within every religious tradition. In the past some of the divisive social issues have been slavery, prohibition, women's suffrage, desegregation, and interracial marriage. Some of today's social hot buttons are abortion, euthanasia, homosexuality, drug and alcohol use, sex, women's rights, and war. Each of these issues can and does cause heated debates, doctrinal discussions, and sometimes a religious group will split as differing factions try to decide what Deity wants people to believe about the worrisome problem.

Wicca, as a rule, doesn't have dogma. No councils or conventions decide how all Wiccans are supposed to behave, think, or react to any social issues. Wicca is based on a personal experience of the Divine. As such, people must decide for themselves how they feel about each issue based on their own understanding of Divinity. People must look within themselves and examine the motivations for the decisions they have made while listening to the voice of the spirit within them to decide whether that decision is the best one for them.

When counseling people who are trying to make a difficult decision in their lives, I try to help them explore all choices and their possible consequences so they can see how each decision will impact not only them but those close to them. If they feel they are unable to pursue a certain course, we discuss why they are hesitant. If they say they want to dash toward another path, we also examine why they believe that is the correct direction to travel. The goal is not to push them toward the path I want them to choose but to aid them in considering their options and making an informed decision that they can live with once the fear and anxiety have passed. My personal beliefs are not important because I don't have to live with their choice; they and those close to them do. Once they have decided what they wish to do, I assist them with whatever steps are necessary and help them decide who they should speak to next, which could include their significant other, parents, doctor, lawyer, or psychologist.

Wicca doesn't have a set policy outlining our stance on social issues, and I hope there is never an attempt to establish one. Wiccans usually believe choices of this magnitude are between the individual and their perception of Deity. If one had to make a characterization of Wicca's views on social issues for most Wiccans, the description would be *choice*. Whether each individual Wiccan is personally for or against issues such as abortion, euthanasia, medical marijuana use, the death penalty, same-sex marriages, or a host of other social issues, most Wiccans want the ability to make these decisions for themselves and to allow others the freedom to make these decisions based on their own conscience or religious beliefs.

Consequently, there is great diversity in how Wiccans feel about any given subject. There are Wiccans in the military and in antiwar rallies. There are vegans, vegetarians, and those who are willing to attempt to eat anything that slows down long enough for them to dump barbecue sauce on it. Every political party has members who are Wiccan, as does, I would suspect, almost every organization in existence. There are Wiccans who have had abortions, and those who would never consider it. Some Wiccans would consider euthanasia an option if they were terminally ill and painfully approaching death, while others would heroically fight for every last breath.

Wiccans may hold very different opinions about many social issues, but we accept that people have different viewpoints. If given the chance, I think very few Wiccans would attempt to pass laws forcing others to conform to their personal beliefs.

If Wiccans think their beliefs are correct, why don't they try to convert others to their beliefs?

Buddha, Allah, Krishna, and Jehovah are all names for Deity as it is perceived and worshiped by various cultures around the world. Each one has its own persona and devotees, code of conduct, and list of social mores. There is, however, one thing all of them have in common. Their devotees are absolutely committed to their worship. Most people, no matter what religion they follow, usually believe their form of worship is the purest and most perfect method of devotion to Deity on the planet, and it *is* the purest and most perfect form of devotion to Deity on the planet—for them.

Throughout time, from a Wiccan perspective, saviors, redeemers, prophets, poets, and saints have suddenly glimpsed a part of the grand cosmic mystery that is Deity. Some shard or drop of the truth of Divinity fills their soul with enlightenment, and from this state of Divine rapture, they are compelled to try to relate to others what they have seen. The problem is that even though each drop of the sea contains the essence of the entire ocean, it is still only a drop, and descriptions of that drop, no matter how poetic, will still not make another person understand the enormity of the ocean. That shard of enlightenment is still only a fragment of the majesty that is the Divine. Complicate this by trying to explain with words something that can only be experienced to people who have had no personal experience of the Divine and, therefore, have no point of reference on which to base understanding, and one can begin to see how difficult it might be to explain enlightenment to others.

It's like trying to explain color to people who live with their eyes closed, making them blind to the light. These blind people become inspired by their enlightened teacher and go out to try to communicate the wonder of color, of which they have been told but have never personally experienced, to other blind people. These people, in turn, tell others of the revelation that there is something more to life than we are experiencing, and if people only follow the teachings of (insert prophet here), their life will be more complete.

From this example, one may see how the world has ended up with so many religious traditions all passing on to the next generation of the "blind" their own variation of the message of color to devotees who unquestioningly accept the message as true. So few people realize the real truth that most of these teachers were trying to relate. No one is really blind; some people are afraid to open their eyes and see color for themselves. Unfortunately, it's easier to live without sight than to risk the light that may burn away our preconceived notions and show us that Divine color is not exactly as we have been told all our lives—it is so much more.

Religions are often hesitant to recognize the relevance of other religious teachings, insisting that everyone in the world should follow the tenets of their religion. Followers of these religions attempt to convince everyone that they can experience true enlightenment only if they pray to their god, eat their bread butter side up, or crack their eggs on the small end. Devotees of this variety may sometimes become hostile or violent when encountering someone who questions their dogma, whose beliefs are different, or who refuses to change their beliefs or conform to the prevailing dogma.

Other religious adherents, just as devoted to their beliefs, understand that others have differing views of Deity without feeling that their own beliefs are compromised or lessened. This group is secure in its beliefs and tends to view all religions as personal to the individual. They believe the existence of Deity can't be proven one way or the other; therefore, arguing about religion is a futile pursuit, which is only going to cause problems. Another possibility is that they may believe all religions are valid because each religion draws us closer to Divinity; therefore, arguing about religion is not productive because a person is questioning someone else's experience, and someone can't tell another person what is best for their life any more than they can tell you what is best for yours. Wiccans tend to fall into this last category.

Wiccans believe everyone has to choose their own religious path and each person follows exactly the right religious path for them. All religions are paths leading toward the goal of spiritual advancement; some paths may be slow but easy, while others may be quicker but more difficult to follow. If you climb a mountain, the easy paths will take a long time to reach the top, while the more direct routes may be impossible for all but the most advanced climbers. Who are we to say the path someone chooses is correct or incorrect for them? If someone wants to go to Paris, they may choose to take a boat, plane, car, train, or any combination thereof. The traveler may choose to take a direct flight or might decide to get there via China, but sooner or later, they will arrive, and the route they take will be the one most appealing to them. Spiritual advancement is extremely personal, and exactly what each person requires for their advancement during a particular lifetime is unknown, even to the individual's persona, while they are incarnated on Earth.

Wiccans allow each individual to make their own choice of religious paths. If that person chooses a Wiccan path, others will guide them along the widest parts of the path, teaching the individual the lessons that will prepare them to find the narrow path, the one that must be walked alone, that leads to oneness with Deity. However, if a person chooses a non-Wiccan path, most Wiccans believe the choice made is what the individual needs at this point in their lifetime. A different choice means this person has different lessons to learn and other experiences to grow from in this lifetime. Each person's spirit guides one to the religious path that will best facilitate the lessons necessary for continued spiritual growth. The choice of a different path is not a reflection of the validity of any religious tradition, as all are valid for the practitioners of that religion.

Therefore, seeking out converts is not a practice in which Wiccans engage. We may discuss religious beliefs and share our beliefs with those who ask, but we don't actively seek converts. Perhaps we are so adamant on this point because Wiccans, especially Wiccan children, are often the targets of proselytizing by people of other faiths. Therefore, we know what it feels like to have one's religious views attacked and for someone to attempt to turn one's children against them, and we don't want others to be in that position.

If the Universe is an abundant place, why do some people seem to have everything and others seem to have nothing?

If we could stroll across the world as we journeyed, we would see people of every social class, educational level, and monetary spectrum from wealth to poverty. We would see people who exist from week to week earning just enough to feed and clothe their families. These people live comfortably but have few extras beyond what is absolutely necessary for them to live. We would find many people who live from hand to mouth, never knowing when or from where their next meal will come. These people live on the street and in villages without clean water and where food is scarce. These people define luxuries as more than one meal a day and a safe, dry place to sleep. If we step around the corner from those living in abject poverty, we may find people who are living in extreme wealth and luxury. These wealthy households have more than they could ever use and beds that are never slept on. They throw away more food than they eat, and as they already have most luxuries, they must work to come up with creative ways to spend their money.

This discrepancy between the *haves* and the *have-nots* has always been something with which I've struggled. Why would Deity allow one child to be born into a world of starvation and unsanitary conditions where they will probably not live long enough to go to school, assuming schools are available, while another child is born into a life where they will not only never know want but are also virtually assured of going to the best schools and receiving a college education? Why is one child born healthy while another is born with Down's syndrome or any of a host of other genetic maladies? Why are some people born physically beautiful, growing up adored, while others are plain or ugly, growing up as objects of ridicule? Why are some given more opportunities than they can use, while others are seemingly given nothing?

These questions were central to my quest for a religious path. I wanted to understand why Deity would allow these vast gulfs between people. I couldn't accept the idea that children were being punished for deeds committed in past lives or sent to families as punishment for the transgressions of the parents. I believe the Universe is essentially positive in its actions and that everything in the world is arranged with the intention of bringing us closer to our Divine nature. Therefore, something had to be gained from whatever circumstance into which one is born. I think that in each life we live we gain new perspective.

Most Wiccans believe the true person isn't the body but is rather the eternal soul that inhabits the body while on Earth. The soul is reincarnated, living through many different lives, and learns something from the experiences of each lifetime. Because there's no way to understand what it's like to be someone else unless one has lived in similar situations and because it's impossible for a single person to experience everything during one lifetime, people are born into a variety of different lives, each offering a different perspective on the world.

By being reborn into differing lives, we gain the perspective of having lived as a starving child or as a noble. In this way the spirit, which is our true self, learns the anguish of an impoverished mother who has lost a child and the elation of the star athlete when winning a match. Unconditional love can be learned through a lifetime spent caring for a disabled child, and the spirit of the child is given the opportunity to learn to accept help and depend on another by being bereft of the ability to care for itself. Each life has its own lessons to learn and challenges to overcome. If we learn the lessons satisfactorily, we may choose to try a different life with new challenges next time. If not, we may try a similar life again, attempting to more satisfactorily learn those lessons and make better choices this time around.

People not only have their own lessons to learn, but they may also be here to help others learn lessons as well. After all, if a soul needs to learn to give of itself by taking care of a disabled child, another soul has to volunteer to be that disabled child. If a parent is to learn to overcome the loss of a young child, a soul must volunteer to be that child, knowing it will experience life for only a few hours, days, or weeks by living as a dying infant to teach the parents, the doctor, and the nurses lessons they needed to learn during this lifetime. I also tend to think that many people need to learn patience and serenity, so maybe there were souls who volunteered to be the "jerks" in the world whose mission it is to try our patience. Everyone is both a teacher and a student while they are on Earth.

There are those who may wonder, if we choose the life we are going to live, why a spirit would choose a lifetime of hardship; why aren't we all wealthy and powerful? Every type of existence has its own lessons, challenges, and pitfalls, and the spirit doesn't have the same ego concerns the body has. A spirit may pick the type of life that will best prepare it for the lesson it feels it needs to learn. Our spirits might like the challenge of trying to maintain their ethics in harsher surroundings. Can we learn to love and respect others when those we live around are killing to survive? Learning generosity and giving to those in need might be easy for the rich but much more difficult when one has next to nothing themselves. Humility might be a more difficult lesson for the rich, while overcoming despair might be a tougher lesson when one has nothing.

Birth and death have relevance only within our existence on Earth. While we might be horrified by the idea that someone would choose to live their life with a severe physical or mental handicap, the spirit sees beyond the comforts of the body. To the eternal spirit, which is our true self, each lifetime is only a glimmer among hundreds or even thousands of other lifetimes. Our spirit might consider entering a lifetime as we would consider going out to a party, and how many people choose to wear an extremely uncomfortable pair of shoes to a party because they are necessary to make our outfit complete? For a spirit the suffering of one lifetime is a minimal price for the opportunity to learn. A single lifetime is fleeting when compared to eternity, and the spirit wants to experience every joy and hardship in order to understand the human experience from every perspective.

What about sin?

Sin is usually viewed as breaking a law given to us by Deity. The *Webster's College Dictionary* defines *sin* as "transgression of divine law." The Wiccan Rede is an ethical guideline governing how we are supposed to live and relate to others, but Wicca doesn't have a list of Divine laws. Since there isn't a list of Divine laws, there's nothing against which to transgress. The decision as to whether an action is appropriate or not rests with the Wiccan Rede, "An it harm none," and the individual's own ethical code. Doing something that violates one's ethical code is a betrayal of oneself. Every effort should be made to rectify any damage done, but it's not considered sin because we have violated our own ethical laws, not Deity's. When we betray ourselves, both the betrayal and the effort to clean up the mess should be lessons that are learned in an effort to prevent us from repeating those actions. We are each responsible for our own actions and the consequences of those actions.

Wicca also doesn't recognize the concept of Original Sin. Original Sin is the belief that all people are born tainted by the transgression of our original ancestors. This transgression is believed, by some, to have caused a rift, or separation, between Deity and man. Wiccans usually believe everyone and everything is a part of Deity; to us, there is no separation between people and Divinity. From a Wiccan viewpoint, praying for Deity to be with us is like fish in the ocean praying for water to be with them. Wiccans believe Deity is everywhere. The food we eat and the air we breathe are part of Deity, and any separation between us and the Divine is of our own making, not Deity's. People are born pure, unstained by any previous misdeeds, with a clean slate on which to inscribe their life's stories.

Many religions believe if a person is not cleansed from sin, their soul will be consigned to torments in the afterlife. The Wiccan afterlife is viewed as many things. Some see it as the Summerland where our souls rest in an Eden-like environment. Others believe we become the guardian spirits for those we loved until it's time for our rebirth. Still others see the afterlife as a time of reflection on the lessons we learned during the previous life. The afterlife can be viewed as any combination of these things; however, to Wiccans the afterlife is not seen as a place of torment.

Consequently, from a Wiccan point of view, there is nothing from which to be "saved." Each person is born, does the best they can in life, and passes from this world to the next where we are all pure spirits.

Wiccans believe the consequences of our actions are not decided after we die; they are something meted out right here on Earth. Wicca has the threefold law, which states that whatever energy we put out is magnified and returned to us. If people do good things, the positive energy put out comes back to them. However, if people use their energy in a negative way, harmful energy will flow back to them. These aren't punishments for violations of Divine edicts; rather, the negative energy drawn to these people is a result of their own choices and actions. This is just the way the Universe works. Like attracts like, we reap what we sow, and punishing or rewarding people has nothing to do with it. This is a great incentive to live the Rede and try to harm nothing as we walk through this life. The time we spend on Earth is short and precious, and our behavior while we are here affects the quality of the experience for others and ourselves.

Whether the world is a place of wonder or torment is influenced by how we perceive life and how we act on those perceptions. Too many people take the "half empty" view of the world, seeing it as full of sin and evil. Wiccans typically take the "half full" approach, acknowledging that the world can be unpleasant at times but still choosing to see the world as a magical place filled with wonder and beauty and always in contact with the Divine. Wiccans believe Earth is a planet that is unique, and our time here is to be cherished, no matter what circumstances we are born in or whatever our reason for being here.

What would Wiccans consider "sinful" that others might not?

There always seems to be a great deal of conflict not only between religions but also within religious groups that is caused by disagreement about what one should and shouldn't do. Each religion has many of its own ideas about right and wrong, and each thinks it has the best ethical list. This leads to much finger wagging as people tell others how they are doing it all wrong and that the world would be a much better place if everyone would listen to them. Wiccans are frequently subjected to ethical criticism because we don't oppose some things that are frowned upon by other religions.

Wiccans tend to allow people to run their own life, and so long as no one is being harmed, we usually see no reason to interfere. We also don't make a habit of lecturing people when their ethics don't measure up to our standards. This sometimes leads people to think Wiccans don't disagree with the ethics of other religions or believe the activities those religions sometimes condone are, from a Wiccan viewpoint, wrong.

Since the Wiccan Rede "An it harm none" isn't an exact list of do's and don'ts, a great deal of variation exists in what individual Wiccans believe is correct. For example, some Wiccans are vegetarian because they think it's wrong to live off the death of animals, while other Wiccans believe death is a part of nature and humans are intended to eat meat. However, there are a number of activities many religions allow that Wiccans might consider unethical.

The unnecessary harming of animals is generally considered unethical. Wiccans don't automatically have problems with hunting as long as a person is hunting for food, but trophy hunting or other sport hunting, where an animal is killed for the "fun" of killing something, would be viewed as unethical. Other actions most Wiccans consider unethical include testing products on animals where animals are tortured, sometimes to death, with large doses of chemicals; fur farming, where animals are raised and killed solely for their skin; factory farming techniques, like cutting chicken's beaks off, where animals are treated like a commodity rather than as living beings; attempting to restructure the genetics of animals to make them more marketable; and driving species to extinction because they are in some way inconveniencing people.

Polluting or damaging the environment is something Wiccans generally consider unethical. Examples of unethical pollution of the environment include clear-cutting forests, which not only removes the trees but also causes erosion and the destruction of animal habitats; farm or industrial waste being washed into the waterways, polluting the water, and killing the fish; deforestation of the rainforests, which produce most of the world's oxygen; throwing cigarette butts or other trash on the ground; and not recycling when possible. Because each of these harms the Earth and makes living more difficult for those with whom we share the planet, many Wiccans would consider these actions unethical.

A great number of Wiccans consider scientific pursuits where the only goal is to kill greater numbers of people or animals more effectively to be unethical. Just because we can do something doesn't mean we should. We don't necessarily need massive megaton bombs, super viruses, or other bigger and "better" ways to destroy one another. Funds used for such pursuits would be better spent to care for and educate people, to provide health benefits for people's retirement, and to offer prenatal care and youth services for our next generation.

Wiccans typically find bigotry and prejudice based on race, religion, gender, sexual preference, or any other biologic or social difference to be highly unethical. Wiccans believe everyone has the right to live and worship as they please. No one should have to fear losing their job, children, or home because someone else disagrees with how they live their life. People shouldn't be ostracized at work or school because their beliefs are different or because they refuse to convert to another point of view. Also, deliberately spreading malicious gossip intended to harm someone else would be considered wrong. Everyone makes their own decisions in life, and people should not be punished, ridiculed, or endangered simply because their choices differ from our own.

Ethics are personal and tend to be a bit different for each person. Wiccans may debate and otherwise express their opinion about ethical issues, but they also allow others to have differing views. Because of the great diversity in Wicca, we have typically gotten very good at agreeing to disagree on matters of personal opinion. Wiccans are also good at letting other religions do their thing while we do ours. However, this doesn't mean we don't have strong ethical views. It simply means we can allow others to disagree with us without viewing them as a threat and directly or indirectly attacking or harming the individual.

Didn't many of the religions Wicca is patterned after use animal or human sacrifice?

Wicca does not practice or condone animal or human sacrifice; however, in ancient cultures people's relationship with Deity required them to shed blood to show their devotion. People sacrificed animals to honor the gods and to give thanks for the new animals in their flocks and herds. At that time people believed that if a part of their herd was not given back to the gods, the gods in their anger at the ungratefulness of the masses would punish them, blighting their crops and herds. In an effort to avoid this fate, these ancient people would often not only sacrifice an animal, they would sacrifice the very best of their herd. Holding back the best for oneself showed the gods that a person was stingy and miserly. The people believed the gods would be offended by substandard sacrifices, so they gave up their whitest bull, most perfect ram, or purest doves in holocaust to honor, thank, or appease the gods.

In some cultures a person was chosen to represent the land. This "king" was chosen in a voluntary competition in which whoever won would become king or be given a place of honor for a time, often three to seven years. At the end of that time, this king would willingly be sacrificed and often dismembered, the body being buried in the fields to assure continued good harvests and well being for all the people. The king believed his death would ensure continued good harvests and would go to his fate willingly; after all, he had competed for this job. Being chosen as the sacrifice meant being the best the community had to offer. It was an honor, and those who were chosen believed their death would guarantee the continued prosperity of their community, friends, and family. People today don't realize how important it was in ancient times for a community's crops to be successful. Life revolved around their hopes for a successful harvest because without it, many people, if not the entire village, would die from hunger.

Human sacrifices might have been thought to show greater devotion to the gods than the sacrifice of animals and could therefore elicit greater favors. Sometimes, when the gods were thought to be exceptionally angry, a person might have been sacrificed. The hope was that by sacrificing the best person in their community, the gods would be appeased and allow everyone else to live. At other times someone might be asking an aid from the gods in a dire situation, as in the biblical story where the king of Moab sacrificed his firstborn son so the Israelites would be driven from his kingdom.[2] Sacrifices might also be offered in thanks for help already provided. This is illustrated in the biblical story of Jephthah, who was required to sacrifice his virgin daughter, as a burnt offering to God, because he had asked for and received help defeating the Ammonites.[3]

How did these gruesome ceremonies get started? Well, no one actually knows because their beginnings are lost in the mists of humanity's preliterate ages. Perhaps people needed a big favor from their gods. Maybe the harvest and herds had been bad last year, so they sacrificed an animal or two to show their devotion. Lo and behold, their harvest was better this year. The two events were probably completely unrelated; however, as frequently happens with superstitions and beliefs, once the two separate events were locked together in people's minds, they became inseparable. The reasoning might have gone, "I sacrifice an animal, and then the gods are nice to me, so they must like us sacrificing stuff." Once people started performing sacrifices, they weren't going to mess with the system because no one wants to risk angering a god. If one year the sacrifices didn't work, people would blame themselves or find other reasons why the gods were angry; they wouldn't question the sacrifices because people believed they had worked in the past. Also, if the gods liked sacrifices for good harvests, maybe they would be more willing to help out with other things if the community offered them a few more sheep. Once people were in this mind-set, the applications could be endless.

Sacrifices of animals or people were considered appropriate and necessary in those days and in those cultures. In this time and in this culture, the sacrifice of people, animals, or pets is neither considered necessary nor appropriate. The Wiccan Rede tells Wiccans to harm nothing, so sacrificing an animal would violate our only rule. In modern Wicca, the harming or killing of any living thing is considered vile and reprehensible. Ancient people often viewed the gods as jealous, angry, and vengeful; therefore, sacrifices were necessary to keep the gods on one's side. Wiccans don't believe sacrifices are necessary to keep the Divine on our side. Wicca views Deity as something that gives to people, freely pouring out Divine energy to all who want it and never expecting anything in return. Wicca may be based on the religions of ancient cultures, but it isn't an attempt to reproduce them exactly. Portions of ancient religious practices have no place in our modern world, and human or animal sacrifice is one of them.

Doesn't it bother Wiccans that so many people disagree with them?

Years ago, people believed Earth was the center of creation and the sun, moon, and planets all revolved around the Earth in fixed spheres. People felt a sort of curtain existed that separated Heaven from Earth and the stars were the light of Heaven shining through that curtain. Most people in the "civilized world" held this belief, and anyone who disagreed with this universal view was branded a troublemaker and a lunatic. Galileo was tried and convicted of heresy for teaching that the sun was the center of our solar system. If he hadn't recanted his views, he would have been executed for teaching ideas contrary to the natural law. Did the idea that Earth was the center of the universe harm anyone? No. Was it correct? In some ways, yes, it was correct. It acknowledged planets and that the planets orbited something, but it was incomplete.

The reality of the universe was more than people at that time could have imagined. It was more than Galileo imagined it, and I am sure the reality of the universe is even more than we currently imagine it to be. There have been many ideas throughout history with which most people disagreed. If everyone had waited for consensus, people would have never sailed around the world, flown in airplanes, or traveled to the moon. The popular opinion isn't always correct, and the correct opinion isn't always popular. People have asked me before if ten million people can be wrong? I always answer, "Yes, frequently."

As a Wiccan, my viewpoints are my own, and it doesn't matter to me whether anyone else agrees with me or not. To Wiccans, religious beliefs are based on a personal experience of Deity, and since no two people will ever experience anything, especially Deity, in quite the same way, I would expect each of us to have a different view of the Divine. Each of us, regardless of religion, views Deity in a way appropriate to us.

Like Galileo peering through his telescope and discovering the universe was more than he had previously imagined it to be, there was a point in many of our lives where we peered into our souls and understood that Deity was so much more than we had ever previously conceived It to be. It's like being inside a box labeled Deity and suddenly finding a lid where one thought there was only space. Pushing that lid open, we find ourselves staring out enraptured at Deity in ever-greater clarity and majesty. Once people have experienced this revelation about Deity, there is no way for them to return to their previous box, which now seems cramped and confining. The danger is in feeling superior to others because, just as Galileo broadened his understanding of the universe but didn't come close to understanding it completely, our new viewpoint of Deity is expanded but woefully incomplete. The box we have crawled out of is itself contained in a bigger box, and only through exploring our soul and examining the limits we place on Deity can we hope to find the edges of this larger box. Like an infinite set of Russian nesting dolls, each one we escape gives us a greater perspective of the Divine but leaves us trapped in a larger container.

None of the various perspectives from which Deity can be viewed are wrong, just as none are completely right. Each simply provides a differing viewpoint of the Divine, and each of us, no matter which religion we practice, experiences Divinity in the way most appropriate to us at this point in our lifetime. No matter how big or complete we think our concept of Deity is, there are other concepts even bigger and more complete, which we aren't yet ready to understand.

Everyone has their own beliefs and limitations for Deity, and everyone is entitled to those. No one should be forced to make one's views of Deity conform to mine and vice versa. We each understand Deity in our own way and as something that is appropriate to where we are in life. It should never matter how many people do or don't agree with a person. Everyone should experience Deity to their fullest extent and find joy in Deity in whatever way It is revealed to them.

A Deeper Understanding about Wiccan Life

Aside from Sabbats and Moons, what other rituals do Wiccans observe?

While Moons and Sabbats are performed monthly or seasonally, other Wiccan rituals are meant to celebrate the seasons of a person's life. Every religious tradition has rites of passage that celebrate the growth and change in a person's life. These rituals honor events so profound that they mark the death of one way of life and birth into another. Rituals of this type are performed to welcome a person into a new way of living, ritually opening a new door leading to a pathway untrodden by their feet and symbolically closing another door behind, sealing off a portion of their life to which they will never be able to return. The birth of a child, death of a loved one, and other significant events change a person's life forever, causing them to be mentally and sometimes physically altered from that point forward. To honor these moments of change and to help ease the transformation from one way of living to another, these events are celebrated with rituals.

Wiccaning

The first ritual of a young Wiccan's life will probably be their Wiccaning. This ritual serves two purposes: it is a ritual of welcoming and blessing a new child, and it marks the change for the mother and father from being a couple to the responsibilities of parenthood. Wiccaning welcomes the child to the world by honoring the spirit that has chosen to be born to these parents. It is a ritual of blessing the child and presenting it to the Goddess, the God, and the friends and family of the parents. People often bring the child some token representing a blessing on the life of the child. A coin for prosperity, an owl figure for wisdom, or a rose quartz pendant for love are possible tokens presented to the child. These treasures are gathered into a special place and put aside for when the child comes of age.

The second purpose of the Wiccaning ritual is to mark the change in the lives of the parents. If this is their first child, the parents may be used to spontaneously going to movies or out to dinner, sleeping all night, and running to the grocery store without twenty pounds of baby essentials in tow; those days are gone. From now on they have another life who depends on them and will be in the house needing to be cared for and fed for at least the next eighteen years. In the Wiccaning ceremony, the parents and community members pledge to guard and nurture the child and raise it in a loving environment. The parents swear to teach the child to think for themself and values consistent with Wiccan ideals so that when the child is old enough, they will be able to find the path that is right for them.

Coming of Age

When children get to a certain age, they reach an awkward stage where they are no longer children, but neither are they adults. They want parents to tuck them into bed at night but not to be seen with them at the mall. They want the privileges of adulthood but none of the responsibilities. This time of too many hormones and too few clues is puberty. The coming of age ritual celebrates the changes in their lives, saying to them, "We no longer view you as a child, so you will now have some of the privileges and responsibilities of adults."

Coming of age rituals are usually performed with family and friends who are the same gender as the child. They are told what it means to be a woman or a man and what will be expected of them in their life. Everyone shares stories from their own growing experience and offers their support as the young woman or man continues to mature. The timing for this ritual will vary. With girls it is usually at the time of her first menstruation and is frequently referred to as a first blood ritual. With boys the timing isn't as obvious, but the ritual is usually performed sometime between the ages of thirteen and fifteen, about the time the boy's voice begins to change.

Handfasting

The Wiccan wedding ceremony is referred to as a handfasting. Like all weddings, it is a celebration of joining two lives together. For the couple, it marks the end of the time when they are concerned only for themselves and the beginning of a time when their actions and decisions also affect another. For their parents, the handfasting marks the point when they must turn over the primary responsibility for the care of their daughter or son to another person. The celebration of a handfasting is a time of beginnings and endings and is, therefore, celebrated with laughter and tears.

The content of a handfasting can vary greatly depending on the couple's wishes. I have performed handfastings where no one in the audience realized it was a Wiccan wedding, and I have performed handfastings that were very obviously Wiccan. Such ceremonies may include unity candles, music, and dance. They may be performed with the audience seated or gathered around the couple in a circle. The couple might jump a broom or ride out on horses. The only thing that is almost always a part of handfastings is a handfasting cord. The handfasting cord is a long piece of ribbon or braided cloth that is wrapped around the joined hands of the couple and tied in a knot. The binding of the couple's hands is a symbol of the binding of their lives and is kept by the couple to be displayed in their home as a symbol of their marriage.

Handparting

As much as everyone would like them to stay together for life, and despite the best intentions of the joyous couple at the time of their nuptials, many marriages end in divorce. While Wiccan clergy usually urge counseling or other amiable possibilities to heal a wounded relationship, we typically also recognize that a couple whose wounded relationship has grown gangrenous and begins to hemorrhage anger and bitter resentment may be better off ending that relationship before any further damage is done.

Most religions permit divorce, although it is often accompanied by shame, guilt, and a sense of failure. In these cases, divorces are usually carried out quietly with the announcement of the event being made through an unofficial grapevine where stories grow more colorful as they are passed from person to person. While the legal divorce severs the civil bond that joined the couple, it does nothing about the emotional and spiritual bonds that formed when they fell in love and became ritually solidified by the wedding. The civil divorce addresses the division of property but not the broken promises, feelings of failure, and shattered dreams the couple once shared.

In Wicca there is a ceremony for beginning the marriage and another to officially mark the severing of the relationship and return to single life. The handparting is a bit like a handfasting in reverse and can be simple and plain or extremely elaborate. Both the husband and wife may be present, or the handparting might be performed for only one of them if a lack of civility between the couple will not allow both to be in attendance. There may be music and guests, though not usually as many as attended the wedding. Rings are returned to their original owners, and the handfasting cord is cut in half and, on occasion, burned. This ceremony severs the energetic bonds and helps the couple adjust to again being single.

In some areas a tradition has arisen in which the friends of the newly divorced person take them out for what is called a rebachelor/ rebachelorette party. Like its counterpart on the happier end of the marriage, this emerging tradition has no religious connotations but copious psychological significance.

Croning Ritual

This ritual, although not universally performed, is a rite of passage growing in popularity with many groups. The croning ritual celebrates the changes a woman goes through during menopause. It is said that in ancient times the flowing of a woman's blood was a sign of power. In many cultures it was, and sometimes still is, taboo to touch a woman during her cycle, because it was believed her power would overwhelm the person touching her. When the monthly cycle stopped, the woman was viewed as keeping her blood and, therefore, her power within. This was a sign of wisdom, and she was now viewed as representing the Goddess in her aspect of crone. The purpose of the ritual is to mark the physical changes in a woman's life and aid in the psychological readjustments of menopause. The ritual is meant to help a woman find her power in this phase of life and remove the stigma that some in society have associated with this stage of womanhood. There is no real male counterpart to this ritual. I have heard of some groups doing retirement rituals for men, which would be similar in psychological significance and very valid but not quite the same.

Final Passage

The only thing sure in life is that eventually it will end. Humans are said to be the only animal that knows it will die. I don't believe this because animals will defend their lives and mourn the death of one close to it. If an animal will defend a life, it would seem to understand death. It can be argued, though, that humanity makes the biggest production out of someone's passing.

The Wiccan funeral service is intended to celebrate the life of the person who passed and to comfort the friends and family who remain, mourning their loss. We remind everyone that the body is only a vessel that transports the soul, which, being a part of the Divine, is immortal. As such, even if we shed the body, the essence of that loved one never perishes. Even though we can no longer physically touch those who have passed, they will be with us, their soul being as close as a thought. Death only separates bodies; it can't separate spirits. Those we love will be with us always, in one form or another.

Initiation

When a person enters a Wiccan coven for clergy training, there is some form of initiation ritual. The purpose of the ritual is to mark the beginning of the student's study of the specific mysteries of that Wiccan tradition. Most covens are more than a church; they are much like a family. While never intended to replace the member's actual family, members care for and help each other in times of crisis and celebrate each other's accomplishments.

The elements of initiation rituals vary widely and will be different from tradition to tradition. Many things might happen during an initiation, but there are also things that should not happen. The Seeker's Bill of Rights (Appendix A) lists the rights someone has when seeking to study with a group. If a coven violates any of these rights, the student should seriously consider finding a different group.

Healing

Magick can be used for many purposes, and one of its more common uses is for healing. To aid in the healing of minor injuries and routine ailments, Wiccans often perform individual healing spells, lighting candles or otherwise sending healing energy to someone who is a bit under the weather. However, if a person is seriously sick or injured and asks for help, covens may get together to perform a healing ritual. Using the ritual format for healing raises and directs the energy of the entire coven, which is more healing energy than could have been raised individually. Music, chanting, meditation, or other means may be employed to generate healing energy that will be focused on the ailing person. If it is the will of the Divine for the person to recover, a healing ritual combined with solo efforts by concerned individuals can often speed recovery to miraculous levels.

Wiccans perform rituals for many reasons, but these are a few of their more common uses. However, different Wiccan traditions may have other rituals specific to their tradition. Like the rituals of every religion, Wiccan rituals are intended to mark life's turning points, to inspire, and to bring us closer to the Divine.

Does Wicca have a sacred text?

People often want to know if Wicca has a sacred text, some holy scripture on which we base our faith. The answer to this question is yes; Wicca does have a sacred text which is ancient but always new and fresh. Wicca's sacred text has been studied by more people than any other work in history. This text is almost universally viewed as being not Divinely inspired but actually written by the hand of the Divine. It is frequently referred to but never quoted. Every person reads it in their own language, but it has never been translated. To the casual reader, it is honored for its beautiful poetry, which has inspired people throughout the ages. However, those who meditate and delve into its depths may find there the answers to the mysteries of life that perplex and confound humanity. This Divinely written sacred text, which has been an inspiration to all other sacred texts and has guided the human soul since the dawn of time, is—nature.

Now at this point, I can hear people protesting that nature is not a text, it's only images. People are saying a text requires words, pages, and colorful artwork on the cover; texts are bought in stores and placed artistically on shelves in the home. How can something that we walk around in, try to change, and build cities to get away from be a sacred text? When we were young, the first books we read were picture books that used images to tell us stories and teach us lessons. We were given picture books because, as children, we lacked the ability to comprehend on an adult level. Our minds couldn't understand the complexity of written language, and more complex works would have been of no use, only frustrating and confusing us. Wicca believes Divinity gave us our sacred text—nature—in images to help reveal life's secrets, explain the mysteries of Deity, and give us clues as to how we should live since we lack the ability to comprehend on a Divine level.

What are words but simply symbols people have created to represent nature. If someone says the word *apple,* do you picture a fruit or see the word? People think in pictures, and words were created to convey those images in a portable fashion, allowing us to use them to relate our inspirations to others. However, words are static and cold. No matter how lovely the language or how poetically the words are crafted, they are only feeble attempts to convey the wonder of the original inspiration. No words will ever adequately capture spring, a rose, or love. Only by experiencing each of these the way the Divine originally intended do we understand their majesty.

With words one experiences problems with definition because two people might be using the same word and yet have very different meanings assigned to the word. This can lead to misunderstandings and difficulties, especially when translating or trying to relate religious or philosophical concepts. The definitions of nature are concrete; if one points to a tree or river, everyone defines the term in the same way because they are looking at the same object. However, how one interprets the meaning of nature and how its lessons are applied can be varied and wonderful, allowing all people the freedom to apply the lessons of nature to their own time period or part of the world. Some of the greatest religious teachers have been poets who were inspired by nature and then interpreted and conveyed the lessons of nature in beautiful ways, attempting to communicate those lessons in a way that captures a bit of the wonder they perceived in the source. The lessons of nature are both ancient and modern and apply to people living in the Tropics as well as in the Arctic Circle.

The leaves of a book are where the prose of the text are recorded. Jots and titles, the musings of the mind, are inscribed on sheets, preserving them for future generations to read and interpret. The pages organize the paragraphs and chapters in an order so the flow of the words will not be lost or their order scrambled. The poetry of nature is also organized with every day being a new page; sunrise and sunset are emblazoned with inspirations for that day. Nature's daily pages are organized into seasonal chapters, each with its own mysteries to discover. Nature's metaphors are jewels lying there waiting for those people to recognize their value and claim the treasure for their own. Wiccans believe these metaphors were given to us by the Divine to teach us about life, birth, death, and our purpose for being here.

Wicca is an experiential religion; that is, we believe Deity is revealed through the experiences of life. Deity talks directly to everyone every day; we choose if we want to listen. Deity speaks in the blowing of the wind and the howl of the wolf, through the smell of the flowers and the songs of the birds. The rivers teach us patience as they slowly carve canyons through stone, and from the waves on the shore, we learn persistence. The soaring eagle gives us perspective, while day and night remind us that things change and that no matter how black life seems, there will always be another sunrise. Wiccans believe we have the choice of heeding the voice of Deity or blocking it out, covering our senses and looking for the Divine in buildings or books.

From a Wiccan perspective, Divinity gave us nature as our spiritual text, and it serves us well. However, after a time people developed the written word, preserving our own thoughts for others to read. The vanity of humanity made us believe we were superior to the natural world around us and convinced us the thoughts we had recorded on paper were more important than the original manuscript written by the Divine. This isn't to say there's no validity or value in religious documents. People are free to find religious inspiration where they will, and written religious texts serve many people well. For Wiccans, though, the first text will always be the Divine lessons and metaphors of nature.

How can prayer be like magick?

Ohm Mani Padme Hum, "the jewel is in the lotus," is a prayer to the Buddhist Bodhisattva of compassion, Avalokiteshvara. *Hare Krishna, Hare Krishna, Krishna Krishna, Hare Hare / Hare Rama, Hare Rama, Rama Rama, Hare Hare* is a prayer to the Hindu God Krishna, and "Our Father who art in Heaven, hallowed be Thy name" begins a prayer to the Christian God. Across the world prayers go out to a multitude of deities offered by supplicants who seek a connection to their gods. Troubled souls cry out for healing of mind and body, assistance with life's trials, or comfort when the process of living becomes more than they feel they are able to bear. Every prayer offered, regardless of which faith group asks, is offered by someone expecting a response, some answer to their entreaty or comfort from the Divine, and amazingly, all of them receive one.

In each instance, throughout every culture in the world, prayers poured forth to numerous deities are answered. From Bombay to Sydney, people are healed, receive assistance, and are comforted no matter how they view Divinity. Prayer is a force that seemingly knows no religious boundaries, is unaffected by denomination or creed, and freely flows from the Divine to all who ask.

The only prerequisite is faith, a belief that requests made will be freely answered. Prayer takes on many forms, from loud verbal requests to silent contemplative meditation; for healing, boons, wisdom, and understanding, people pray. The form may vary, but the concept is the same: people communicating with Deity through prayer.

Prayer works; research conducted on the effects of prayer show it functions in the way it is directed by the person offering the prayer. For good or bad, to heal or harm, like rubbing a genie's lamp, prayer flows out to fulfill the request of the supplicant. In his book *Healing Words: The Power of Prayer and the Practice of Medicine,* Larry Dossey, MD, documents research on prayer.[1] Research shows prayer heals people, prayer heals animals, prayer heals bacteria, prayer harms bacteria, prayer can alter genetic mutations of bacteria, and even water appears to become more beneficial when prayed over. Prayer works when the prayer is offered in person and when the prayer is offered from a great distance. No one has shown *why* prayer works, but there is a great deal of evidence to support the claim that it *does* work. There would also seem to be no Divine monopoly on prayer. Hindus, Wiccans, Buddhists, Christians, and others all pray to different concepts of Deity, and yet all of them receive answers to their entreaties. Since each of these different faith groups pray and all of them can offer anecdotal evidence to the miraculous effects their prayers have, prayer would seemingly not rely on the intervention of a particular divine entity, at least not Deity as perceived by any one religion.

Wicca has prayer, and Wicca also has spells; it is my view that prayer and magick are simply two different ways to tap into the same Divine energy. The main difference between prayer and spells seem to be one of perception. Prayers are seen as petitions to the Divine for assistance in achieving a desired effect, while spells are perceived as working with the Divine to reach a desired goal. To me, prayer and magick both tap into a universal Divine energy that surrounds us constantly. This Divine energy flows around and through us all our lives, and as creatures of the Divine, we are entitled to use this energy if we choose. Jung's concept of synchronicity is a use of this Divine energy. Synchronicity is often viewed as coincidence, chance happenings that are unrelated leading up to some event. However, nothing actually happens by chance—it only seems to. We think about our mother calling, and when the phone rings and it's her, we shrug it off as chance as we walk away whistling *The Twilight Zone* theme.

People pass magick off as chance because it's easier to believe in random occurrences than to believe our thoughts somehow affect the world around us. Thoughts are things. Divine energy is directed by our thoughts for good or ill, and whether it helps or harms is our choice. For example, if we sniffle and think, "Oh no, I'm getting sick," we will probably come down with the flu. If we think, "It's my allergies," we will continue to sniffle for quite some time. If we sniffle and think, "Must have been a bit of dust," the sniffles will end. In this way our thoughts can affect our bodies; however, thoughts can also affect the world around us. The only requirement is faith—the absolute belief that it will work—and therein lies the problem. How many people pray for a miracle and would faint dead away if it happened? People tend to pray for miracles with little faith their prayers will be answered, and it's very difficult to gather or focus energy with no belief that the prayer will work.

Witchcraft uses spells as a ritual means of directing the same Divine energy used in prayer. The various parts of a spell serve to aid a person in focusing their thoughts while gathering, shaping, and directing Divine energy. The chanting, colors, herbs, ritual attire, candles, tools, and crystals all serve to aid in the collection of the Divine prayer energy available to us all. Each component of the spell adds more energy to the spell, and a person wants to gather as much energy as possible, since the more energy gathered, the more effective the prayer or spell will be.

This is why a hundred people praying for a single cause is usually more powerful than the prayers of a single person—the prayer energy is cumulative. This is also why some people's prayers seem to be more powerful than others—they are more adept at gathering the energy and focusing it toward their goal, or their need may simply be greater. For example, a person who has complete faith their prayer will be answered is more powerful than a dozen people who pray absent-mindedly, and the prayers of a single mother for her dying child hold more power than the prayers of a hundred of her acquaintances.

With a spell the energy has to be gathered, the goal clearly seen, and the energy released, allowing it to flow outward to fulfill its purpose, and prayers are the same. When one prays or casts spells, one should see the ultimate outcome clearly. If a friend is in a bad car accident and you pray while picturing your friend alive but in a hospital covered with bandages, you are only sending that person enough prayer energy to keep them going. How much more effective might your prayers be if you prayed for their healing while picturing them fully recovered and enjoying an activity they love? When people pray, many of them don't pray for what they want—they pray for an intermediate step, not picturing what they truly want but rather for what they will settle. Then they may think their spells don't work or their prayers haven't been answered. In reality they are getting exactly what they prayed for. Without realizing it, we rob ourselves; by visualizing and praying more effectively, we can live closer to our full potential.

Prayer and magick should both be approached with the proper attitude, one of compassion, humility, and absolute faith that we can affect change in the world around us. Neither magick nor prayer are about seizing Divine power and forcing it to do our bidding; one does not force Divine energy to go anywhere the Divine doesn't want it to go or force it to do something outside of the Divine order. The power of magick is in yielding to the Divine, where the humble are given strength and the egotistical denied.

Those who seek Divinity with humility and reverence are given more than they can imagine, while those who grab in arrogance and pride are given little. Respect for all life and the humility that comes from recognizing that we are a part of all living things is essential to the practice of magick. Divine energy should be approached with the desire to help or heal, not with the desire to seize power as if we were above the world. We collect energy as a child gathers flowers, release it as a mother gives birth to new life, and direct it with the wisdom of a grandmother who knows that sometimes unpleasant situations must happen for people to learn and loved ones will still die eventually no matter how much we wish they wouldn't.

The order inherent in nature will always have the final word, and we learn from life's pains as well as its pleasures. The Divine has a reason for all actions. Some events we can't change, but we can sometimes postpone them or make them easier to bear. However, to understand what can or can't be changed requires wisdom, and that wisdom comes from always being open to the Divine. We must search for Divine guidance even when our lives are wonderful, not simply when we are troubled.

Sometimes people seem to wall the Divine part of themselves off into a corner of their being behind a little sign reading, "In case of emergency, break glass." People seem to have an unfortunate tendency to pray only when they are in trouble or feel they are in dire need. Occasionally they even pray for something while doing nothing to help facilitate their request. For example, if someone prays earnestly for a job, then sits back, watching television, waiting for the job fairy to knock on the door, can they honestly expect their prayer to be answered? How often do people's prayers fit into the previous scenario? Meister Eckhart said, "Some people want to see God with their eyes as they see a cow and to love him as they love their cow— they love their cow for the milk and cheese and profit it makes them."[2] I think a more current example is that people tend to view God like Chinese takeout: we call and place our order, then sit back and wait for our spiritual dim sum to show up. However, to be fair to Meister Eckhart, Germany didn't have phones in the fourteenth century, or Chinese takeout for that matter.

The typical energy flow in prayer is outward with people sending Deity their wish lists of wants and needs. People don't stop to consider that the Divine already knows what everyone needs, which is often very different from what we want. If we desire to be closer to

Deity, the flow of energy in prayer should be inward from Deity to us. We can pray for Deity to make itself more manifest in our lives by asking what It wants for our lives. If we were to treat the Divine less like fast food and more like a garden, we would pray more effectively. People don't go to a garden to make demands; people go to a garden to be part of nature, take in the beauty of their surroundings, and refresh their spirit. If, in prayer, we simply open ourselves up to the Divine by asking Deity what It wants for our lives, Deity will fill our lives with things we never knew we wanted or needed. If we let the Divine fill us with Its energy, allowing It to change us and bring to our lives what we need most, we would be energized with Divine energy and given the peacefulness that comes with a closeness to Deity.

In this way meditation is also a form of prayer. I was told once that prayer is talking to God and meditation is shutting up and listening. When we don't feel the need to pour forth our words to the Divine and instead simply open ourselves to the Divine, maintaining a calm, meditative, prayerful attitude throughout the day, we stay in constant contact with that fount of Divine energy. Literally we are praying without ceasing, letting this God-force fill us, directing our actions, and allowing us to direct sacred energy outward to help others when necessary. If we could only maintain this prayerful attitude, we would be walking in the light of the Divine, and our faith could literally move mountains.

Can children and teens be Wiccan?

I would like to answer this question with another question. Can a child be any religion? If one believes a child can be Muslim, Buddhist, Christian, or Baha'i, then a child may also be Wiccan.

I have always had trouble with young children being labeled a certain religion. Children are wonderful, free spirits who really have no personal religious views. They may be taken to religious services by their parents and may repeat back words and ideas they have been told, but they have no concept of religion. To a child everything exists in concrete reality; there is no abstract. Kids have no concept of why things happen: to them the sun sets because it's time to go to bed.

They think that Big Bird is real, and Deity is way too abstract a concept for four-year-old children to wrap their minds around. To a young child, the only image they have of God is their mother because that is who nurtures and protects them.

Later, as a child grows and matures, the family's religion helps shape the children's ethical development, their views of the world, and how they see their place in that world. At this stage the child typically practices the religion of their parents because they know no other. I know that until I was twelve I didn't even realize there were people who practiced religions other than the one in which I was raised.

It's not until their teen years that children truly begin to understand the abstract concepts of Deity and religion. This is a time when a child may begin to seriously ask religious questions as they attempt to rationalize the concrete images in their head with the abstract concepts being presented to them. They want to know and understand what Deity is, why they are here, and what is beyond the world they can physically touch. The teen years are a time of exploration where this former child wants to rise and take their first unsteady steps using adult feet. Frequently teens will retain the religious traditions of their childhood while seeking to delve ever deeper into that religion's mysteries. Sometimes, though, they begin to seek out other religious traditions to find differing points of view, alternative ways of seeing the world that might supplement or even replace their existing religious structure. In Wicca children, teens, and adults all have their own reasons for being Wiccan.

Wiccan children are Wiccan for exactly the same reason any child follows a religion: because their parents follow it. As children they are taught Pagan ethics, such as respect for the Earth, respect for others, respect for themselves, and the equality of all people. Parents may walk with them in nature, teaching them about flowers, trees, and animals while showing them the world is something to cherish, not consume. As a family, children are taught to live with the seasons and celebrate the Sabbats, making the holidays full of fun and joy. Children are taught the myths of the Goddess and God as metaphors for living. They may also be taught short Goddess mantras for when they are scared, lonely, or worried. These are the concepts at the heart of

Paganism; there will be time when they are older to teach them the more involved aspects of Wicca. Parents should live as an example to their children and include them in their religious practices, when possible. This teaches children what it is to be Pagan and live with the Goddess and the God. Most Wiccans wouldn't teach their children that Wicca is the only valid religion because Wiccans respect all religious paths and, in time, want their children to make their own religious choices. Wiccans often want their children to grow up understanding all religious beliefs, and it is not uncommon for Wiccan parents to tell their children the religious teachings and stories from a variety of traditions.

The only children who are usually Wiccan are those who have Wiccan parents because there would be few other opportunities for a child to learn about Wicca. Wiccans don't even proselytize adults, and we would view any group attempting to convert children as highly unethical. Most Wiccans agree that the religious foundations of a child's life are best laid down by their parents. Wiccans will not allow a child into any religious class, even one intended for Wiccan children, without the consent and preferably the presence of their parents.

When children reach their teen years, they begin to get a better understanding of religion and might choose to seek out Wicca for several reasons, although the two that seem to be most common are as an act of rebellion and to seek answers to their own spiritual questions. There are teens who adopt Wicca for its shock value. Some teens want to rebel against their parents and society, and popular vehicles for this rebellion are clothes, music, friends, and religion. It's usually obvious when teens become involved in Wicca simply for the shock value of saying they're Witches. Getting most of their information from movies, these teens usually know little about actual Wiccan teachings. They seek to draw attention to themselves by wearing all black and pentagrams so large they can neither be overlooked nor mistaken. They may also threaten to put a curse on anyone who offends them, speaking loudly enough to be overheard at a Metallica concert. Wiccans typically try to gently encourage these teens to learn what Wicca is all about or to use something other than representing themselves as Wiccan to upset their parents and make themselves seem "weird" to their classmates. Wiccans have enough problems with undeserved propaganda without teens who are clueless as to Wicca's true nature perpetuating movie stereotypes in some misguided attempt to get attention.

In contrast to teens who become Wiccan for the shock value are those who are truly searching for their own special path and believe they have found it in Wicca. These teens are typically less religiously demonstrative, preferring to avoid confrontations and don't parade their spirituality down the halls of their schools. They will hungrily devour any source of information that will help them find out more about Wicca, scanning the Internet, reading books, and trying to attend public rituals. Most Wiccan covens teach people how to be clergy and will not allow anyone under eighteen to join, so finding qualified teachers is frequently difficult for teens. However, because many Wiccans have children, many groups and covens also conduct family rituals so children can honor Deity with their family and friends. When looking for a teacher, people of any age should read the Seeker's Bill of Rights (Appendix A) to help them understand what a Wiccan priestess and priest should and should not require of them.

Some Wiccan communities, recognizing the difficulty teens have in finding community support and legitimate sources of information, have organized Pagan groups for teens. International groups like Spiral Scouts (www.spiralscouts.org) have formed for Pagan children and teens, as well as kids from other minority religions, to learn about nature, mythology, and life skills. These groups afford Pagan teens the opportunity to socialize with other like-minded teens while learning Pagan principles at an appropriate level and in a safe environment. Pagan youth groups are usually nonproselytizing in nature, welcoming everyone without attempting to change their religious beliefs.

How much free will do we have in life?

"All the world's a stage, / And all the men and women merely players; / They have their entrances, And one man in his time plays many parts."[3] How much choice we actually have in the parts we play throughout life is a subject that has been often debated but rarely answered satisfactorily.

Some people say our lives are completely our own and all events are random, occurring by chance based on millions of previous choices made by oneself and others. Any little change in the way the events of one's life happened could lead to a person ending up with a different job, different spouse, or being hit by a truck; the possibilities are endless.

Each choice is a passage that leads to other passages. Once we have made a choice, all possible futures that could have been reached by differing decisions are now sealed, closed to us forever. This argument makes us masters of our fate and captains of our soul.[4] We are responsible for our existence, and there is no unseen force mucking about with our lives. Nothing in our life is set in stone, and if we don't like the way things are, we have the freedom to take steps to alter our situation as we see fit.

However, from this perspective, a person could be considered either incredibly lucky or woefully unlucky to be where they are now. This view of life's events can cause problems because many people agonize over their choices, trying to guess what is around the corner in each possible tunnel. This can make even the smallest decision in life excruciatingly difficult.

Also, if a person is unhappy with their current life, they might begin to analyze past decisions, looking for the point at which they made a misstep. People can get caught in the trap of thinking, "If only I had gone to that party, I wouldn't be so alone now" or "If only I had gone to a different college, taken a different job, not broken up with Sally"; the regrets can mount up until one begins to see life as a collection of might-have-beens and missed opportunities. If this continues, the should-have-beens pile up so high that a person begins to drown in them. Depression at the thought of so many missed opportunities can eventually keep a person from functioning, and they quit living the life they have, fretting about the should-have-beens.

The opposite extreme in this debate espouses a hypothesis where every tiny detail in a person's life is planned out and preordained. Every event in people's lives, from the time they stretch in the morning to the time they lay down on their pillow and all things in between, are preordained. Come to think of it, their dreams are also already determined, so sleep time is covered as well. If one steps in gum, meets the girl of their dreams, or falls off a ladder and breaks an arm, there is some higher plan behind it.

Now, seeing the world in this way takes all the pressure off people because they know no matter what decision they make, it will be the one they were supposed to make. If our life is falling apart, it's not really our fault because we are just the tragic heroes in a divine soap opera where everything happens as it should and we bear no personal responsibility for our actions.

However, the downside to believing everything is preordained is that it means we have no personal choice. With our life completely scripted, we are no more than characters in a play or movie, with some of us in supporting roles while others are destined to be comic relief. With no one having any decision power in their life, why even bother getting out of bed in the morning, except if you *don't* get out of bed, it was preordained that you *wouldn't* get out of bed. This line of thinking can drive one nuts, except a person can't even go crazy without it being in the script, so we had better jump this train of thought before it crashes.

Both viewpoints leave much to be desired. Both are possibilities, however, I choose to see a middle path between unbridled chaos and draconian order. This is the possibility that some events are put in place to set others in motion or to give us an opportunity, while others are simply random occurrences. If we view that, as souls, we're attempting to learn something by being on the Earth, then certain events will present themselves, which give us the opportunity to learn these lessons. Events of the learning sort will be arranged for us; however, how we react to the event will be our choice. For example, if in this lifetime a person is supposed to be learning patience, events will spring up that will cause waits, delays, and general holdups, thereby providing that person with valuable opportunities to learn patience. The slowest-moving line at the grocery store, the inept salesperson, and rubbernecker traffic jams are all teachers instructing us in the fine art of patience. If we say to those teachers, "Thank you for this lesson;

I will use this extra time to enjoy this wonderful day," or some other nice, calm response, the Universe may smile, check that lesson off, and life will no longer seem so full of hang-ups. However, if every time a person is offered this opportunity for growth, they begin to swear like a sailor on shore leave, blow the horn, and give everyone a one-fingered salute, the Universe will say, "Not there yet. Better try that lesson again later. I know, let's throw in a broken elevator with a screaming baby." The lessons will keep coming until they get it, which may take more than one lifetime. This is not to say that after one learns the lesson there will be no more holdups in their life. I think the Universe sometimes gives us pop quizzes, or maybe we get to help out with someone else's lesson, so try to set a good example or you might end up as a horrible warning.

I feel some occurrences are just serendipity and arranged in such a way that a person is in the right place at the right time to be given the opportunity to find the ideal mate, the perfect job, or have their life changed by some unforeseen chance. However, the decision is always ours and we may choose to seize these opportunities or let them pass. Who knows, one of my lessons this lifetime could be learning to deal with sudden wealth, and I am supposed to win the lottery. However, if every time I think about the lottery I decide not to buy a ticket, I will never win. Of course, if I do buy tickets, it's also possible I will never win anything because my lesson is to learn to calculate odds and quit throwing away money on lottery tickets. Therein lies the burden of personal choice.

At this point, I can hear many of you asking, "Who sets all these situations up for us?" The significant events in our life may be orchestrated by the Universe, our higher selves, guardian angels, Deity, or perhaps fifth-dimensional beings—who knows? Maybe all of these and more, probably none of them, or at least not as we want to perceive them. My personal favorite is our higher self, but anyone who thinks they have a better answer is free to jump in with their opinion at this point.

It doesn't matter what one calls the guiding force or even if one believes there *is* a guiding force. In the end, what matters is that we live our lives to their fullest, making the best decisions and choices possible. Think of it like parenting. People do the best they can and hope they don't screw the kids up so much that therapy can't fix them.

From our perspective, we can't see where each decision will take us. The path is always a bit foggy in the distance, but if we act as if every decision matters and every adversity is an opportunity for personal growth, life will remain positive and full of possibilities. We can either choose to live life fully, not knowing for sure whether or not our choices ultimately matter, or we can hide in the corner watching life pass us by. The choice is ours to make. If all the world is a stage, choose your character and go for an Academy Award.

Why do Wiccans use altars?

The first rays of a new sun break over the horizon on Winter Solstice morning, illuminating a woman sitting beside a table, draped in white and adorned with holly and mistletoe, which is positioned before her eastern window. The light strikes a wand of crystal in her hand, shattering the beam into hundreds of tiny rainbows. These prismatic fairy lights play tag around a pinecone, a silver bowl of water, and an ornate brass bell, each carefully arranged around a bright orange pillar candle burning in the center of the table. The lights chase across the room touching other items. They play across a group of family photographs—some recent, others featuring people wearing the clothing and expressions of bygone eras—arranged on the piano; the lights flit over a table in the corner, draped in blue, holding a green candle, a small doll, and a photograph of a man; they flutter across the mantel, where amid a sprinkling of rice stand a small bride and groom, flanked by candles and surrounded by a green-and-rose cord; they also dazzlingly caress a display where male and female statues stand before a small fountain surrounded by stones, feathers, bells, and a myriad of other small items. Each of these places shimmering in the prismatic splendor is part of the woman's home, has special significance to her, and is an altar.

Most people seem to think of altars as something that exists only in churches or temples, places that hold sacred relics or are used to show devotion to a Deity. However, altars are so much more than shrines relegated to religious buildings; they are personal sacred spaces people use to give focus and a sense of the Divine to their everyday life. The desire to construct altars seems to be part of the human make up. Evidence of their existence has been found dating back possibly seventy-five thousand years, and we don't seem to have stopped yet.[5] Even those people who don't consciously strive to construct altars often group pictures or arrange knickknacks in a way that is significant to them and is reminiscent of an altar.

Wiccans use altars for many different purposes. Altars can be constructed to honor the Divine, bring healing, assist in worship, honor ancestors, celebrate rites of passage, protect the home, assist in transforming one's life, or dozens of other reasons. The possibilities are limited only by one's imagination. Each of the altars described earlier is a different sort of altar that one might find around a home. As we explore these altars, see how they help the individual focus on some aspect of their life. Also, notice how many of these altars are similar to displays found in the homes of friends or family members, even if they may not think of them as altars.

The table before which the woman sits as she welcomes the rising sun on Solstice morning is a ritual altar. Ritual altars are usually temporary altars used to help facilitate a particular ritual. These altars are often decorated with flowers, holly, pumpkins, fresh vegetables, or whatever might be appropriate for that ritual. This altar might also hold the chalice and bread for the feast, any tools used during the ritual, and often candles or statues representing the Goddess and God. The ritual altar serves a practical purpose, holding all the items one will need during the ritual as well as becoming the focus of the ritual, giving everyone a point on which to fix their attention.

The pictures on the piano form an ancestor or family altar. Many households have some form of a family altar, which could be as simple as a few family photos grouped on a wall in the hallway to something as elaborate as those used to celebrate the Day of the Dead. Ancestral altars connect us to our past, reminding us that our life and the way we live is due to a long line of people who lived, loved, triumphed, and made mistakes, just as our actions will become part of our children's and grandchildren's legacy. In this way one can visibly see how a piece of the web of life binds us one to another, giving us a feeling of eternity and showing us how we live on in others.

The table draped in blue is an altar constructed for a magical purpose; this one is being used for healing. Magical altars are used to help bring about a transformation in life. They may be built as part of any ongoing magical working to aid in healing, prosperity, protection, job searches, weight loss, or any one of hundreds of reasons one might wish magical help in day-to-day life. The magical altar serves as a focal point for that spell where candles or incense may be burned and the spell may be renewed daily.

The bride and groom on the mantel form a part of a wedding altar. Our lives, like the seasons, change almost imperceptibly as one part of our lives fades into another, and sometimes we seem to lose special occasions in the tumult of our daily lives. Altars established for life-changing events, like a wedding, help people celebrate, remember, and mourn the important events in their lives. Such altars can help keep those events alive and fresh for the people who use them, or they can be a source of healing for those who are mourning a loss. For example, as years pass and problems arise, a wedding altar becomes a daily reminder for the couple of their love and the happiness on the day of their wedding for those times when the couple may begin to get on each other's nerves.

The altar probably created most often and designed with the greatest diversity is the personal altar. Personal altars are an expression of an individual's unique relationship with the Divine. It can be an intricately created space with statues and incense, a knickknack shelf, or a child's window ledge strewn with colored pebbles, feathers, and flowers. Any space that a person creates to calm their nerves, create an atmosphere of beauty, or help them feel the presence of the Divine could be construed as a personal altar.

Even when we don't consciously construct them, altars seem to spontaneously arise in our surroundings. They remind us of our past, give us inspiration to strive toward our future goal, or provide an oasis of calm and serenity in our busy lives. Altars seem to be a part of the human psyche, and consciously constructing them brings us more in touch with our lives, the world around us, and the Divine.

Why would Wiccans perform charity?

Once, during a discussion with an evangelist about Wiccan-sponsored charity projects, I was asked why Wiccans would perform charity. He seemed puzzled; "Christians are commanded to perform charity," he said, "but why would Wiccans?" His underlying thought seemed to be that without a rule requiring us to care about others, humanity's base nature would assert itself, driving us to utter selfishness. I had to ponder this question because my initial response would be "because I think people are basically good, and helping those in need is the right thing to do." However, this answer sounds like a parent answering, "Because I said so"; it answers the question but seems trite and unsatisfying.

From the Wiccan perspective, Deity is part of everything; this is easy to say but more difficult for some people to truly grasp. When someone really feels the Deity within them, they also see the Deity within everyone and everything else. Therefore, if one wishes to serve Deity, they should serve others who are in need and work to make the Earth a better place. If someone needs their tire changed, help them change it. If someone is stranded and needs a ride, take them home. If someone needs to talk, listen to them. In these ways we serve Deity. So much of the good we receive every day we have no direct way of repaying, so helping out others, even in little ways, helps "balance out" the karmic books and repays humanity, as a whole, for the kindness it has shown to us. People should help others because that's what they would like others to do for them if they were in need, or as Gandhi said, "Be the change you wish to see in the world."

To me, Wicca is a path of service: we are in service to Deity and, therefore, in service to the Earth, protecting the environment, plants and animals, and also other people. Being in service to all these things could mean working with large, high-profile aid projects like volunteering with the Peace Corps, working for a local homeless shelter, or organizing food and clothing drives. However, it's the little things, offering no recognition, that are more critical: picking up trash lying on the ground, pitching in to help set up or put away tables and chairs for an event, or serving water to everyone at a meeting. If a person feels they are too good to clean up a mess or serve others, then that person has missed the point about Deity being in all things.

Altruistic acts of service for those around us display not only a willingness to help others but also compassion. Compassion is a key point in spiritual growth, the balancing of one's own ego, seeing oneself as neither above or below everyone or everything else because one sees oneself as a part of the Earth rather than separated from it. Every person is a critical component of the planet, and lessening the burden of any individual is a service to the Earth and to Deity. If one is blinded by their own self-importance, that person will never find Deity in others, and it's through our service to others we serve Deity in whatever form we perceive It.

Isn't the pentagram a Satanic symbol?

When Anton LaVey founded Satanism on April 30, 1966, several different symbols were incorporated into its religious iconography.[6] Two of these symbols were the inverted cross and the inverted pentagram. The cross in its inverted form is sometimes called Saint Peter's Cross because Saint Peter was supposedly crucified upside down.[7] The form of the pentagram chosen as the symbol for the Church of Satan is also the inverted image of the symbol with the single point down and two points up. The image chosen was from an image of Baphomet allegedly drawn by Alphonse Louis Constant, known in occult circles as Eliphas Lévi. Constant is credited by some as the first person to separate the pentagram into good and evil uses. Constant used the inverted image of the pentagram drawn over the head of Baphomet, with points corresponding to his horns, ears, and beard, to represent evil.[8]

Wicca teaches that the top point of the upright pentagram represents the element spirit; this pentagram usually symbolizes the dominance of the spirit over the physical form. The inverted pentagram with the spirit point downward indicates that the spirit is subservient to the physical world and that people are subservient to their carnal desires. The inverted pentagram is not used by most Wiccans, although a few groups may use it for one level of students who are learning to face and master their inner darkness.

The reaction to these two symbols by the Church and the general population has been very different. The inverse image of the cross is seen as something abhorrent and repulsive, an evil symbol. However, the pentagram has not been given the same consideration. Rather than simply regard its inverted form as heinous, people began to view the entire symbol and all who use it as evil. So the pentagram, a symbol of light, has been viewed by the public with fear and suspicion while the cross retained its original meaning, even though the pentagram itself is no more Satanic than is the cross.

What rights do Wiccans have at school and work?

The Founding Fathers of the United States felt so strongly that all citizens should have the right to choose the way they worship that the first words added to the Constitution guaranteed our religious freedoms. The first ten amendments to the Constitution are collectively known as the Bill of Rights. The First Amendment to the Constitution begins, "Congress shall make no law respecting an establishment of religion, or prohibiting the free exercise thereof." The Founding Fathers knew religious conflicts could easily shatter the fledgling union. Many of the early American colonists fled to the New World because of religious persecution. As a result, the American colonies had the most diverse religious mixture in the world. The Founding Fathers feared that if the United States established an official religion, the followers of the unofficial religions would be subject to the same persecution many of the early settlers had fled to America to escape. By not recognizing any one religion, our founders sought to establish an environment of religious diversity where people could explore Divinity in whatever way they wished without fear of losing life or liberty. Unfortunately, not everyone shares the viewpoint of America's founders; there are groups who believe religious diversity will destroy their way of life.

I have heard people complain that public schools are trying to strip away students' rights to express their religion; this isn't true. The regulations concerning public schools are intended to allow individual religious expression while protecting the rights of students who are in the religious minority. The rules pertaining to religious expression in public schools are reasonably clear. The United States Department of Education has said students are free to pray, read religious literature, discuss religion, and wear religious jewelry or clothing to the same extent they can engage in comparable nonreligious activities.[9] Students are even allowed to "express their beliefs about religion in the form of homework, artwork, and other written and oral assignments free from discrimination based on the religious content of the submission."[10] This means that any student is free to privately pray whenever they wish, wear religious T-shirts, give reports about their religious beliefs, and even discuss religion with other students as long as they don't disrupt school activities or use it as a means to harass other students. The problem arises when schools say all religions are equal but behave as if some are more equal than others.

Wiccan students should have the same rights to read religious books, wear religious jewelry, and write about and discuss their religious beliefs as do any other students. However, many school districts ban the wearing of pentagrams, Wiccan books are frequently confiscated, and students are often not allowed to present class projects if they choose a Wiccan theme. Schools know this is discriminatory and illegal, but they typically take a "so sue us" attitude. Some students have fought the school district to regain their rights and usually win, but many students don't want the trouble and exposure involved in fighting the system. Wiccan students don't want special rights; all they want are the same religious rights other students enjoy.

Workplace policy should ideally be almost the same as the policy in public schools. Any form of religious expression that is allowed in the workplace should be allowed equally for all religions. If other workers are allowed to wear religious jewelry, Wiccans should be allowed to wear pentagrams or other religious images. If people are allowed to display religious quotes, signs, or books on their desks or in their offices, Wiccans should have the same privileges.

Everyone should have the right to feel safe in the workplace regardless of their religious beliefs. A Wiccan employee shouldn't have to endure incessant proselytizing or any other form of religious harassment. Religious harassment creates a hostile work environment where a person begins to dread going to work not because of their job but because someone is constantly trying to convert them or belittling their beliefs. A person should also never feel their job is in jeopardy because their religious views are different from their employer's. Religious bigotry happens frequently and is even condoned by many groups. However, a person shouldn't fear losing their means of supporting their family because someone else is a bigot.

Every religion teaches approximately the same ethics and values, and every religion has members who aspire to those ethical standards and those who ignore them completely. There is no religion that is inherently immoral or whose existence should inspire fear in others. All people, regardless of their differences in religion, race, or gender, want to be treated with fairness, equality, and respect. These rights are legally promised in the Constitution; however, nothing can assure that the hearts and minds of people will allow others to have the rights promised in the Constitution. Too many people are willing to violate the law and their own religious teachings by promoting bigotry and fear. Wiccans, and members of any religious group, have the right to equality, to respect, and to feel safe at school and work. When dealing with members of other religions, the best thing for people to do is treat them as what they are—people. People should give everyone the same courtesy and respect they would like to receive from others.

How does the military feel about Wicca?

When a person joins the military, they sign away certain rights and freedoms, but the freedom to practice the religion of their choice isn't one of them. The United States military is home to an estimated forty thousand Wiccans. These soldiers, like their civilian counterparts, want to be able to practice their religion free from fear and prejudice. While in the military, people retain the right to worship as they choose, and most military bases seem to be making every effort to accommodate Wiccan soldiers. The *Religious Requirements and Practices of Certain Selected Groups: A Handbook for Chaplains* has a section on Wicca that describes its ethics, summarizes beliefs, and explains to chaplains how to accommodate the worship of Wiccan soldiers, just as it does on most religions. Many bases allow large Wiccan rituals to be held, and soldiers may maintain small individual altars. Soldiers may also wear pentagrams and list Wicca as their religion of preference on their dog tags, although some list no religious preference for fear of discrimination. In general, as long as it doesn't violate other regulations or interfere with order and discipline, Wiccan soldiers may worship as they wish.

The right of soldiers to practice the religion of their choice has been established in court.

> In Katcoff v. Marsh (1985), the Second Circuit Court of Appeals concluded that the government's practice of hiring military chaplains did not violate the First Amendment's ban on religious establishments because of the need to support military personnel in the free exercise of their religion. The court indicated that the military's religious program should be "neutral," should limit competition among religious groups, and should leave the practice of religion solely to the individual soldier, "who is free to worship or not as he chooses, without fear of any discipline or stigma."[11]

In an effort to maintain this neutrality, "The Department of Defense does not evaluate, judge, or officially sanction any religious faith."[12] The military chaplaincy provides for the religious needs of the soldiers on their base whatever those religious needs are.

However, there are people who are more comfortable with certain religions than others. Wicca breeds a great number of highly colorful and usually horrific rumors that, although completely fictitious, some people are more than happy to believe. The Reverend Jack Harvey, pastor of the Tabernacle Baptist Church in Killeen, Texas, is quoted in the *Fort Worth Star-Telegram* as saying, "I've heard they drink blood, eat babies. They have fires, they probably cook them. This is unbelievably wrong."[13] If people are led to believe this is what Wicca is, how could they not be irate?

Speaking at a Pluralism Project symposium in 1999, Captain Russ Gunter of the Armed Forces Chaplains Board said that after an article discussing Wiccan worship at Fort Hood appeared in the paper, his phone rang for six weeks. "Captain Gunter recalled a typical phone call, this one from a Roman Catholic woman who asked, 'are you telling me the Department of Defense recognizes Wicca?' I responded to her, 'It may come as a shock to you, madam, that the Department of Defense does not recognize the Roman Catholic Church.'"[14] The military does not pick and choose which religions are acceptable for their soldiers. Religion is a personal decision, and if soldiers are in combat, they are going to pray to Deity in whatever form they perceive it. The job of the military chaplain is to help provide whatever religious support that soldier needs, not judge their choice of worship. After all, the purpose of the military is to defend the Constitution and the rights of Americans, and the first right guaranteed by the Constitution is the right to freedom of religion.

Why do Wiccans sometimes use different names?

A popular story that has become part of Wiccan folklore tells how hundreds of years ago Witches covered their faces and used assumed names when they attended rituals to protect their identities from witch-hunters. While this is an interesting story, it cannot be authenticated. Maybe hundreds of years ago people concealed their identities this way, but it's probably no more than a folktale.

Today, Wiccans are often known in the Wiccan community by "magical names." I have a magical name, but I only use it for e-mail. Other people use their magical names so frequently that people they encounter don't realize it's not their legal name. The use of magical names is completely optional in most groups, but there are several reasons why someone might choose to be known by a different name.

Some people say they are using a new name as a way of paying respect to Witches who suffered to practice their religion, but this reason is uncommon. More commonly, Wiccans choose a new name to help conceal their identities from the outside world. Whether there were actual Witches or Wiccans persecuted hundreds of years ago is not historically proven, but there is no doubt many Wiccans are discriminated against today. In an effort to protect their jobs and families, some Wiccans use only their magical names at Pagan events. This prevents someone from accidentally using their real names somewhere else and thereby accidentally "outing" them. This practice is also a great help when a person bumps into someone they know but can't quite recall where they know the other person from; the name this person uses can place them and help prevent an embarrassing faux pas. The third reason people give for taking a magical name is simply because they like the name. We had no hand in choosing our legal name, as our parents assigned it to us at birth. By the time we get old enough to legally change our names, we've been using it for fifteen or sixteen years and, for better or worse, feel attached to it. When a person becomes Wiccan, sometimes they wish to take a spiritual name of their own choosing. They want a magical name to connect them to their spirituality, and they choose a particular name because they feel it symbolically connects them to their inner nature.

Magical names may be chosen from many different sources. From a Wiccan viewpoint, everything has its own unique energy, and people usually choose a certain name because they feel some connection to its energy. The name epitomizes a quality to which they aspire, or the name is intended to represent a characteristic they wish to develop more fully. Wiccans may choose names that relate to nature, such as Summer, Sky, or Rain. Other Wiccans may feel more of a connection to the energy of a tree and may choose names like Thorn, Rowan, or Ash. Flower names like Rose, Iris, or Jasmine or plant names like Thistle, Rosemary, or Yarrow might be more to the liking of others. Animals are the inspiration for some who may choose Raven, Coyote, or Otter, while others will choose the names of stones or gems, such as Amber, Jasper, or Ruby. Wiccans who want a more exotic name may look to a magical creature like Griffin, Dragon, or Phoenix. Some groups also allow their members to choose the names of deities to which they wish to connect while other groups believe using deity names is egotistical and presumptuous.

The magical name becomes a sort of Wiccan nickname a person can use when or if they feel it appropriate. Some people keep the same name for years. Others may choose a new name when they feel their life has changed and their energies are moving in another direction. Whatever the source, people who choose a magical name select one special to them. It may represent their connection to Deity, purpose for being in the world, or qualities they wish to embody. If you're curious about what a person's magical name means to them, ask. Most Wiccans are willing to share what their chosen name means to them.

What do Wiccans believe about dreams?

On average we spend about one-third of our lives asleep, which means that by age sixty (assuming we live that long) we have spent approximately 175,320 hours, which is 7,305 days or 20 years, of our lives asleep. A question most people have is whether this dream time is random entertainment of an otherwise bored and stressed mind or if there is more to it than that. This question becomes more difficult because many assume just one choice is correct when in actuality the possibilities are several.

Dreams may have many purposes. Shakespeare said, "We are such stuff as dreams are made on; and our little life is rounded with a sleep."[15] In Hinduism we—the universe and all within it—are the dream of the God Vishnu. Different people have conflicting ideas about dreams. Wiccans, being people who already use magick, often assign mystical qualities to dreams. People's experiences in dreams range from ecstatic pleasures to eldritch horrors. It's hypothesized that there is not merely one type of dream but several varieties. Dreams are said to be not simply nighttime cinematic fun but prophetic visions, bringers of self-awareness, and ships that send us sailing on the stormy seas of the astral plane. Psychologists use dreams to gain insight into a person's psyche. Many people use their dreams as a topic of conversation at work. Some people remember their dreams, others don't, but everyone dreams. Psychologists have shown dreams to be necessary to the mind. Deprived of one's dreams, a person may become irritable and enter a dream state quicker when next sleeping.

When we dream, our mind is released from the clutter of our consciousness. When we are awake, we plan meetings, organize schedules, and have daydream fantasies all while somehow paying enough attention to what is going on around us to function in the world. While sleeping, our mind is freed from the everyday clutter and is able to move about unencumbered by the restrictions of the rational mind and its views of what can and can't be done. Freed from these logical shackles, our spirit can seek information from other sources. Sleeping gives us clear contact with our higher self, Deity, the collective unconscious, or something else entirely. We can then be given information intended to help us in some way. We may be guided through a problem that has confounded us, shown our true feelings in an emotional struggle, tormented by an unethical action, or given insight into our personality. Most people have been advised to sleep on a problem. Often we wake from slumber knowing our course of action or with a plan fully formed in mind. Sleeping on a problem can work great; however, difficulties may arise when the answer given by a dream is abstract and not as concrete as ideas in the physical world.

The drawback with insight and revelations received while we sleep is that dreams don't communicate with memos, voice mail, or even e-mail. There is no absolutely clear directive saying, "Hey you, dump the bum you're dating who you know is cheating on you, and ask out that cute girl you met at the bookstore, and call your mother more often." Life would be so much simpler if dreams communicated directly, but then again, that would take all the fun out of deciphering the twisted little dramas.

Dreams communicate on the level of myth, in symbols and metaphors. It's up to us to interpret these symbols and apply them to our lives. A cheating boyfriend might be seen as a spy or a figure shrouded in a dark cloak who sneaks away with your jewelry and gives it to someone else, while a lonely mother could be dreamed as a bird in a nest gazing forlornly at broken fragments of shell. The images give us the clues, but we have to decide what those images mean to us. Unfortunately, while some people view their dreams with mild curiosity, most disregard their dreams to the point where they don't remember having them. Even when a dream pounds on the walls of our consciousness so hard we are compelled to remember it, we shun its message, passing the experience off as "just a dream."

Throughout history, dreams have been viewed as having a prophetic nature. Even religious texts are full of stories in which people are warned of future misfortunes in dreams, so this would seem to give credence to the idea that people's dreams can be omens of future events. Many people view dreams as warnings of future catastrophes, and experiences of déjà vu are often thought to be events we have foreseen in dreams. How many people have been woken from a sound sleep at 2:00 AM by some frantic friend or family member who just dreamed you were terribly hurt and wanted to make sure you were all right, or is it only my grandmother who does this? People change travel plans, reschedule meetings, and get into screaming fights with spouses because of some dreamed vision being interpreted as a prophesy.

Are dreams actually prophetic? Dreams would seem to have that possibility; however, the problem is distinguishing the dreams that foreshadow future events from the more garden variety ones. Most dreams are the more normal variety, and prophetic dreams are extremely rare, but the decision as to the future possibilities of any dream can be judged only by the dreamer. So, if you have a dream about a fiery plane crash the night before your big trip to Kenosha, it will be up to you to decide if that dream was an urgent warning to change your travel plans, a product of an overly nervous subconscious, or a result of that late evening burrito. Just ask yourself: do you feel lucky?

How many times have you had a dream about someone you know? Have you ever had that person call you the next day and say they were also dreaming about you? Most people think of astral projection as something performed only by yogis who have dedicated years of their lives to serious navel contemplation. For those who don't know, astral projection is a discipline in which one causes their spirit to leave their body, zip off to other places, and return safely. Performing this feat consciously is tricky for many people possibly because they have trouble believing in the possibility of the soul leaving the body. Sometimes the difficulty is caused by the person's poor motivation for wanting to astral project: "Dude, I could totally be invisible in the girls' locker room." However, more frequently this problem arises because people tend to consider their body and spirit as the same thing rather than viewing themselves as a spirit who wears a body. If we see ourselves primarily as a body, then it's difficult to conceive of the spirit leaving it. However, if we perceive ourselves primarily as a spirit wearing a body, then exiting the body should be no more amazing than stepping from a car. While conscious projection may be difficult for most people, doing it in one's sleep would seem to be much easier. While we sleep we don't have that nagging little sabotaging gremlin "you can't do that" running through our head.

If we are concerned for or thinking about someone when we fall asleep, our spirit can reach out to them, and we perceive this as a dream. In this way we can comfort a person, let them know someone cares, or give advice spirit to spirit. Only rarely do we remember visiting the person, and even less often does the person we visit remember our stopping by. While we are asleep, it may also be possible to more readily converse with spirits who have crossed over, though we may still perceive the discussion to be a dream. In this way we may be able to receive comfort and closure from loved ones with whom we would otherwise have no means to converse. If one wakes up in the morning still feeling tired, maybe their spirit was out all night helping or being helped by others.

"In your dreams" is a popular phrase, expressing one's opinion that the only way a person will achieve that particular goal is while sleeping. We are the stars of our dreams, and we spend our evenings waiting for Mr. DeMille to give us our close-ups. Dreams become our ultimate playland where anything and everything is possible. Every desire, fantasy, or fear can be played out in splendid 3-D Technicolor with surround sound. While we are in them, dreams are indistinguishable from reality. There is a Taoist story about dreams: "I slept and dreamed I was a butterfly. When I awoke, I wasn't sure if I was a human who had a butterfly dream or a butterfly who was having a dream of humanity." All pleasures and terrors seem absolutely real no matter how fantastical or illogical they would appear in the waking world. We can fly, walk through walls, seasons can instantly change, and one person can transform into another or even an animal while we watch. Every event is taken completely in stride and seems completely logical to the sleeping mind.

Dream events are often transformed into physical reactions as we thrash and flail against an opponent. Our heart pounds in fear while we sweat profusely. We dream of the Arctic and wake up cold, or maybe we had the Arctic dream because we kicked off our blanket. We dream a friend betrayed us, and we wake up mad at them. Life in a dream is so real that people say if one dies in a dream he will die in real life, which isn't absolutely true, because I've died in dreams and I'm still here, or maybe this is a dream. Dreams could be just our hopes and anxieties rampaging through our sleeping mind with no real meaning other than we shouldn't worry about work so much or shouldn't eat chili before bed; after all, it is possible for that dream cigar to be just a cigar.

Everyone dreams, and we dream for a variety of reasons. Each individual must ultimately determine for themselves which type of dream they are having. That flying pig dream could be a symbol of a recent business venture, a prophetic dream about an upcoming plane trip, angelic reminders of those heavenly pork chops, or maybe they just look funny—the correct interpretation is up to the dreamer.

Many wonderful books have been written on how to interpret dreams, so I'm not going to address how to tell one type of dream from another here. However, if you have trouble remembering dreams, here are a couple of tips. When you are going to sleep, tell yourself you will remember your dreams. Keep a notebook and pen beside your bed so if you wake from a dream, you can make notes before you lose the details. Making notes is helpful because the ethereal world of dreams frequently fades quickly in the harsh glare of the physical world, and the notes will help jog your memory later. See if these techniques help, and even if you don't discover any deep psychological insights or prophetic stock tips, you might at least get some fun stories to tell your coworkers.

Doesn't the belief in reincarnation promote suicide?

Periodically in everyone's life, a person feels down or stressed; at these times people often turn to their religion to find comfort and renewal. However, sometimes a person may get so depressed that life ceases to seem worth living and death begins to seem a better option than continuing to wallow in the mental anguish they feel their life has become. At these dark points, people also turn to their religious beliefs, but occasionally, in the darkness they perceive their lives to be, a person finds not reassurance that life will become better but rather comfort that they will be better off after they have died.

Every religion has some view of the afterlife. Whether that religion believes we go to a place of perfection, go to a place of rest, or are reborn into another life, these choices could seem, to a severely depressed or anguished individual, better options than continuing on in what they perceive to be a miserable existence. Heaven, Nirvana, or even starting over in a new life could seem a viable, even logical option to someone who feels they have nothing left for which to live, but every religion, that I know of, teaches that suicide is not an acceptable choice when dealing with life's problems, and Wicca is not an exception. However, even though religions don't approve of suicide, a few people of every faith try to find out what's on the other side of death's door a bit earlier than expected.

When I lecture about Wicca, I am sometimes asked whether reincarnation doesn't promote suicide by giving a person a way out if they think life is becoming too difficult. Their reasoning seems to be that if someone has that option and they don't like their life, they'll just get out and start over with a better one, as if life were some type of video game that could be restarted if we don't like the level we're on.

Wicca teaches that life is sacred and is something to be cherished. The Wiccan Rede says we are to harm none—this includes ourselves—so suicide is inherently against Wiccan doctrine. However, let's just look at suicide from the perspective of reincarnation. Wicca teaches that through reincarnation our soul learns and grows through the experiences of each lifetime. Reincarnation is not some cosmic reset button someone pushes if they don't like the way their life is going. To learn life's lessons, we have to live with and deal with life's problems as they present themselves, not bail out of life when the going gets hard. It's commonly believed in Wicca that if someone commits suicide, that person has tried to dodge their lesson, but the Universe is a persistent teacher, and if we don't learn the lesson this lifetime, we will be presented with similar problems again in our next lifetime. So, simply put, if a person doesn't learn the lesson in this lifetime, they will repeat it over in future lifetimes until they get it right.

Therefore, from the point of view of reincarnation, suicide doesn't make sense because someone isn't avoiding the problem—they are simply delaying it to the next lifetime and having to redo everything that led up to that point. It would be like someone halfway through the eleventh grade deciding that it was too difficult and that they would just pull themselves out of school and come back the next year. Well, when the next year rolls around, they would find themselves back in the eleventh grade again with different friends, different teachers, and maybe even a different school but with the same lessons to learn. They would be back at the beginning and would have to repeat all the lessons and encounter all the problems that got them to the point at which they quit the last time.

It's a tragedy when a person of any age or religion feels their life is so cataclysmically wrong they wish it to end, especially when it's a teen who has just started to experience life. No religion promotes suicide, and neither reincarnation nor any other religion's view of the afterworld justifies suicide.

A Deeper Understanding
of Misconceptions about Wicca

Are Wiccans discriminated against?

> In Germany, they first came for the communists, and I didn't speak up
> because I wasn't a communist. Then they came for the Jews, and I didn't speak
> up because I wasn't a Jew. Then they came for the trade unionists, and I didn't
> speak up because I wasn't a trade unionist. Then they came for the Catholics
> and I didn't speak up because I wasn't a Catholic. Then they came for me—
> and by that time there was nobody left to speak up.
>
> —MARTIN NIEMÖLLER

IT HAS BEEN said that what we don't understand, we
fear, and what we fear, we seek to destroy. Fear is the foundation on
which towering edifices of discrimination are built. Any time there
is a lack of understanding or misinformation about something, discrimination usually follows, and there is a lot of misinformation
about Wicca. Why would someone hire a person when he's convinced
this professional-looking applicant will perpetually show up for work
stoned, wearing all black, and placing hexes on everyone who gets in

her way? Why would parents let their children play with someone they think will be sacrificing animals and drinking blood? The misinformation about Wicca not only could fill libraries but has done so, and most people don't care to learn the truth when the lies are so colorful. It's so much easier to believe the propaganda than to get the facts, easier to discriminate against others than to educate oneself.

I am on the Discrimination Task Force at Dallas's Betwixt & Between Community Center, and as such, I try to help the people who come to us with complaints of discrimination. The instances we see range from blatant discrimination and unintentional slights to cases where a Wiccan got a little too touchy and saw discrimination where there was none. I have seen a case where the Waxahachie Independent School District suspended a student for wearing a pentacle even though other students are allowed to wear religious symbols. A community college's world religions professor told a Wiccan student, and his class, that according to his research, Wicca was a Satanic cult, and he had the student removed from the class. I have seen children taken from their parents because a contractor at a woman's house saw Wiccan symbols and reported it to Child Protective Services (CPS). The CPS caseworker thought the child was in danger of ritual abuse because the parents were Wiccan and removed the children from the home. A child was taken from his parents while the child was still in the maternity ward because the parents put Wicca as their religion on the hospital admission form. The parents in both of these cases had their children returned to them, but they all endured weeks of court hearings and accusations of religious abuse. People have been subjected to perpetual proselytizing to the point it created a hostile work environment. I was in the local news when the Dallas City Council canceled the opening invocation I was scheduled to deliver because a local religious radio station found out I was Wiccan and asked its listeners to call the mayor's office to complain. Even though the misunderstanding was worked out and handled extremely professionally, several of my business clients cancelled contracts, and some parents told their children they could no longer play with my then nine-year-old daughter, all because they had seen the news and found out what our religion was.

Should discrimination happen because of religion? No. Does discrimination happen because of religion? Yes. It's easy for any minority group whether religious, sexual, or racial, to become "those people," and everyone knows what "those people" are like. When a group becomes "those people," they are no longer individuals; they are a group. People are more comfortable discriminating against a group where all group members can be passed off as strange, demented, or dangerous. The group is reviled and made to seem somehow dangerous to others, a social cancer that, if allowed to exist, will infect all of society by destroying morality with unclean ideas. When former Republican Representative Bob Barr (Georgia) was pushing to have all Wiccan worship services banned from military bases, both he and then-Texas Governor George W. Bush stated that Wicca isn't a real religion and is, therefore, not entitled to constitutional protection. By portraying Wicca as unreal or scary, people create an atmosphere of fear, and people will go to great lengths to combat something of which they are afraid. Fear and ignorance drove the Inquisition, the Nazi attacks on Jews, the slaughter of Native Americans, and the oppression of former slaves. Fear and ignorance now drive the discrimination against Wiccans and other minority religions.

The unique thing about discrimination is that it requires the consent of the individuals in society in order to flourish. People must choose to be hostile to another group of people or at least apathetic to others' hostility toward them. If people stand up and say, "No, we will not permit others to be oppressed simply because they are different," then the whole system of discrimination begins to fall apart.

The discrimination I have seen and personally experienced has led me to examine my own beliefs and feelings about others. Whether I agree with them or not, no one should be discriminated against. As long as people can live in harmony with others and the world around them, people have the right to be themselves no matter what religion, race, creed, nationality, sexual orientation, political persuasion, or interesting personality trait they have.

Do you have to be special to do magick?

Lightning flashes around a spindly tower in the moonless dark of the night. A woman's screams rise over the howling of the wind as she cries out in the last stages of labor. Monks in robes chant in some long-forgotten language as they circle her bed. The clouds seem to boil as the storm outside rises to a shrieking crescendo matching the first wail of the child as it enters the world. A monk takes the baby, searching its tiny body until with an expression of rapture he finds what he is searching for. Raising the infant high for all to see, the monk proclaims, "This baby, born the seventh child of a seventh child, in the seventh hour of the night, bears the mark of power—this will be a magical child." This is the vision many people have of what is necessary for a person to be born with the ability to perform magick, and they have been watching too many old science fiction movies.

Many people have the idea that to perform magick, one must be born under some auspicious star with all the planets in the right place and have a peculiar birthmark on one's butt. All right maybe it's not *that* bad, but people often believe that to have the power to do magick, one must be either born special or make some deal with an evil being. These erroneous beliefs keep many people from consciously using magick in their life.

Everyone does magick. It happens around us all the time. Most people just don't realize it's magick. Magick isn't something sinister or evil. It doesn't come with light shows, smoke, or other special effects. It's something natural and part of life.

Magick is consciously using Divine energy to cause changes to oneself or surroundings. Divine energy surrounds us constantly, and we pay about as much attention to it as a fish probably does to the water in which it swims. If it were suddenly gone, we would be looking around wondering what happened, but otherwise, we ignore it.

Everyone can and does do magick. Most people just don't believe in themselves enough to use it effectively. If you have ever been in desperate need of money and you received an unexpected bonus at work for the desired amount, that's magick. If you envisioned meeting someone special and, rounding the corner at the bookstore, you bump into someone and you begin a conversation that hasn't stopped years later, that's magick. If your car needs to be fixed, but you can't afford it, and the new guy on your bowling league says he can help you out with the repairs, that's magick. Now many people are saying, "That isn't magick; those are coincidences." My response is, "No, those incidents show synchronicity, which is one way magick frequently manifests itself."

The psychologist Carl Jung wrote about synchronicity, which is a seemingly random series of events all coming together to make something happen. For instance, Joe, a friend of mine (true story and, yes, that is his real name), bought a house in Texas in October. When summer rolled around, it got hot, and in Texas, *hot* means the kind of hot that makes other hots look cool. Anyway, his grass quickly begins to turn from a bright kelly green to khaki, and he decided it was about time to turn on his fancy in-ground sprinkler system. Now, Joe's house was a bit old, and it had a few issues with which he had been dealing, so when he turned on the sprinkler, he found it had developed a leak in one of the pipes. So, he did what any good male with absolutely no knowledge of plumbing does: he grabbed a shovel and dug up the pipe to have a look. After this, he determined that duct tape couldn't fix the problem and dragged the old-fashioned oscillating sprinklers from the garage. The company that installed his sprinkler system had been out of business for years, so he and his wife were sitting in the living room debating how they were going to take off work to get the problem fixed and how they were going to afford fixing it—when the doorbell rang. Joe answered the door, and there on the porch stood a neighbor from down the street holding a beer. He introduced himself and said he had noticed Joe was using the oscillating sprinklers and asked if Joe knew the house had a really good in-ground sprinkler system. Joe said, "Yes, I know, but it is currently broken, and how did you know we have a sprinkler system?" The man answered that he used to work for a sprinkler company, and he had installed the system. Joe was dumbfounded when the man said he would come over and fix the leak for free on Monday while they were at work if Joe left the back gate unlocked. Most people write off this kind of event to random chance or happy coincidence, but I believe there are no coincidences in the universe. Events usually happen for a reason.

Wicca teaches that thoughts are things. Everything we think about sends energy out into the world that changes the world in some way. Most thoughts don't have enough energy behind them to actually do much, but some will have just enough to tip that first domino, setting a chain of events into motion that will lead to something magickal happening in one's life.

Magick is like kismet, those fortuitous chances we blow off as random events because we are uncomfortable thinking we might have had something to do with them: while thinking about your sister, the phone rings, and it's her; a parent who is miles away from their child suddenly, and correctly, senses that the child is sick or hurt. Those are a type of magick.

I believe there are three levels of magickal use, each requiring a bit more trust in Divinity and belief in oneself. To illustrate the levels, let's say you are walking through the park, and you think, "I would like an apple." The first level of magick would be to look around for a store, walk in, and buy the apple. Now, there are people out there saying, "That's not magick; anyone can do that." This is my point: anyone can do magick. People have just become extremely good at rationalizing events so that they're not perceived as magick. There was a thought, and that thought was made manifest in reality. The person could have ignored the thought or talked themselves out of acting on that thought, but they followed through and transformed an intangible thought into a real thing. Just because we consider the act commonplace doesn't make it any less incredible. Plants don't shape their environment. For the most part, other animals don't decide what they want to eat; they eat whatever presents itself. If people don't like the way something is, we find a way to reshape the environment to our whims, and that is a form of magick.

The second level is the synchronicity level, where you think, "I want an apple." Then some guy on the park bench says, "Hey, I brought more food for lunch than I can eat; you want my apple?" Now most people see more possibility for magick at this level but may still try to explain it away as chance. The last level of magick is when you think about the apple, and it appears in your hand. I think everyone has the possibility of doing this. However, we just don't because of that nagging little voice in our heads constantly playing the "you can't do that" track. As long as any part of our mind believes this track, we won't consciously manifest items. Also, if our ego jumps in and thinks, "Move over, David Copperfield; I could make a bundle doing this on stage," it's not going to work either.

This is the way I see the Divine functioning in the universe, and I have used this explanation of the three levels of magick for years. However, I recently saw a PBS special with Dr. Wayne Dyer in which he used a similar list to illustrate synchronicity, so I guess I'm not the only person who sees the Universe working in this way. Maybe if everyone saw these steps as the way the energy of the Universe functions, we would all live a bit more magically. Therefore, all people can do magick whether they have a birthmark on their butt or not. Magick is a gift from Divinity and has nothing to do with religion. Most people use magick unconsciously, but when one opens oneself up to the possibility, magick becomes a conscious part of life. When life is magickal, there is no room for the humdrum or commonplace.

Is there an official Wiccan dress code?

"But you don't look like a Witch!" This is one of the most frequent exclamations I hear—and the funniest. I usually chuckle and tell them that my wart is on order but doesn't arrive until next week. People laugh and the conversation continues, but this does bring up a serious subject: what is the public perception of what a Witch looks like?

Many people cling to the idea that all Witches wear black gothic clothing, have warts, and a few people even believe we run around in pointy hats. However, none of these stereotypical images are true for most Wiccans. There is no list of acceptable clothing for the fashionably dressed Witch, although I have known a few people who've volunteered to put one together. Wiccans aren't usually required to wear anything that would distinguish them from the general public, including pentagrams or black clothing; the pointy hats are also usually considered purely optional attire. Wiccans actually have exactly the same wardrobe options as anyone else and a few more than some.

Even when attending rituals, Wiccans have a wide variety of clothing options. People of most faiths usually have special clothing set aside for worship, and Wicca is no exception. Many Wiccans prefer to wear special robes or jewelry to ritual, and some Wiccan traditions have colored cords that are worn around the waist to indicate at what level a student is studying. Most Wiccans have at least one robe they wear for ceremonies and gatherings where robes are appropriate. Some covens have a specific style of ritual attire, but for most Wiccans, ritual robes may be tailored in a variety of styles and colors. The robes worn for ritual are usually only worn for religious purposes and are intended to help put the person in the proper mental attitude for the service. However, for many rituals, especially public gatherings, people wear whatever it is they had on in the car as they drove over. Then why do people think Wiccans dress in a certain way?

Most misunderstandings concerning Wiccans happen because there are, at the time I'm writing this book, fewer than a million Wiccans in the United States, and most of those don't advertise their religious beliefs. This means that of the two or three Wiccans most people know, they probably don't realize more than one of them is actually Wiccan. No one notices a Wiccan in business attire, but everyone gravitates to the Wiccan who has a more unique and individual look. So if the only Wiccan a person thinks they know always wears green fingernail polish, they tend to overgeneralize and assume *all* Wiccans wear green fingernail polish. They tell this imagined "fact" to a couple of friends, who have no clue this information isn't accurate, and then they tell two friends, who tell two friends, and so on. Eventually a whole group of people begin to think green fingernail polish is a code sign for Wiccans. This is the usual way most bizarre rumors about Wiccans are spread, and they will continue to be spread this way until people realize they know more Wiccans than they think they do and that Wiccans typically dress the same as everyone else.

Wicca doesn't encourage people to discover new and unique

looks, but neither does it discourage an individual's self-expression. Wiccans, as a group, tend to have a high percentage of people who are not only naturally eccentric but who actually strive to be different. Wicca allows for freedom of expression, so if one wishes to dye their hair a color that has never been found in nature, we don't care. If a Wiccan wants to have various anatomical tidbits punctured with metal objects, most Wiccans wouldn't look at them twice. There is also a contingency of Wiccans who are into gothic fashion, which translates into dressing like Morticia Addams at her prom. All Wiccans don't dress in black, but since Wiccans who dress in a more gothic style tend to look like the public's idea of a witch, they're the ones who tend to get their pictures published and thereby unwittingly help perpetuate the stereotype.

Even many, usually conservative, members of the Wiccan community are sometimes responsible for perpetuating this stereotype. Every Halloween the media rediscovers Wicca, and reporters want to interview a Witch and photograph a ritual. Many Wiccans are eager to help because they see this as an opportunity to dispel much of the negative propaganda about Wicca, so they jump at the opportunity to be interviewed. As the day approaches, they are so excited about being on television that when the reporter says they want to do the interview in a graveyard, with the Wiccans dressed in black robes and holding skulls, somehow this sounds like a good idea.[1] Personally, I only wear my robes for public rituals when I am the High Priest, and any interviews I do are in at least a shirt and tie and are not in, shall we say, exotic locations.

Therefore, for the most part, people aren't able to distinguish Wiccans from anyone else, and most people probably encounter a dozen Wiccans a day without ever realizing it. A few Wiccan groups may encourage their members to wear certain colors during specific times of the year, and a very few groups may ask all their members wear a special ring or they may all agree to get matching tattoos. These requirements, when present, only apply to the dozen or so members of that group. Their requirements don't extend to the entire Wiccan population.

Are Wiccans psychic?

One of the common public perceptions of Wiccans is that as Witches they are psychic. Movies and television often depict witches as having the power to read minds, levitate objects, teleport, and otherwise do extraordinary things with their minds. Some Wiccans consider themselves to have psychic talent, but nowhere near Hollywood standards. Other Wiccans wouldn't consider themselves to be psychic at all. Being Wiccan doesn't give a person any more potential for psychic ability than anyone else. What Wiccans have that many others don't is—belief.

There is a saying that some things have to be believed to be seen. This statement also applies to psychic experiences because if a person doesn't believe psychic abilities exist, that person will never open themselves up to even the possibility of experiencing them. Wiccans believe that to some extent we create our own reality. We allow some things to exist in our reality and disallow others because of our beliefs. For example, people who believe themselves to be strong and healthy will become ill less frequently and for shorter duration than people who perceive themselves to be fragile and sickly.

My mom always said, "Can't never could do nothing." People hate to be proven wrong, so when they think they can't do something, one can bet they will go to any length to prove themselves right. I often hear people say things like, "I can't sing; I can't play the guitar; I can't juggle; I can't speak in front of people." The list goes on and on as people limit themselves, telling themselves what they can't do. In reality anyone can do any of these things if they put the time and effort into learning how and practicing the skill. It only requires a little bit of time for anyone to acquire a skill they perceive to be difficult; impossible skills take a bit longer.

People have been told psychic skills are impossible and are, therefore, unwilling to even believe in their existence, much less consider the possibility that something they're feeling might in any way be paranormal. Wiccans tend to believe psychic abilities are possible and give more credence to nagging hunches, sudden thoughts of danger, and tingly feelings zipping up and down the spine than would many people. When someone begins paying attention to those odd feelings, they begin to develop their natural psychic abilities just as athletes train their bodies. Now, I'm not saying all Witches can bend bars with their minds or track down fugitives from the psychic vibrations left at a crime scene, but I have met a few priestesses, and mothers, who could look right through a person and tell when they had screwed up.

So to answer the question: no, Wiccans as a group are no more psychic than anyone else. Wiccans just tend to be more in tune with their feelings and more acutely aware of those Divinely given psychic nudges everyone gets but most people deny. By acknowledging these feelings and hunches, Wiccans, as a group, do tend to develop their natural psychic potential more than many other groups. However, that would be a natural by-product of their belief.

Can Wiccans tell the future?

There seems to be a human fascination with wanting to know the future. People want "insider information" to help them decide what's going to be the most productive course of action for their lives. Psychic chum's lines and Madame Dejour's phone-in tarot readings do a booming business off people who want the assurance that their lives will get better. Personally, I always thought knowing what's going to happen would spoil the surprise, but that doesn't seem to bother all those people who peek at birthday presents, read the last chapter of books first, and try to divine their future.

Throughout the ages, a veritable cornucopia of divination (future telling) methods have been developed. Wiccans, if they wish, are free to use almost any divination method they desire. Tarot cards, runes, crystal gazing, coin flipping, astrology, and the ever-popular tasseography (tea leaf reading) are but a few of the hundreds of divination methods. Now, with saying, "Yes, Wiccans do employ methods of telling the future," comes the inevitable question: "So if you can tell the future, why haven't you won the lottery?" I always chuckle at that question because while the person asking is dead serious, it shows a lack of understanding about divination.

Using divination to predict the future is an imprecise science to say the least. At its best, divination predicts what is going to happen to a person if they maintain their present course of action; however, every minute we have the power to change our actions and alter the outcome. The best use of divination is as an aid to personal and spiritual growth. In this case divination is used as a tool to help a person spot bad habits, destructive trends, and areas of their life that need improvement. Among those who believe divination works, differing opinions abound as to why it works.

Few readers will take personal credit for the information communicated in a reading. Most will say one's higher self, the Divine, the collective unconscious, or simply Spirit causes certain patterns to form in whatever divination tool is being used. The patterns are presented in such a way that the reader will deliver the intended message. Usually the answers come in the form of general information to be interpreted by the person and applied to their life. For example, a reader would be more likely to say, "You need to be careful of an abusive male figure in your life who has been deceiving you for years about his relationship with you," rather than, "Your husband, Bob, is cheating on you again, this time with your friend Mary, and you need to get out before the drunken bully hits you again." The person asking the question receives the information from the person doing the reading, interprets it, and chooses whether or not to act on the information. In this way divination is intended to help a person navigate some of the problem areas of life; it isn't intended to give out lottery numbers, pick race horses, or decide if Friday is a good night for poker, although it might tell a person to find a more stable form of income and quit trying for easy money.

Divination is intended for occasional help when life seems especially difficult. There is sometimes a danger of people becoming so dependent that they lose the ability to make their own decisions. This can be seen when someone refuses to get out of bed because Mercury is in retrograde or has to call their tarot phone pal every time they meet someone in a bar. Divination isn't intended to be a substitute for common sense or act as a crutch for those who are afraid to take responsibility for their own actions. For those people, the cards would probably read, "Live your own life and accept the consequences of whatever decision you make."

Aren't male Witches called warlocks?

A little knowledge is a dangerous thing. Often when I am at some public event where people are discussing religion, someone will hear I am Wiccan and, wanting to appear knowledgeable, will say, "So, you're a warlock." After all, they've seen every episode of *Bewitched;* the first three seasons of *Sabrina, the Teenage Witch;* several episodes of *Charmed;* the movie *Warlock,* and both of its sequels, so they think they know this is what someone calls a male Witch. At this point I have to pause to take a deep breath because the person speaking really doesn't know how insulting that statement is. Unfortunately, this is a point where Hollywood views reality through opaque glasses or possibly through sunglasses that are mirrored on the inside, reflecting back only images Hollywood has created, giving the illusion of reality while seeing nothing of the actual world.

Not all Wiccans refer to themselves as Witches. Witch is sometimes said to be one of the "scary words" because it leads people to leap to many unpleasant, scary, and completely incorrect images that have been perpetuated over the years. Therefore, rather than risk looks of revulsion usually reserved for mass murderers, many Wiccans choose not to characterize themselves as a Witch. Of those who do call themselves a Witch, the women and the men are both called Witches. *Witch* is a word used to describe someone who uses magick. Witch is a gender-neutral word, no matter what Hollywood says to the contrary.

The word *warlock* comes from the Old English word *wærloza,* which means oath breaker or traitor.[2] Therefore, if a Wiccan says someone is a warlock, they are saying that person has been found to be dishonorable, untrustworthy, and unethical. Also, when someone is expelled from a Wiccan coven or tradition because of ethical violations, that person is sometimes said to have been warlocked from the group. So, while the term *warlock* is used in Wicca, it's not used the way everyone thinks it is. Warlock is not a desirable thing for a

Wiccan to be called, unless one likes being referred to as a liar and a cheat, and it's definitely not used as the word for a male Witch.

Is Wicca Satanic?

Satanism has become the boogieman of the late-twentieth century. Urban legends of Satanic human sacrifices abound to the point where people think they happen all the time. During psychological counseling, some people have reported repressed memories, usually later proven to be false, of being ritually abused as a child in Satanic rituals. Women who were later proven to have never been pregnant claimed to have given birth to children who were sacrificed during black masses. Movies depict Satanists stealing people's pets and children to sacrifice them on black obsidian altars as giant demonic forms take smoky shape from foul-smelling braziers. People hear these stories all the time, but none of them apply to Wiccans; in fact, none of these stories even apply to Satanists.[3] In a 1989 report, the FBI said they have been unable to identify even one Satanic murder in the United States.[4] Ritual Satanic murders are an urban legend spread by people who seem to want some tenuous attachment to anything that will make their lives less boring, so they are willing to believe any lurid tale they come across no matter how unlikely that tale is.

This question comes up so often that I was forced to take the time to research Satanism so I could accurately contrast Satanists' beliefs with the beliefs of Wiccans. Even though both Wiccans and Satanists may call themselves Witches, there is no relationship between Wicca and Satanism. Wiccans don't like to be referred to as Satanists, and I would be willing to bet Satanists don't like to be called Wiccans. According to Magister Peter H. Gilmore, modern Satanism is "a brutal religion of elitism and social Darwinism that seeks to re-establish the reign of the able over the idiotic, of swift justice over injustice, and for a wholesale rejection of egalitarianism as a myth that has crippled the advancement of the human species for the last two thousand years." This is not a definition one would ever apply to Wicca. Neither Wiccans nor Satanists practice or condone the abuse of children or the sacrifice of animals. Both groups expect their members to obey the law; however, past those points, there are few similarities.

Satanism and Wicca are two completely different religious philosophies that share the dubious distinction of being portrayed by some religious groups, as well as in film and in the media, as purveyors of heinous acts. Because most people understand neither group, they are lumped together and become the scapegoats for sensational, bizarre, and twisted actions of demented individuals in society. They shouldn't be linked together, and neither group deserves the infamy that some try to thrust upon them.

Wicca and Satanism have completely different views of Deity. Although Wiccans may honor Deity in many ways, Wiccans frequently honor and worship an archetypal Goddess and God that can be anthropomorphized into many differing perceptions of Deity. Satanism "does not subscribe to the notion of an anthropomorphic deity and, by extension, some being who must be worshiped." They believe that "in Satanism there's no Deity to which one can sacrifice" because Satanists are their own gods.

Wicca has an ethical structure that allows complete freedom to explore life with the exception that one can't harm others in their exploration of life. On the other hand, Satanism teaches "Satan represents vengeance, instead of turning the other cheek!" and that "Satanists must strive to apply the dictum of 'Do unto others as they do unto you.'" Also, in the *Satanic Rules of the Earth* (on the Church of Satan's Web site), Anton LaVey states, "If someone bothers you, ask him to stop. If he does not stop, destroy him."

Wicca teaches that everyone is part of the Divine and deserves respect because of the divine spirit we all share. Every person is seen as serving a purpose, and no one should let their ego convince them that they are better or worse than anyone else. Satanism believes in stratification and teaches "There can be no more myth of 'equality' for all—it only translates to 'mediocrity' and supports the weak at the expense of the strong."

Both Wicca and Satanism have been overdramatized in the media to the point of making them unrecognizable to anyone who actually practices the religion. People who have no valid information about Wicca are easily convinced that the bogus information fed to them by the movies is true. There is no connection between Wicca and Satanism other than in the minds of some extremely misinformed individuals. Therefore, the next time you hear someone say Wiccans are Satanists, please keep in mind that person has absolutely no idea what they're talking about.

For Those of You
Who Still Want More

What if I don't agree with my
friend or loved one's religious choice?

If you want to keep things civil, never discuss religion or politics. This is advice I have often heard given, though I rarely follow it myself. Even so, for most people, this is usually good advice because, unless handled diplomatically, no other two topics are more likely to spark animated discussions, heated debates, or bloody fistfights. Many people tend to think their own religious and political views are the most lucid and reasonable, and if everyone else would only listen to them, the world's problems would vanish. Even those who are more open to differing opinions often view those opinions as bizarre or misguided. I would be willing to bet there are no two people on the planet who have all the same religious and political views. They may be close but not the same. So how do we work, play, and live with others in such a diverse environment? The three most obvious answers are that we can surround ourselves only with people who have ideas similar to our own, try to convince everyone else to conform to our own ideas, or allow everyone to have differing opinions, enjoying the exploration of new ideas without judging them.

Choosing to associate only with people who have religious views similar to our own is a choice many people make. In fact, many religions actively teach their followers not to have dealings with members of other religions. On the plus side, this does considerably cut down the possibilities for religious arguments, as one would have much in common with everyone around. This is part of the idea behind a monastic life. If one associates only with others of their own faith, one can grow spiritually without having to contend with the possibility of other religious views pulling a person away from their path. However, in the modern world where we work in diverse environments, go to public schools with people from all cultures, and watch television programs that show many differing viewpoints, shielding ourselves from outside influences is difficult.

Isolating oneself limits one's opportunities and choice of friends and often causes difficulties within families. Even when possible, isolating oneself from the world may have an effect different than the one we intended. Buddhism teaches that when the prince Siddhartha, who would later become the Buddha, was born, his father was told the child would become either a great king or a great spiritual leader. The king isolated him in the palace so the young Buddha would never experience any unpleasant thoughts that might make him question life and prevent him from becoming king. This worked fine until eventually the prince was exposed to old age, sickness, and death. These were outside his experience and, instead of becoming king, the prince set his feet on the path to becoming the Buddha, the very path his father was trying to avoid.

People can sometimes be convinced to change their religious viewpoints, and many religions encourage their followers to persuade others to convert to their religious ideas. This may help people in need of religious guidance to find a path away from self-destructive behavior. However, what happens when someone says, "Thanks, but I am very happy with my own religious choice and see no reason to change?" Can someone stay friends with that person in spite of the religious differences, or will they be abandoned as a hopeless cause?

Are their wishes to be respected, or does this mean one needs to try even harder to convince them? I think the way people are treated after they have made it clear they don't want to change religions tells a lot about the individual who is trying to convert them. One finds out how genuine and caring the person truly is and how much of their previous behavior has been an act. Respect and consideration should not be doled out only to those who agree with our worldview; they should be given to everyone whether they share our beliefs or not. This is part of the reason why Wiccans don't proselytize; we believe everyone's faith is deserving of respect. Living our faith is enough, and if people want to know about our religious views, they will ask.

The world is a big place with lots of differing viewpoints. Each of us views the world in a different way. A multitude of religions, denominations, and sects reflect that diversity of religious thought. Wicca views Deity as something powerful enough to encompass all those possibilities and still not be completely explained. However, even if a person believes their religion is the only way to view Deity, shouldn't everyone be treated with respect and compassion regardless of their religious choice? A basic respect for people is not something that must be worked for and earned. It should be something freely given, and our actions can either increase or diminish the respect we have for one another. By respecting everyone as individuals regardless of our religious differences, we illustrate the compassion, love, and charity taught by most of the world's religions. Even if one views all other religions as wrong, don't people have the right to be wrong? Allowing people to have different opinions should in no way diminish one's own view of Deity. Many families who have Wiccan relatives choose to still love the individual for who they are in spite of their religious differences.

When someone is around people of differing religions, the actions of those people communicate the message of their religion more effectively than do words. Admonitions and rejection may make someone think that a religion is more about anger and control than peace and love. Respecting others and honoring them as individuals in spite of their religious differences illustrates a religion's love for humanity, which any individual filled with the Divine should possess.

This leaves a person with a positive impression of that religion and is a better witness of faith than a dozen arguments.

How do I find a Wiccan Circle?

There may be several reasons why someone would want to attend their first Wiccan Circle. Some people simply want to learn more about other religions and are curious about Wicca. Others want to see for themselves the form of worship their friend or family member has chosen. Some might be sure I'm omitting something diabolical from my description of Wicca and may want to attend a Circle to prove me, or someone else, wrong. However, many want to attend because they are curious to see if Wicca is an appropriate spiritual path for them.

Most Wiccan clergy understand that many people are unsure about Wicca and will continue to be suspicious as long as Wiccan groups remain secret and hidden. Therefore, open Circles are held not only to give solitary Wiccans a place to worship with others but also to give people curious about Wicca a place to experience a Wiccan Circle firsthand. Even if you're not interested in Wicca as a religious choice and are just curious to see what Wiccans do in Circle, you will usually be welcome if you let the priestess and priest know that information up front and if you enter the Circle with a respectful attitude. Most public Circles have several new people in attendance, so don't worry about sticking out. Anyone who wishes to attend and enters the Circle in perfect love and perfect trust should be welcome at open rituals.

Sometimes the most difficult part of attending a Circle isn't deciding whether or not you want to experience a Wiccan Circle; it's finding a Circle to attend. Wicca isn't like many religions where one simply opens up the phone book and looks for the proper religious institution. Wiccan groups are typically small, don't tend to advertise their presence to the general public, and frequently only allow people initiated into the coven to attend. In the late eighties, a person had to have connections to even find out about public Circles. Today, however, with the number of Wiccans in the United States increasing, it's getting easier to find public gatherings where everyone is welcome. In my area, announcements of public Circles often appear in the religion section of the newspaper.

If you know someone who is Wiccan, that's probably your best starting point. Tell them you want to attend a Circle, and see if they know of any in the area that welcome interested people. If you have no one to ask, check for a local metaphysical store and ask the owner. Literature about public Circles is often posted at metaphysical stores, and the owners usually know several people in the area who might be good contacts. You might also try going online and checking for groups that meet in your area. Good Internet resources are the Covenant of the Goddess (www.cog.org) and the Witches' Voice (www.witchvox.com).

On the Covenant of the Goddess's Web site, there are links for local councils that will take you to a page where you can contact various local councils around the country, and the local council contact person might be able to put you in touch with someone in your area who holds public Circles.

The Witches' Voice is a wonderful resource for people looking for Wiccans in their area or circles they can attend. Their Web site is divided by state and has ways to contact individuals, adult groups, family groups, teen groups, college groups, local circles, and local events. The Witches' Voice provides a valuable service for the Wiccan community, but their contact information is so extensive that there is no possible way for them to screen all the information to determine whether the people posting are legitimate or not. Anyone can post on this site, so please be cautious. There are many great people listed on the Witches' Voice, but some may be more ethical than others, so ask questions about their Circle and make sure you are comfortable with them before you agree to meet. Any legitimate coven will completely understand a person being cautious and will not mind answering a few questions to put your mind at ease. They will also probably have questions for you because as much as they are a stranger to you, you are also a stranger to them.

As with any group, use your head to evaluate any information you are given. Don't do anything you are uncomfortable doing. Listen to your instincts; that's why we have them. Even if everything appears fine, if you have a bad feeling, walk away! I would suggest using the Seeker's Bill of Rights (Appendix A) as a guide to ethics.

What do I need to know before attending a Wiccan Circle?

"But I don't have anything to wear." As strange as it sounds, this and many other worries arise as a person approaches their first ritual. When going to any religious service, there are an incredible number of embarrassing mistakes a person can commit without realizing there has been an error, and when one is attending a ritual and is completely in the dark as to what will happen, their mind may begin to go into overdrive, concocting bizarre, worst-case scenarios. A person can lose sleep with visions of erring so badly that everyone turns and stares as someone taps them on the shoulder, telling them they had best leave now.

To put your mind at ease, short of leaping unbidden into the middle of the circle and announcing that you are channeling some multidimensional deity, you will not mess up that badly. If you are attending a public Circle, chances are you won't be the only new person present, so relax. Wiccan rituals are celebrations of life and the Earth. They can be fun and/or informative, and most rituals, especially public rituals, are difficult to ruin.

Let's begin with that first concern: what to wear. If this is your first public ritual, unless you have been instructed otherwise, show up dressed casually. If it's like most public rituals, people's dress will range from shorts and tank tops to elaborate robes or other ritual wear, so anything casual will usually fit in nicely. A suit and tie might be considered overdressed, and showing up naked is a bit too casual.

Many public Circles ask that everyone bring food to share. If everyone brings food, then after the ritual there is sort of a "Pagan potluck" where people have the opportunity to eat and chat with one another. This can be a great time to get to know people in your local Pagan community. Some rituals want everyone to bring food, but others don't, so try to find out before the Circle whether or not the ritual you are attending asks people to bring snacks. If you can't find out, don't worry; no one should be angry if you don't bring something to share to your first ritual. However, if you are concerned, throw a bag of Oreos and a two-liter bottle of Coke in your car just to be on the safe side.

There are two types of open rituals. The first type is a completely open Circle that is usually held in a park or some other public location. These rituals are publicized, and anyone who wants to may attend. The second type is a semi-public ritual that is often held at a person's home. These rituals will welcome new people, but they are not publicized and are by invitation only. If you didn't find out about the ritual in the newspaper, on a flier, by a general online announcement, or some other public source, then someone is probably bringing you as their guest. Unless you are positive the ritual was announced to the public, don't invite anyone else to come with you unless they are cleared by the hosting group.

Whether the ritual is in a public space or at someone's house, please respect the surroundings. Be courteous, and try to leave the place cleaner than when you arrived. This means making sure trash gets thrown away, spills are cleaned up, smoking is done only in appropriate areas, and the butts are disposed of properly. If there is food to share, help yourself to what is out, but don't rifle through the host's refrigerator or pantry looking for something different if you get the nibbles. Respect the host's space; don't wander around closed rooms or snoop through cabinets. Also, helping to clean up by picking up plates, glasses, or cans that others may have left out is always a nice gesture.

My rituals are family rituals where kids are always welcome. The natural, genuine, free-flowing and slightly chaotic energy that children bring is, to me, the essence of life. Other people view children as a distraction to their meditative state and find it difficult to fully experience a ritual if kids are moving around, asking questions, and just being kids. Therefore, if you are considering bringing a child or a pet with you to Circle, it is best to ask whether kids or animals are welcome at whatever Circle you are planning to attend. My viewpoint is that the spiritual experience should be shared as a family. Others may disagree with me, so it's best to check first. Also, even if kids are allowed in the ritual, please be respectful of others and quickly step out of Circle if the child becomes a disturbance.

Don't be late! Most ritual announcements list two times: the first is for gathering, and the second is for ritual to begin. Attempt to show up as soon after the gathering time as possible. Don't be late because for most Circles, once the ritual starts, no one is allowed to join in. Besides, if you're early, you can introduce yourself to the hosting group. Tell them it's your first ritual, that way they can tell you a little about the ritual, answer questions you might have, and give you any specific information you might need to know. They might also introduce you to several more experienced people who can answer any other questions that might occur to you and help guide you through any rough spots.

Most rituals last thirty to forty-five minutes, and if you think you may not be physically able to stand for the duration of the ritual, let someone know before the ritual starts; for most rituals chairs are handy for people who have problems standing for long periods of time. Please don't torture yourself because you are afraid others will think less of you. If you have problems, let someone know.

Often when someone is new, they fear everyone will look down on them for being a novice, that they, like the sorcerer's apprentice, will be consigned to carry water while everyone else shares arcane knowledge. In an attempt to avoid this perceived fate, people sometimes try to make themselves seem more impressive than they feel. People start going on about how psychic they are, how they were burned as a witch in a past life, or that their great-grandmother was a Witch, and it was from her that they inherited their powers. People may also try to impress others with how knowledgeable they are and begin quoting from the books they have read. The problem is, the person they're talking to may have been studying Wicca for two days or twenty-five years. Heck, they could have written the book being quoted. More often than not, this behavior makes the person look silly rather than impressive. Just be yourself, ask questions, and learn from those around you. Everyone in attendance was new at one time, and no one is going to make you haul water.

There are several things people frequently do before ritual begins, but each group may have a slightly different list of things to do in preparation for Circle. It's best to either ask (most people won't be offended by polite questions about precircle activities) or pay attention to what others are doing to prepare for Circle. Although, as I said, specific precircle preparation may vary from group to group, here are some preparations that are fairly universal.

Turn off cell phones, pagers, watch alarms, electronic pets, or anything else that might make noise during Circle. It's a bit disconcerting when a phone rings and even worse when someone answers one, and the fact that someone has a really cute ring doesn't help. If there is a possibility of an imminent medical emergency or you are on call, set your phone or pager to vibrate. Otherwise, please shut it off or, better yet, leave it in your car for the duration of the ritual.

Watches are one of our connections to the nonspiritual world, with its hectic pace of time schedules and meetings, so there is a tradition of removing watches during ritual—one less distraction for people.

Some groups prefer people didn't eat or drink before ritual; other groups don't mind. However, if you are eating, drinking, or smoking before ritual, please don't take your snacks or smokes with you into Circle. Wiccan Circles are religious observances, not movies, and someone crunching popcorn, smacking gum, or blowing smoke can be very distracting. Also, don't come to the ritual under the influence of alcohol or illegal drugs. Everyone entering the Circle should be sober and alert.

Many groups also prefer people remove their shoes during Circle because it puts them in direct contact with the Earth, helping shift their mindset from the mundane to the spiritual world. However, this tradition may vary with location and seasonal considerations.

Before ritual begins, take some time to ground and center yourself. That means letting go of all the day's worries for a little while: drop all the distractions, clear your mind, and try to find a place of peace and calm within you. I know, you're probably saying to yourself, "If I could do that, I wouldn't have this ulcer or need the Valium, and I could sleep without my sounds of nature machine." Although it may sound difficult, it gets easier with practice, so just relax and do the best you can. Clearing your mind lets you enter the ritual peacefully and focused on what is going on rather than being distracted by what happened earlier in the day or worrying about what will happen later. This allows you to fully experience the ritual in which you are participating.

When it's time for the ritual to begin, one of two things usually happens: people either begin forming a circle in the ritual area, or they start lining up outside the ritual area. If everyone begins to form a circle in the ritual area, just join in with everyone else, stay close to anyone you came with or anyone with whom you may have made friends, and wait for the ritual to begin.

If people line up, however, everyone is going to be brought into the ritual in some way. Sometimes people enter the Circle in a certain order. If this is the case, an announcement should be made before the Circle begins as to how people are supposed to line up. People could be put in order by how long they have been practicing; by age, height, gender; or by any other order the group conducting the ritual feels is appropriate. However, at public rituals this is uncommon, and if no one specifies an order, just get in line wherever you fancy.

As you approach the ritual area, one or more things will probably happen. A person may ask, "How do you enter?" to which the usual response is, "In perfect love and perfect trust," although this response may vary. The best thing to do is listen to whatever the person in front of you says and repeat whatever they said, but don't say "ditto," as the group might not be amused.

For spiritual cleansing, someone may anoint your forehead with oil, offer you a bowl of water in which to wash your hands, or waft sage smoke over you. These are some of the more common practices used by groups to bring people into Circle, but there are others, each with its own magical or symbolic significance.

After everyone enters the Circle, you might notice one person who stays outside the Circle. Often one person is assigned to stay outside the Circle to act as the guardian or the "Green Man" for the ritual. The Green Man's job is to make sure nothing disturbs the Circle, and this job is especially important when rituals are being conducted outdoors or in other public locations. The Green Man greets those who are late, letting them know when they may enter the Circle or if they must wait until the Circle is finished, and will answer the questions of any curious people who might happen to stroll past the ritual area while keeping them at a distance that won't disrupt the Circle.

Once people begin to enter the Circle, extinguish cigarettes and don't chat with anyone; there will be time after ritual to finish conversations. This is a religious service, and people go to a lot of trouble to prepare a meaningful ritual for everyone involved. It's extremely disrupting for the energy and the focus of the ritual when someone is complaining about their Aunt Edna or chatting about this cute guy at work while everyone else is attempting to pay attention to the ritual and connect with the Divine. There is time both before and after the ritual for conversation, so please stay focused during the Circle.

After the Circle begins, don't leave the Circle unless you have a medical emergency, screaming baby, or the equivalent. People are usually not allowed to enter a Circle once it has begun, and leaving the Circle before it is finished is frowned upon. If you must leave, please try to do so as unobtrusively as possible and at a time when you are less likely to be noticed; don't wave good-bye or blow kisses as you go. If everyone is holding hands, bring the hands of the people on either side of you together as you step back. Some groups have a specific way they want people to leave if they must exit the Circle area early, so if there is a Green Man or other member of the group hosting the Circle standing nearby, let them help you leave the Circle or assist you with any medical problems or emergencies.

There will probably be chanting and other activities during the ritual, but don't panic—you will probably not be the only one who doesn't know the words. Most chants used in public rituals are short and easy to pick up, so just do the best you can and have fun with it; no one should critique your singing voice. If you follow along with what everyone else is doing, you will be fine.

Toward the end of the ritual, there is usually a ritual feast. The feast usually begins with blessing wine, or some other drink, and bread of some type. Then the group hosting the ritual passes the food or drink around the circle, offering a bit to each person. When they arrive at your spot, take a sip from the chalice and a bit of whatever food is being used, and either return the chalice to whomever offered it to you or pass it to the next person, whichever is being done in that ritual. Many people have food allergies, have dietary restrictions, or may not be feeling well and not want to risk infecting others. If for some reason you don't want to partake of the chalice or bread, either kiss the chalice or hold it up to honor the Goddess and God and pass it on.

Don't do anything you are uncomfortable with or feel unable to do. If everyone starts dancing around the circle and you have a bad knee, don't dance. If everyone is sharing events that have happened in their lives and you're not comfortable sharing, don't. People shouldn't force you to do something you're not comfortable with, but don't make a big deal out of refusing. If you quietly and respectfully decline to participate in a part of the Circle, no one should be upset with you.

At the end of the ritual, people may sometimes solemnly leave the way they came in, or everyone might start hugging each other and heading for the food. As with the rest of the ritual, just watch what everyone else is doing, and you will be fine.

Attending a Wiccan ritual can be a very spiritual experience. Academic discussions and lists of beliefs tell a person what a religion believes, but it's only through experiencing a worship service that one gets a glimpse into the heart and soul of the religion. Even if you aren't Wiccan, attending a Wiccan ritual will give you a much better understanding of why someone might practice the Wiccan religion.

Seeker's Bill of Rights
By Charles Mars

SEEKERS OF THE Pagan path are often extremely vulnerable. In their quest for teaching and fellowship, they risk encountering those who use our faith to prey on others. Since Paganism is still struggling for public acceptance, there is little sympathy from authorities. Neither can the elders of our communities effectively address this issue. The most they can do is denounce these predators, and they are usually accused of starting a "witch war" when they do. The answer to this dilemma is to empower those most vulnerable, the Seekers. To this end, the Seeker's Bill of Rights has been drafted. This tool will help to alert seekers of a problem if a group or teacher violates any of the ten rights described. It will also serve to remind seekers that while they may not have "degrees," they are still human beings with rights and dignity.

    I. THE RIGHT TO VERIFY CREDENTIALS: Seekers shall not be obstructed from contacting persons who can substantiate or disavow claims made by a group or teacher. In the case of elders who were inspired to create a new tradition, the seeker has a right to know the circumstances surrounding the inception of that tradition.

II. THE RIGHT TO ANONYMITY: Seekers have the right to keep their involvement in the occult a secret to preserve their personal and professional lives.

III. THE RIGHT TO FINANCIAL STABILITY: Seekers shall not be required or coerced to take on financial burdens on behalf of a teacher or a group.

IV. THE RIGHT TO COMPENSATION FOR PROFESSIONAL GOODS AND SERVICES: Seekers have the right to be paid for goods produced and/or forskilled labor from which they would normally receive an income. Seekers shall not be required or coerced to provide "freebies" or discounts on behalf of a teacher or group.

V. THE RIGHT TO SEXUAL FREEDOM: Seekers shall not be required or coerced to have sexual relations with unwanted persons. Nor shall seekers be restricted from sexual relations with consenting adults.

VI. THE RIGHT TO PHYSICAL WELL-BEING: Seekers shall not be required or coerced to submit to any form of physical injury.

VII. THE RIGHT TO ABIDE BY THE LAW: Seekers shall not be required or coerced to commit any illegal act.

VIII. THE RIGHT TO CONSISTENCY: Seekers have the right to expect consistent policies from a teacher or group. Seekers should be formally informed in a timely manner of any policy changes.

IX. THE RIGHT TO SEPARATION WITH IMPUNITY: Seekers have the right to discontinue association with any teacher or group without fear of harassment or reprisal.

X. THE RIGHT TO BE AT PEACE WITH ONE'S CONSCIENCE: Seekers shall not be required or coerced to commit any action contrary to their own sense of ethics and morality.

APPENDIX B

Resources and Suggestions for Further Reading

Beginning Wicca Books

Each of these books contains information helpful to someone who is starting to practice Wicca. Each book is that author's opinion of how Wicca should be practiced; therefore, no single book should be taken as the only way Wicca should be practiced. If you want to learn more about practicing the Wiccan religion, read several of these to get a feel for the variations in how Wiccans practice.

The Craft: A Witch's Book of Shadows: Includes Rituals, Spells, and Wiccan Ethics, by Dorothy Morrison (St. Paul, MN: Llewellyn, 2001).

Green Witchcraft, by Ann Moura, 3 volumes (St. Paul, MN: Llewellyn Publications, 1996–2000).

Living Wicca: A Further Guide for the Solitary Practitioner, by Scott Cunningham (St. Paul, MN: Llewellyn, 1993).

To Ride a Silver Broomstick: New Generation Witchcraft, by Silver RavenWolf (St. Paul, MN: Llewellyn, 1993).

Wicca: A Guide for the Solitary Practitioner, by Scott Cunningham (St. Paul, MN: Llewellyn, 1989).

Wiccan Beliefs and Practices: With Rituals for Solitaries and Covens, by Gary Cantrell (St. Paul, MN: Llewellyn, 2001).

Wiccan Warrior: Walking a Spiritual Path in a Sometimes Hostile World, by Kerr Cuhulain (St. Paul, MN: Llewellyn, 2000).

Beginning Books for Children and Teens

Each of these books is written for teenagers who want to practice the Wiccan religion or for parents who are working with children. Just as with the beginning Wicca books, no one book is "THE" book to read, and each should be taken as the author's opinion of what teens need to know. It is best for teens who want to study Wicca to have a parent or adult with whom to discuss what they have read.

Circle Round: Raising Children in Goddess Traditions, by Starhawk, Diane Baker, and Anne Hill (New York: Bantam Books, 1998).

A Little Witch's 1-2-3's, by L. B. Hazel (Euless, TX: Dreaming Hazel Studios, 1999). Available at *www.dreaminghazel.com.*

Spellcraft: A Primer for the Young Magician, by Lilith McLelland (Chicago: Eschaton Productions, 1997).

Teen Witch: Wicca for a New Generation, by Silver RavenWolf (St. Paul, MN: Llewellyn, 1998).

Where to Park Your Broomstick: A Teen's Guide to Witchcraft, by Lauren Manoy (New York: Fireside, 2002).

More Information about Magick

Be Careful What You Pray For . . . You Just Might Get It: What We Can Do about the Unintentional Effects of Our Thoughts, Prayers, and Wishes, by Larry Dossey M.D. (New York: Harper Collins, 1997). (This book is actually about prayer not magick; however, if you substitute the word *magick* for *prayer,* it becomes a great book on magick ethics.)

Everyday Magic: Spells & Rituals for Modern Living, by Dorothy Morrison (St. Paul, MN: Llewellyn, 1998).

Magical Use of Thought Forms: A Proven System of Mental & Spiritual Empowerment,
by Dolores Ashcroft-Nowicki and J. H. Brennan (St. Paul, MN: Llewellyn, 2001).

The Ritual Magic Workbook: A Practical Course of Self-Initiation, by Dolores Ashcroft-Nowicki (York Beach, ME: S. Weiser, 1998).

True Magick: A Beginner's Guide, by Amber K (St. Paul, MN: Llewellyn, 1990).

Other Books

Not all of these are Wiccan books, but they are books I have enjoyed greatly and have helped me along my spiritual path.

Ethics for the New Millennium, by the Dalai Lama (New York: Riverhead Books, 1999).

Illusions: The Adventures of a Reluctant Messiah, by Richard Bach (Boston: G. K. Hall, 1977).

Myths to Live By, by Joseph Campbell (1972; New York: Arkana, 1993).

Out of the Shadows: Myths and Truths of Modern Wicca, by Lilith McLelland (New York: Citadel, 2002).

The Power of Myth, by Joseph Campbell (New York: Doubleday, 1988).

The Spiral Dance: A Rebirth of the Ancient Religion of the Great Goddess, by Starhawk (1979; San Francisco: HarperSanFrancisco, 1999).

Tao Te Ching, by Lao Tsu, trans. Gia-Fu Feng and Jane English (New York: Vintage Books, 1972).

Triumph of the Moon: A History of Modern Pagan Witchcraft, by Ronald Hutton (Oxford, NY: Oxford University Press, 1999).

Wiccan Internet Resources

A Google search for *Wicca* reveals over half a million Internet sites devoted to some aspect of the Wiccan religion. Some of these sites are very good, while others contain little, if any, legitimate information. Obviously I can't list all the good sites here, but what follows are a few of the better Internet resources for people wanting online information about Wicca. All of these Web sites were valid at the time of printing; however, I can make no promises about the current status of any site. Each site has its own strengths and weaknesses, and they will give you a good place to start surfing.

Ardantane Witch College and Pagan Learning Center: *www.ardantane.org*
Betwixt & Between Community Center: *www.betwixt.org*
Cherry Hill Seminary: *www.cherryhillseminary.org*
Covenant of the Goddess: *www.cog.org*
Ontario Consultants on Religious Tolerance: *www.religioustolerance.org*
Pagan Parenting.com: *www.paganparenting.com*
Pagan Space: *www.paganspace.org*
Teen Witch News: *www.teenwitchnews.com*
Wiccan Ethics Research Project: *www.perfecttrust.org*
The Wiccan-Pagan Times: *www.twpt.com*
The Witches Voice: *www.witchvox.com*

NOTES

Introduction

1. Joseph Campbell, *Transformations of Myth Through Time* (New York: Harper & Row, 1990) 211.

One: The Beginning

1. Joseph Campbell, *The Masks of God: Primitive Mythology* (1959; New York: Penguin Books, 1977), 297.
2. Campbell, *Transformations of Myth* , 31.
3. Ibid., 59.
4. Ibid.
5. "Pagan," *Random House Webster's College Dictionary,* 2nd ed. (New York: Random House, 1997).
6. "Pagan," *Oxford Advanced Learner's Dictionary,* online ed. *<http://www.oup.com/elt/oald/>*.
7. "Pagan," *The Merriam-Webster Dictionary: Home and Office Edition* (Springfield, MA: Merriam-Webster, 1995).
8. Scott Cunningham, *Wicca: A Guide for the Solitary Practitioner* (St. Paul, MN: Llewellyn, 1988), 200.

Two: Deity

1. Voltaire, "The world embarrasses me, and . . ." 2003 Brainy Media *<http://www.Brainyquotes.com/quotes/quotes/v/q118590.html>*.
2. Douglas Adams, *Hitchhikers Guide to the Galaxy* (1979; New York: Harmony Books, 1980), 55.
3. Nordic runes, also called *staves,* are pictographic symbols used by the ancient Germanic people. Each character conveyed esoteric knowledge or lore; runes were used for magickal and probably religious purposes and as an alphabet.

4. Edward Carpenter, *The Origins of Pagan and Christian Beliefs* (1920; London: Senate, 1996), 112–13.

Three: Ethics

1. The use of the word *An* is in its Middle English form and means "so long as," or "provided that."
2. William Shakespeare, *Hamlet, Prince of Denmark. The Complete Signet Classic Shakespeare.* Ed. Sylvan Barnet (San Diego: Harcourt Brace Jovanovich, 1972), 1.3.78.
3. Lilith McLelland, *Out of the Shadows: Myths and Truths of Modern Wicca* (New York: Citadel, 2002), 230.

Four: Living a Wiccan Life

1. Campbell, *Masks of God,* 341
2. Tony van Renterghem, *When Santa Was A Shaman: The Ancient Origins of Santa Claus & the Christmas Tree* (St. Paul: Llewellyn, 1995), 110-116.
3. Silver RavenWolf, *Halloween: Customs, Recipes, Spells* (St. Paul, MN: Llewellyn, 1999), 46.
4. "Pentagram," *DK Illustrated Oxford Dictionary* (New York: Oxford University Press, 1998).
5. Barbara Walker, *The Women's Dictionary of Symbols and Sacred Objects* (New York: Harper Collins, 1988), 72.

Five: Misconceptions about Wicca

1. "Pope delivers broad apology for sins of the Catholic Church: Unprecedented homily welcomed as appeal for reconciliation," *Dallas Morning News,* 13 March 2000: A1.
2. Ibid.
3. Walter Stephens, *Demon Lovers: Witchcraft, Sex, and the Crisis of Belief* (Chicago: University of Chicago Press, 2002), 366.
4. Nachman Ben-Yehuda, "The European Witch Craze of the 14th to 17th Centuries: A Sociologist's Perspective," *American Journal of Sociology* 86.1 (1980): 18.
5. Stephens, *Demon Lovers,* 366
6. Ben-Yehuda, "European Witch Craze," 5.
7. James A. Connor, *Kepler's Witch: An Astronomer's Discovery of Cosmic Order Amid Religious War, Political Intrigue, and the Heresy Trial of His Mother* (New York: Harper San Francisco, 2004), 234.
8. Helen Ellerbe, *The Dark Side of Christian History* (1995; Orlando: Morningstar and Lark, 1998), 131.
9. Barbara Walker, *The Women's Encyclopedia of Myths and Secrets* (Edison, NJ: Castle Books, 1996), 1079.
10. Stephens, *Demon Lovers,* 126.
11. Ellerbe, *Dark Side of Christian History,* 118, 121.

12. Ben-Yehuda, "European Witch Craze," 3.

13. Connor, *Kepler's Witch*, 237-238.

14. Compare the Biblical NIV version of Proverbs 30:16—"There are three things that are never satisfied, four that never say, 'Enough!': the grave, the barren womb, land, which is never satisfied with water, and fire which never says, 'Enough!'"—with the version of Proverbs 30:16 found on page 47 of the *Malleus Maleficarum*, which makes it seem that the Bible supported their premise that women's lust is insatiable and states: "There are three things that are never satisfied, yea, a fourth thing which says not, It is enough; that is, the mouth of the womb."

15. The *Malleus Maleficarum*, "Hammer of Witches," is a manual for identifying and hunting witches written by two Dominican inquisitors, Heinrich Kramer and James Sprenger, under the authority of Pope Innocent VIII and first published around 1486 CE. Heinrich Kramer and James Sprenger, *The Malleus Maleficarum*, trans. Rev. Montague Summers (1928; New York: Dover Publications, 1971), 66.

16. Anne Llewellyn Barstow, *Witchcraze: A New History of European Witch Hunts* (San Francisco: Pandora, 1994), 109.

17. Kramer and Sprenger, *Malleus Maleficarum*, 47.

18. Ibid., 121.

19. Stephens, *Demon Lovers*, 366.

20. Kramer and Sprenger, *Malleus Maleficarum*, 44.

21. Ibid., 52–53.

22. Ibid., 47.

23. Ellerbe, *Dark Side of Christian History*, 119.

24. Kramer and Sprenger, *Malleus Maleficarum*, 107.

25. Rosemary Ellen Guley, *The Encyclopedia of Witches and Witchcraft* (New York: Facts on File, 1989), 37.

26. Ibid., 388.

27. "Albigenses," *Grolier Multimedia Encyclopedia*, Version 7.0, CD-Rom (Novato, CA: Mindscape, 1995).

Six: The Personal Experience of Spirit

1. John Godfrey Saxe, "The Blind Men and the Elephant." *Read-Aloud Poems for Young People: An Introduction to the Magic and Excitement of Poetry*, ed. Glorya Hale (New York: Black Dog and Leventhal, 1997), 30.

A Deeper Understanding of Wicca

1. Letter taken from public Internet discussion group.

2. "Witch," *Oxford English Dictionary* (New York: Oxford University Press, 1970).

3. Marcia Rudin, MA, retired as director of the International Cult Education Program of the American Family Foundation. "Marcia Rudin's 14 Common Characteristics of a Cult" were provided courtesy of the American Family Foundation, *www.culticstudies.org*.

4. "Witch," *Oxford English Dictionary*, 1970 ed.

A Deeper Understanding of the Wiccan View of Deity

1. Campbell, *Transformations of Myth*, 1.
2. Joseph Campbell, ed., *The Portable Jung* (1971; New York: Penguin, 1976), 150.
3. Campbell, *Transformations of Myth*, 12–14.
4. Ibid., 54.
5. Ibid.
6. Joseph Campbell, "Volume 3: The Eastern Way," *The Joseph Campbell Audio Collection* (St. Paul, MN: High Bridge, 1997) Tape 1: Oriental Mythology.
7. "How Many Wiccans Are There in the U.S.?" *www.Religioustolerance.org*, ed. Ontario Consultants on Religious Tolerance, 1995 to 2003 <http://www .Religioustolerance.org/wic_nbr.htm>.
8. Campbell, *Power of Myth*, xvi.
9. Ibid., 31.
10. All discussions of the purposes of mythology are a summarization of information from multiple audio and video recordings of lectures by Joseph Campbell with some of my own additions.
11. *Christian Wicca*, ed. Nancy Chandler-Pittman, 2003 <http://www.christianwicca .com>.

A Deeper Understanding about Wiccan Ethics

1. Larry Dossey MD, *Be Careful What You Pray For . . . You Just Might Get It: What We Can Do about the Unintentional Effects of Our Thoughts, Prayers, and Wishes* (New York: Harper Collins, 1997) 1.
2. 2 Kings 3:15–27.
3. Judges 11:30–39.

A Deeper Understanding about Wiccan Life

1. Larry Dossey M.D., *Healing Words: The Power of Prayer and the Practice of Medicine* (1993; New York: Harper Collins, 1997).
2. Meister Eckhart, *Meister Eckhart: A Modern Translation*, trans. Raymond B. Blakney (New York: Harper & Brothers, 1941), 241.
3. William Shakespeare, *As You Like It. The Complete Signet Classic Shakespeare*. Ed. Sylvan Barnet. (San Diego: Harcourt Brace Jovanovich, 1972), 2.7
4. William Ernest Henley, "Invictus." *Modern British Poetry*, ed. Louis Untermeyer (New York: Harcourt, Brace and Howe, 1920).
5. Campbell, *Masks of God*, 339–41.
6. *Church of Satan*, ed. Magus Peter H. Gilmore, 14 July 2003 <http://www. churchofsatan.com/home.html>.
7. Walker, *Women's Dictionary of Symbols and Sacred Objects*, 60.
8. "Eliphas Lévi: The Man Behind the Baphomet," *TemplarHistory.Com*, ed. Stephen Dafoe and Alan Butler, 25 July 2003 <http://www.templarhistory .com/levi.html>.

9. U.S. Department of Education. *Religious Expression in Public Schools: A Statement of Principles* (Washington: GPO, 1999), 7–8.

10. Ibid., 8.

11. Mark Silk, "Something Wiccan This Way Comes," *Religion in the News,* Summer 1999, Vol. 2, No. 2 <*http://www.trincoll.edu/depts/csrpl/RINVol2No2/wicca.htm*>.

12. Diana L. Eck, *A New Religious America: How a "Christian Country" Has Now Become the World's Most Religiously Diverse Nation* (New York: Harper Collins, 2001), 358.

13. Barry Shlachter, "Bothered and Bewildered; Wiccans at Hood Shrug Off Media Hubbub," *Fort Worth Star-Telegram* 8 Aug. 1999: A1.

14. Eck, *New Religious America,* 359.

15. William Shakespeare, *The Tempest. The Complete Signet Classic Shakespeare.* Ed. Sylvan Barnet (San Diego: Harcourt Brace Jovanovich, 1972), 4.1.156–58.

A Deeper Understanding of Misconceptions about Wicca

1. McLelland, *Out of the Shadows,* 132.

2. "Warlock," *Oxford English Dictionary,* 1970 ed.

3. All information on Satanism and quotes taken from the official Church of Satan Web site. *Church of Satan,* ed. Magus Peter H. Gilmore, 14 July 2003 <*http://www.churchofsatan.com/home.html*>.

4. Curt R. Bartol, *Criminal Behavior: A Psychosocial Approach,* 4th ed. (Englewood Cliffs, NJ: Prentice Hall, 1995), 262.

BIBLIOGRAPHY

Adams, Douglas. *Hitchhikers Guide to the Galaxy.* New York: Harmony Books, 1980.

Barstow, Anne Llewellyn. *Witchcraze: A New History Of European Witch Hunts.* San Francisco: Pandora, 1994.

Bartol, Curt R. *Criminal Behavior: A Psychosocial Approach,* 4th ed. Englewood Cliffs, NJ: Prentice Hall, 1995.

Ben-Yehuda, Nachman. "The European Witch Craze of the 14th to 17th Centuries: A Sociologist's Perspective." *American Journal of Sociology* 86.1 (1980).

Campbell, Joseph. "Volume 3: The Eastern Way," The Joseph Campbell Audio Collection. St. Paul, MN: High Bridge, 1997: Tape 1: Oriental Mythology.

———. *The Masks of God: Primitive Mythology.* New York: Penguin, 1977.

———, ed. *The Portable Jung.* New York: Penguin, 1976.

———. *The Power of Myth.* New York: Doubleday, 1988.

———. *Transformations of Myth through Time.* New York: Harper & Row, 1990.

Carpenter, Edward. *The Origins of Pagan and Christian Beliefs.* London: Senate, 1996.

Christian Wicca. Ed. Nancy Chandler-Pittman. 2003 <*http://www.christian wicca.com*>.

Church of Satan. Ed. Magus Peter H. Gilmore. 14 July 2003 <*http://www .churchofsatan.com/home.html*>.

Connor, James A. *Kepler's Witch: An Astronomer's Discovery of Cosmic Order Amid Religious War, Political Intrigue, and the Heresy Trial of His Mother.* New York: Harper San Francisco, 2004.

Cunningham, Scott. *Wicca: A Guide for the Solitary Practitioner.* St. Paul, MN: Llewellyn, 1988.

DK Illustrated Oxford Dictionary. New York: Oxford University Press, 1998.

Dossey, Larry M.D. *Be Careful What You Pray For . . . You Just Might Get It: What We Can Do About the Unintentional Effects of Our Thoughts, Prayers, and Wishes.* New York: Harper Collins, 1997.

———. *Healing Words: The Power of Prayer and the Practice of Medicine.* New York: Harper Collins, 1997.

Eck, Diana L. *A New Religious America: How a "Christian Country" Has Become the World's Most Religiously Diverse Nation.* New York: Harper Collins, 2001.

Eckhart, Meister. *Meister Eckhart: A Modern Translation.* Trans. Raymond B. Blakney. New York: Harper & Brothers, 1941.

"Eliphas Lévi: The Man Behind The Baphomet." *TemplarHistory.Com.* ed. Stephen Dafoe and Alan Butler. 25 July 2003 <*http://www.templarhistory.com/levi.html*>.

Ellerbe, Helen. *The Dark Side of Christian History.* Orlando: Morningstar and Lark, 1998.

Farrar, Janet, and Stewart Farrar. *The Witches' Goddess: The Feminine Principle of Divinity.* Custer, WA: Phoenix Publishing, 1987.

———. *The Witches' God: Lord of the Dance.* Custer, WA: Phoenix Publishing, 1989.

Grolier Multimedia Encyclopedia. CD-Rom. Novato, CA: Mindscape, 1995.

Guley, Rosemary Ellen. *The Encyclopedia of Witches and Witchcraft.* New York: Facts on File, 1989.

"How Many Wiccans Are There in the U.S.?" *www.Religioustolerance.org.* ed. Ontario Consultants on Religious Tolerance. 1995 to 2003 <*http://www .Religioustolerance.org/wic_nbr.htm*>.

K, Amber, and Azrael Arynn K. *Candlemas: Feast of Flames.* St. Paul, MN: Llewellyn, 2001.

Kramer, Heinrich, and James Sprenger. *The Malleus Maleficarum.* Trans. Rev. Montague Summers. 1928; New York: Dover Publications, 1971.

Linn, Denise. *Altars: Bringing Sacred Shrines into Your Everyday Life.* New York: Ballantine Wellspring, 1999.

"Marcia Rudin's 14 Common Characteristics of a Cult." Provided courtesy of the American Family Foundation. <*http://www.culticstudies.org*>

McLelland, Lilith. *Out of the Shadows: Myths and Truths of Modern Wicca.* New York: Citadel, 2002.

The Merriam-Webster Dictionary: Home and Office Edition. Springfield, MA: Merriam-Webster, 1995.

Oxford Advanced Learners Dictionary. Ed. Sally Wehmeier. 6th ed. 2000. <*http://www.oup.com/elt/oald/*>.

Oxford English Dictionary. New York: Oxford University Press, 1970.

"Pope delivers broad apology for sins of the Catholic Church: Unprecedented homily welcomed as appeal for reconciliation." *Dallas Morning News,* 13 March 2000: A1.

Random House Webster's College Dictionary, 2nd ed. New York: Random House, 1997.

RavenWolf, Silver. *Halloween: Customs, Recipes, Spells.* St. Paul, MN: Llewellyn, 1999.

Saxe, John Godfrey. "The Blind Men And The Elephant." *Read-Aloud Poems for Young People: An Introduction to the Magic and Excitement of Poetry.* Ed. Glorya Hale. New York: Black Dog and Leventhal, 1997: 30.

Shakespeare, William. *The Complete Signet Classic Shakespeare.* Ed. Sylvan Barnet. San Diego: Harcourt Brace Jovanovich, 1972.

Shlachter, Barry. "Bothered and Bewildered; Wiccans At Hood Shrug Off Media Hubbub." *Fort Worth Star-Telegram* 8 Aug. 1999: A1.

Silk, Mark. "Something Wiccan This Way Comes." *Religion in the News.* Summer 1999, Vol. 2, No. 2 <*http://www.trincoll.edu/depts/csrpl/RINVol2No2/wicca.htm*>.

Stephens, Walter. *Demon Lovers: Witchcraft, Sex, and the Crisis of Belief.* Chicago: University of Chicago Press, 2002.

Telesco, Patricia. *Future Telling: A Complete Guide to Divination.* Freedom, CA: Crossing Press, 1998.

U.S. Department of Education. *Religious Expression in Public Schools: A Statement of Principles.* Washington: GPO, 1999.

van Renterghem, Tony. *When Santa Was A Shaman: The Ancient Origins of Santa Claus & the Christmas Tree.* St. Paul: Llewellyn, 1995.

Voltaire. "The world embarrasses me, and . . ." 2003 Brainy Media <*http://www.Brainyquotes.com/quotes/quotes/v/q118590.html*>.

Walker, Barbara. *The Women's Dictionary of Symbols and Sacred Objects.* New York: Harper Collins, 1988.

―――. *The Women's Encyclopedia of Myths and Secrets.* Edison, NJ: Castle Books, 1996.

ACKNOWLEDGMENTS

THE WRITING OF this book has been a path which wound and forked and appeared to be unending; however, the further along the path I went, the heavier this volume became, until finally I had to say "enough" and turn this journey over to others for printing and binding. Nothing is accomplished in a vacuum, so I walked with many other people along the path leading to this book. These people aided me in refining my thoughts and honing my presentation, and I am grateful to each and every one of them. There are many people who helped with this book, more than I can possibly remember, but I would like to take this opportunity to thank a few of them here.

First I would like to thank my mother Linda, my father Wes and my other family members, who have not always understood or agreed with my choices but have always loved me anyway; I appreciate your tolerance as I found my own path. I will be forever indebted to my wife, Anastasia, for proofreading all my revisions and for not throttling me when I wanted to revise the text one more time; I love you more than you can know. I want to thank my daughters, Peri and Lucina, for their patience when I had to work and for at least trying to keep the interruptions to a minimum; you are both the light of my world. I appreciate the support given to me by all of OIC coven, especially Mikhail for suggesting the book format and Joe for the synchronicity story. You're all more than friends;

you're family. Thanks for your encouragement and for making it your mission to keep me from getting a big head. Juli and Amy, it's your turn now. I could not have finished this book without the input of the Texas Local Council of the Covenant of the Goddess, especially Thorn, Gaelen, Chuck, J'Ann, Robert BlackEagle, SilverMoon, Susan, Georgia, Charles, and Mark; you were all invaluable in helping me to be inclusive of the great diversity of Wiccan traditions. Bob, I'm sorry I didn't finish this before you had to leave, but wherever you are, thanks for keeping an eye on us. Thanks to Maeven, Angela, and everyone at Betwixt & Between Community Center for giving me the opportunity to teach and refine the ideas presented in this book. To Theresa, Christine, Reverend Harrell, Prajapati, my brother James, my Aunt Carolyn my stepmother Lynn, Marty, and all the others who read through the early drafts of this book, thanks for your input and for being honest enough to tell me when sections were awful. Next time I see her, I owe Lilith McLelland a huge hug for her help with the book proposal; you're one of my heroes too. Jennifer, thanks for the input on Odin; you are my Nordic expert. I am in reverent awe of the artwork created by Hazel and Clovis of *www.Dreaminghazel.com;* your talent and vision has always been an inspiration to me. Thank you, Brenda, for your perceptive input on the final draft. My eternal gratitude goes out to Shanna for looking at the text from an outsider's perspective; your keen insight helped me smooth out many areas that might have been confusing to a non-Wiccan reader. You are amazing, and I'm so glad our paths have once again come together. Thanks to my agent, Andy Zack, for his work in finding a publisher and negotiating the contract; I'm just glad you're on my side. Thanks to my publisher, Matthew Lore, for seeing the potential in this book when so many others lacked that vision, and to his assistant, Peter Jacoby, for working with me on all the little details necessary in getting this book through the publishing process. Thanks to Robin Yown for her photographic prowess; you rock girl! Thank you, thank you to all the people who, over the years, have asked me questions about Wicca and hung around to listen to my answers. You shaped this book by letting me know what aspects of Wicca people were interested in and by providing the questions for the second half of this book.

These people and many others have helped me find the philosopher's stone, that magical talisman that gives its owner unlimited life and riches. This stone is found inside oneself when one realizes unlimited life is not measured in years of existence but in how well we live the life we have, rather than waiting around to die, and unlimited wealth is not found in collecting possessions but by finding the richness in the world around us and in the love of friends. I thank all of you for the joy of life and wealth of love you have given to me.

INDEX